Know Hunting

Truths, Lies & Myths

By

Dr. David E. Samuel

Dave Samuel

Illustrated by Michael Watson

Know Hunting
Truths, Lies & Myths
By Dr. David E. Samuel

Published by:
> Know Hunting Publications
> PO Box 18115
> Cheat Lake, WV 26507

1st. Edition: September, 1999

Cover design by Jamie Bouquot
Cover illustration and interior illustrations by Michael Watson
Interior design by Kay L. Richey
Electronically created camera-ready copy by:
> KLR Communications, Inc.
> PO Box 192
> Grawn, MI 49637

Library of Congress Cataloging in Publication Data
Samuel, Dr. David E.
Know Hunting, Truths, Lies & Myths, By Dr. David E. Samuel
Hunting --- North America
ISBN 0-9672689-0-7 Softcover

Table of Contents

Acknowledgments

This book was several years in the making. At least six years ago several hunters requested the need to put the various types of positive information on hunting together in one place. I too thought there was such a need, and began to file and store information that could be used in such a book.

Outdoor writer and friend, Bob Robb, read my first draft of 11 chapters and gave me strong encouragement to write this book. Jay McAninch, then wildlife biologist with the Minnesota DNR and now Executive Director of the Congressional Sportsmen's Foundation in Washington D. C., and Dr. Ben Peyton, wildlife professor at Michigan State University, provided extremely important comments and editing of the first 11 chapters. Their insight gave me direction on how to proceed and how best to develop the text. Ken Mayer, wildlife biologist with the California wildlife agency, provided very important editing and comments on chapter 11. Kay and Dave Richey made the book possible. Kay did the layout while Dave edited the entire text. Thank you both for being so patient and so helpful.

Candi Jennings gave me some preliminary sketches that led to some of the ideas for art work. Mike Watson put those ideas, plus many of his own, into his fantastic art work. Mike, your talent gave this effort some life, and you captured the meaning of the book with your art. Thank you.

Many friends in the bowhunting community, and many friends in the wildlife community, gave me insight and ideas for years preceding, and during the writing, of this book. For over 25 years I taught a course on wildlife attitudes at West Virginia University. Thus, my students also assisted with their input in content. Dr. Steve Hollenhorst, a vegetarian and, in general, an antihunter, would lecture every year in that course. Our values differed on hunting, but those differences enriched the classroom and our relationship. My thanks to this outstanding professor and friend.

Four people have had a special influence on my wildlife and writing careers. In the text you will read about my grandfather, Jacob

Hoffman. He not only exposed me to the values of the woods at a very young age, but he kindled that interest by quoting the Bible, Thoreau, Burroughs, and others at a time when I did not fully appreciate the lessons. However, those lessons were not lost nor forgotten. Life in a home with four children and limited resources was rough at times. My parents made many sacrifices that enabled all four children to attend college. Without that education I could not have pursued my wildlife career. While growing up I had a neighbor, Bill Eash, who found the time to help my brothers and me get into the woods. That friendship remains today. Len Cardinale is a friend and bowhunter from New Jersey. He knows people as well as anyone I've met and his advice and counsel has been helpful over the years. And finally, my good and trusted friend Steve Fausel, in recent years, has introduced me to many new interests in efforts to conserve our heritage in hunting and natural resource management. Thanks Steve for the insights that I hope are reflected herein.

Thanks to friends and associates at Bowhunter magazine. A special thanks to my long-time editor, M. R. James. For 28 years M.R. edited and assisted me with my writing. Dwight Schuh and Rick Cochran have also been a great help to me. And a special thanks for allowing me to use the title of my column in Bowhunter as the title of this book. I also want to thank Carol Rushford, my creative and thoughful sister-in-law, for coming up with the title for my column and this book.

My family has been supportive of my work, for which I am truly blessed. Cathy, my wife, helpmate, and friend, has always believed in me...sometimes when I did not believe in myself. There is no way to measure this. Know that it is appreciated more than I can ever express.

Foreward

Thirty years ago, when I was out bowhunting for deer, trapping for muskrats or 'coon, or hunting for pheasants, rabbits or squirrels, I had nothing on my mind but the thrill of the pursuit and some great times shared with my best friend, Jim Braden. If, when we were hiking out of the woods and headed to our car, someone had thrust a microphone under our noses and asked Jim or me, "Why do you hunt?" we would have first been stunned that anyone would ask such a dumb question, and second, would have been tongue-tied over a question that would have seemed similar to, "Why does the sun come up in the morning?".

Today, thousands of bowhunters hunt throughout urban neighborhoods, helping private landowners and city and county governments control overabundant deer populations. Although hunters initially felt these "city" deer hunting programs were inferior to hunting in rural areas, many hunters now flock to these opportunities as a way to extend their time in the woods. At the same time, nearly all hunters have learned they had better become involved in an advocacy organization in order to protect their hunting way of life. Loss of hunting opportunities in several states as a result of ballot initiatives or in local areas due to animal rights threats and intimidation, are not uncommon and have left an indelible imprint on today's hunters.

Yet, hunters needed more than threats and panic to respond to the public's interest in hunting. Hunters needed to learn more about hunters, hunting, wildlife management and society, and needed to realize that most Americans did not hunt and certainly didn't equate hunting with the sun coming up in the morning.

The fact that hunters, today, not only know why they hunt but are unafraid to answer on camera, is because most have spent the last 30 years reading the works of Dr. David Samuel, or, as he is known to bowhunters, Dr. Dave. In his column in Bowhunter magazine, aptly named Know Hunting, Dr. Dave has taught people about the spirtual, cultural, scientific, environmental, legal, political, social, economical, philisophical, religious, and ethical aspects of hunting. Through tireless reporting of the most recent scientific work, local and national antihunting activities, and wildlife management controversies throughout the country, Dr. Dave has molded many of today's modern hunters into sportsmen and women who are as comfortable in their treestand as they are at a city council meeting.

This book is a comprehensive look at the changes that have occurred in the world as well as the way hunting and hunters have related to those changes. Pulling from his vast background in the published works on the science and art of hunting, Dr. Dave provides provocative perspectives on the many issues that swirl around the hunting question. Here and there you will experience the wit and sensitivity of a man who has hunted the world over but continues to care about every last one of his students at West Virginia University. As you read, you will catch glimpes of his humor and, on occasion, he will tell you exactly how he sees it.

A book of this breadth and depth, on the topic of hunting, has been sorely needed. Dr. Dave has provided hunters, housewives, corporate executives, artists, small businessmen and anyone seeking to learn something about hunting, with a primer that will promote thoughtful reflection on one of the difficult issues of our time. Whether you agree with all that Dave has written is irrelevant. The feelings and thoughts that jump from these pages are the passions of a life-long hunter who has enjoyed all that anyone could want out of life - a life where hunting has provided definition, substance and fulfillment.

Jay McAninch, Executive Director
Congressional Sportsmen's Foundation

Preface

I first became aware that antihunting was a growing situation that would negatively impact our ability to manage wildlife on a beautiful spring day in 1971. I was attending the North American Wildlife and Natural Resource Conference in Washington D. C., and was having dinner with two colleagues.

Dr. James Applegate was an old college chum from Penn State University. For the past 30 years he has been a leader in the wildlife program at Rutgers University. My second friend also was a wildlife biologist - Dr. Jack Ward Thomas - a former student at West Virginia University (where I formerly worked). Jack has risen within the ranks of the U. S. Forest Service, and was the Chief of that agency. Today he is a Professor at the University of Montana.

These fine gentlemen have always been held in the highest regard by their peers, and both are keen thinkers. When they speak, it pays to listen and learn, and during our conversation, I did just that.

Jim was discussing new research with the objective of learning how New Jersey citizens felt about deer hunting. The study showed a growing number of people opposed deer hunting in New Jersey (a statistic that was to reverse itself in the late 80's, but more on this study with an update in Chapter 7).

Jack Thomas confirmed what Jim said...society is changing. It is more urban, and people do not relate to the death of animals as they once did.

Both agreed antihunting brought good and bad news. The good news was that this growing area had the potential to improve hunters ethics. The bad news was it would make wildlife management more difficult in the future and that wildlife might well suffer.

Until that time I assumed most people supported deer hunting, especially in areas with too many deer. Boy, was that naive.

A few years later Jim and I bowhunted together in Colorado, and the antihunting topic came up again as we sat around a campfire in the Rocky Mountains. Our discussions caused me to read and study the topic, and made me realize the future of wildlife management was in doubt. If antihunters got their way, all hunting might stop and we would lose our source of funding that keeps wildlife management alive today. Since that meant losing $155 million each year in federal excise taxes on hunting equipment, plus another $420 million in hunting license fees—with these funds going to wildlife management—any loss of hunting would have serious ramifications.

There were several reasons I was upset at the thought of losing hunting. First, I'm a bowhunter and love being in the woods. I wasn't compulsive about hunting, but next to my family and Christian beliefs, bowhunting was the most important thing in my life and losing the opportunity to bowhunt would be catastrophic for me.

Second, I was a Professor of wildlife and fisheries management, and losing hunting would mean a decline of most revenues that pay the salaries of future wildlife professionals. Were there to be a total loss of hunting, we would lose all revenues from license sales and hunting equipment excise taxes which amounts to three-quarters of the budget for most state wildlife agencies. Those agencies would face major lay-offs; biologists, managers, conservation law enforcement officers, etc. would be out of work.

Wildlife management would creep to a standstill, and all wildlife would suffer.

Thus began a life-long interest in this topic. I began teaching a course at West Virginia University on this subject in 1974, hoping to educate wildlife students about the many intricacies of the antihunting movement. That course is still being taught today.

My discussions with Jim Applegate and Jack Thomas led me to begin writing about the subject. Many articles and columns about the antihunting movement have followed.

This book comes in response to requests from hunters and nonhunters to provide information on antihunting. The topics covered will not please all hunters, nor all nonhunters.

Most of what I'll discuss will not be agreed upon or accepted by antihunters, but then it's purpose is not to convince nonhunters or antihunters to become hunters. Nor was it written to convince hunters to stop hunting.

My reasons for writing this book are several. I want to provide hunters with information on this complex subject. In so doing, it is my fervent hope that they will be able to use the information to help keep hunting alive. Even more importantly, I want hunters to be better hunters, more ethical, and more appreciative hunters.

Aldo Leopold once said the more we learn about a subject, the more knowledge we acquire, and the more we appreciate that subject. I want hunters to fully appreciate this subject, to fully appreciate the many values of hunting to modern society and to fully appreciate why we have an antihunting movement.

Secondarily, I want nonhunters to be aware of the values of hunting and some of the issues that surround the antihunting issue. Dr. Robert Muth, a close wildlife biologist friend at the University of Massachusetts, has researched this topic and recently concluded that "...most Americans no longer have direct experience with wild nature, but rather experience it through an urban epistemology characterized by highly mediated and stylized filters, such as nature magazines, television (e.g., the Discovery Channel, Animal Planet), movies (e.g., "Bambi", "Free Willy", "Babe"), zoos and Sea Worlds, and their own backyard bird feeders" (Muth, R. M., *et al.* *"The Future of Wildlife and Fisheries Policy and Management: Assessing the Attitudes and Values of Wildlife and Fisheries Professionals"*, 1998 Transactions of the 63rd North American Wildlife and Natural Resources Conference, pages 604-627.). Hopefully this book will provide nonhunters with material that goes beyond the "stylized filters" mentioned above.

Thus, I hope to provide some perspective on a very complex subject where even the terminology can get confusing. We will discuss antihunting and antihunters. Antihunters usually oppose hunting for recreation, and they usually have never hunted.

Some oppose all hunting. Others support some forms of hunting but not all forms (hunting bear over bait is a good example of a form of hunting not supported by everyone, including some hunters). Some antihunters also believe in the most liberal definition of "animal rights," and that is to give animals the same moral and legal standing as humans.

Thus, all "animal rights" believers are antihunting, but not all antihunters are "animal rightists." We must understand there are gradations of animal rights. Some animal rights believers feel only select animals deserve rights, or that animals should have rights equal to humans only in certain situations. Other animal rightists (including some leaders of animal rights groups), believe all animals should have a standing equal to humans.

There also are gradations of antihunting. Some oppose all hunting, but do not believe in animal rights. And as mentioned, others believe in some forms of hunting, but not other forms.

Another commonly used term that I'll refer to in this book is "animal welfare"....people who are concerned with the humane treatment of animals. Animal welfarists can be hunters, nonhunters, and antihunters. Nonhunters might ask: how can a hunter be concerned about the humane treatment of animals?

Let there be no mistake on this. Most hunters care a lot about the animals they hunt. For the nonhunter, this is not an easy concept to understand, but it is real for hunters and I will cover this topic thoroughly.

One final term I'll use is "animal activists." Animal activists are people concerned about abuses to animals, and they are active in their beliefs. They work hard to see that animals are treated humanely (hence they are also animal welfarists), or that animals are not used by man for any purpose (hence, in this case they are also animal rightists). Some animal activists are animal rightists, and some are antihunters. It is a complex subject and the water often gets muddy. Some antihunters say that they believe in "animal rights" yet do not seem to understand what that term actually means. While many antihunters are concerned about animals, a few are caught up in a "cause," and as with all such social movements, some with ulterior motives are attracted to it.

The actions of some antihunting leaders give the impression they care not a twit about animals, but rather are involved to secure funding for their organizations. While most hunters are ethical, honest citizens, a few also do not care a twit about animals.

The ethical hunter does not like to be painted with the same brush that portrays the poacher or unethical hunter. Antihunters are the same. Many...most...are opposed to terrorist tactics and do not want to be linked with them.

I want hunters to better appreciate opposing points of view, to understand the fundamental threats associated with the antihunting movement and, most important, to take action in a manner that will secure the future of hunting and wildlife management as we know it. As my close friend Steve Fausel said recently, "be passionate about your hunting, but do so in such a way as to convey nothing but positive values to nonhunters. Then, and only then, will nonhunters support our position and give us their trust."*

"The root of a human's soul grows from and is nourished by simple activities such as hunting."

Steve Fausel

*Portions of this last paragraph are used with permission of Bowhunter Magazine, excerpted from the article, *The Next 25 Years*, October 1996.

SECTION I

THINGS WILL NEVER BE THE SAME AGAIN

Chapter 1. Introduction*

Growing Up Hunting.—I remember the first animal I shot and killed as if it were yesterday. I felt bad.

It was a starling feeding in our back yard. At 10 years of age, and with a new bow and arrow for my birthday, I never expected the animal to die...I never expected to hit it.

And I did not associate shooting a bow with killing a bird until I held that warm feathered creature in my hand. Prior to that moment, I thoroughly enjoyed the excitement of my backyard hunt. Killing that starling ended my pot shots at birds...but not my desire to hunt.

I grew up in a home where hunting was the norm. As boys, me and brothers Bill and Earl were very interested in wildlife, in nature, in being in the woods and in hunting. They all went together. My friends' fathers hunted and they also looked upon the chance to hunt with anticipation.

When we could not hunt, we read about it as much as possible. We knew the approximate delivery date for my father's subscription to Outdoor Life, and raced from the school bus to the mail box to get first dibs on it. That magazine provided a vicarious way for us to be in the woods hunting while we awaited our chance to participate.

During those years we would watch my dad and his friend empty their game bag on Saturday evenings. There were always a few gray squirrels to clean, because my father was a squirrel hunter. There would occasionally be a rabbit, even less often a ruffed grouse, and once I recall the celebration of a wild turkey in his game bag. The squirrels were cleaned, placed in salt water overnight, and then put

*portions adapted (with permission), "On Your Side" columns, Bowhunting News, June & July, 1992 and Bowhunter Magazine, "The Next 25 Years," Nov. 1996.

Chapter 1

in the freezer. We always listened with excitement, and a twinge of jealousy, to every detail of their hunt. The food was important because our family had to struggle to come up with enough money to feed four hungry children; no wild game ever went to waste; a situation not atypical for hunting families. Securing that food was an important part of our lives, and finally, at age thirteen, my twin brother and I went hunting.

I remember our first hunt well. We went with my father and his friend to a State Game Lands near Rainsburg, Pennsylvania. We arrived an hour before legal hunting time, so my brother and I went for a short walk near the parked car. We hadn't gone 100 yards before spotting a gray squirrel so we picked out a log to sit on. Rustling leaves caused me to turn to the right, and there, not 20 yards away was an eight-point buck.

The hearts of two 13-year-old boys could be heard beating yards away. Any woods-loving boy whose heart doesn't jump out of his chest when seeing a buck that close isn't quite normal.

The buck walked closer and soon was only 15 feet away, feeding on red maple twigs. When he winded us, snorted, and ran we were left with an indelible image that is still vivid 42 years later. To this day, the magic and excitement I felt that morning has been the defining reason I hunt—to feel that rush, the thundering heartbeat, the shortness of breath and the tingling feeling of being so close to such a majestic creature. So began my first hunting day in the woods.

Later I killed a gray squirrel. There was no mental torture for me in killing the animal. I wanted to do it, and I did. It wasn't sordid or sick; it was a small part of a much bigger hunt, and a hunting tradition.

The squirrels my brother and I took that day brought smiles from my dad and mom. My dad praised me in having a successful hunt. Mom appreciated that her sons were now helping to provide food for the table. Maybe it wasn't the food that stimulated moms response; perhaps it was seeing her boys start to grow into manhood.

Don't be misled here...one doesn't have to kill to reach manhood, but in our home, and in thousands of others, hunting was a part of growing up. And being a good hunter gave you a sense of belonging.

I grew up where hunting was a way of life. There was an air of

20

excitement as hunting season approached, and we were instilled with a respect for wildlife and for the opportunity to be in the woods. Twelve was the legal hunting age in Pennsylvania, but dad felt that was too young for such responsibility so we had to wait. Not a bad idea either, for in the waiting there was nurtured a growing respect and reason for the hunt.

Trudging through the fall foliage with dad brought ethics lessons that can only be given to hunters by their parents. Friends just don't teach the same things, nor do they get the same response, as fathers do. *Example;* for the first three years I gun hunted for deer—age 13-16—dad only allowed us to carry one cartridge. The reason? Safety. If we shot a deer, got excited (as young boys are prone to do), we might forget to put the safety back on after a successful shot. With one shell, there was no way an accident could occur after a shot was taken.

It also taught us to be certain of our first shot...there would be no second chance. Subsequently, I killed three bucks during those years, and all with one shot. I don't think I would have learned that lesson from a friend.

Example: my first deer hunting day took place in McKean County, Pennsylvania. I was given strict instructions to wait for the legal 7 a.m. shooting time. Snow lay on the ground with visible shooting light before legal time arrived. Sure enough, at 6:55 a.m. a very nice eight-point buck walked up to me and stood at 20 yards. I did not shoot, and that night in hunting camp several hunters teased me for not doing so. My dad just looked at me and winked. A great lesson; I took a buck the next day. I wouldn't have learned that lesson from a friend.

Things were very tough for our family, and my dad spent long hours working two or three jobs just so we could survive. There were few father-son activities except hunting and fishing at that time. As I look back on my early life, I can't help but feel those hunting excursions taught me many lessons in life...valuable lessons for which I am forever grateful.

My early days led me down a hunting path that took both me and my twin brother Bill into studies of wildlife management in college. Then it was graduate school, and then long careers as wildlife professors at major universities.

Chapter 1

Things Will Never Be The Same.—I constantly hear hunters talk about what it will be like when all this antihunting stuff goes away. They point out the many positive things they do, the values of hunting, as if all of this will ultimately lead to a time when things will be "like the good old days."

One only has to look at all aspects of human life to realize we can never turn back the clock because things will never be the same again. Almost nothing (except perhaps things that animals do) stays the same; things are constantly changing.

Man is the cause of much of the change. Consider that 10,000 years ago 34 percent of the world was forested. One hundred years ago figures had dropped to 32 percent. Today we are down to 12 percent.

Humans obviously call the shots. Habitat never stay the same, nor do people's philosophies on most issues. It amazes me how hunters fail to see these changes, fail to see them happen right before their eyes. Though I fervently wish that the world would not change, the truth is that we will never return to the "good old days."

In February, 1996, I had the pleasure to participate in the National Shooting Sports Summit meeting in Florida. The keynote speaker was Harvey Schiller of Turner Sports Network. He talked about marketing the shooting sports in a changing world and it was a fascinating speech.

Relative to a changing society, consider the following: the United States population is aging. By the year 2005, the majority of Americans will be mature. Now, older Americans hunt at a higher rate than young Americans. When the old pass away, unless young folks pick it up, hunting will also pass away.

There is a generation gap in other facets of our lives as well. Older people spend money on clothes, cosmetics, books, new cars, meals and entertainment. Young people spend money on upscale retailers, home building repairs, additions and luxury motels.

Today's young people want entertainment; they want to be entertained. Has the shooting sports industry recognized this? Is shooting a gun or bow presented to young people in an entertaining way? If not, then we cannot expect them to enter into the shooting sports.

Dr. Schiller noted other changes. For example, by the year 2005,

63 percent of women will have full-time jobs. Parents once took us into the woods, into the outdoors. Working parents now have less chance to do so.

By the year 2016, the majority of Americans will be minorities. Historically, minorities were less active in hunting so will that carry over into the future? While most American populations grow older, minority populations grow younger. Since young people are less inclined to hunt, will this trend mean fewer hunters? Yes, unless programs are started that get women, minorities and young people into hunting.

Leisure time is very different today. When I was a kid, we spent time walking in the woods, an activity that our ancestors have done for a million years. Suddenly, that has changed.

Today, people sit in front of television sets and computers. One-third of all American families own a computer and the Internet buzzs with activity. How about watching home videos? Americans spend twice as much time watching home videos as they do going to the movies. We eat fast foods and packaged goods. We walk and shop in the malls of the world. The bigger the better.

We eat at theme restaurants. We live in big cities. In addition to all these changes, "the role and social meaning of animals in society are changing. Pets are becoming members of the family, often replacing human beings as friends, companions, confidants and children." (Quote from *Muth et al., The Future of Wildlife and Fisheries Policy and Management: Assessing the Attitudes and Values of Wildlife and Fisheries Professionals'* 1998 Transactions, 63rd North American Wildlife and Natural Resources Conference, pages 604-627).

These are real changes that impact all facets of our life. The question is how these changes will affect our relationship to the outdoors and our relationship to hunting. How much are animal activism and associated antihunting activities a result of these social changes?

Things do not stay the same and relative to the antihunting movement, the battles we are fighting now will always be there to fight. They may ebb and flow, the pendulum may swing back and forth, and things might improve some, but antihunting sentiment will not disappear in the foreseeable future.

Consider that 1991 was the first year when most Americans lived in an urban environment; a majority of us live in cities of over 50,000. We no longer grow up with rural values. This fact alone creates major problems for those who want people to understand basic natural resource management. Urban people have less chance to be exposed to nature, to the realities of death in nature, to the realities of death of animals without hunting.

Cities Change Kids.— I occasionally take my young nephew, Justin, hiking in the woods. When we go, he learns more about nature. Justin is 13, but beginning at age six he learned what a poison oak vine was, recognized duck weed on the surface of the local pond, and knew that certain ducks eat it. He can point out a deer track, and can tell you what direction the animal was walking. He knows a buck rub, and scrape, and can point out spring seeps (and he knows that such seeps are important food sources for wild turkeys in the winter when the rest of the forest is frozen over). Every time we hit the woods, Justin learns more about nature and wildlife.

I recently promised to take him to a new woods where he would see raccoon and wild turkey tracks. His mother said he is so excited he has trouble sleeping. Those walks are as important to me as to Justin. It's good exercise and a fun, learning experience.

Many kids would love to get into the woods as Justin does, but being urban-born they never have a chance to experience nature. They have little chance to learn those things most hunters learn as a child in the woods.

Many who hunt can relate to Justin. Do you remember those early hikes? Do you remember that young excitement, that first buck you saw in the woods? I certainly do.

While the actors may change from dinosaurs to warm blooded mammals, the scripts in nature remain the same. For thousands of years black-footed ferrets ate prairie dogs, and still do. Cold spring rains killed wild turkey and grouse chicks for 500,000 years, and it still happens.

Ospreys still eat fish, deer continue to drown while attempting to swim swollen spring rivers, raccoons still eat crawfish, distemper continues to ravage many furbearers, and hawks still eat mice. For one million years, humans have been at the top of the food chain, and we still are. Some people in today's urban society do not want to be on top of the food chain.

Sorry, that can't be changed. It's the way things are.

Today's kids aren't exposed to nature's life and death events. An urban society won't have the chance to see such things, and cannot relate to them very well at all.

With each new generation in the United States, we become further removed from living off the land. How many generations off the farm are your children? Two, three, or maybe four? When kids grew up on the farm, they saw more of nature, understood that domestic and wild animals die all the time. They understood that animal deaths led to that plastic-wrapped chicken found in local super markets or the Styrofoam-packaged hamburger bought at the local fast-food restaurant.

Those earlier children were active participants in the chain of life, in the realities of life and death. It's not so today, and with each new generation, there is less awareness of what happens in real nature. No wonder young children are so easily influenced by animal rights or antihunting philosophy.

It sounds good, and they have no exposure with nature to make a comparison. It will get worse before it gets better. NO, it may never get better.

Most youngsters today are born and raised in big cities. Compared to their parents, about 20 percent of the kids raised in big cities are opposed to hunting for recreation. They oppose hunting for meat by about 20 percent more than their parents. Unless they have parents or other relatives who hunt, or unless they return to the country regularly, urban backgrounds preclude most children from knowing the difference between a duck and a goose, or deer droppings from those of a grouse or rabbit.

The idea that one animal eats another is a million years normal, and a part of the wild landscape, yet it is abhorrent to many children. It isn't their fault.

They would love to walk in the woods with someone who could show and teach them about nature. They would enjoy those hikes as much as Justin does, but nature is not available to most of them.

I thank God that my dad and my grandfather took time to show me nature when I was a kid. Grandpap took me and my brothers for Sunday walks hundreds of times. Nothing thrilled us more than to be out on a new snow. We became instant animal detectives, following and learning the habits of wildlife from their tracks.

Grandpap knew them all. He wasn't much of a hunter, but he loved the woods. Not only would he show us tracks, sign, droppings, trails, etc., but he could quote the Bible, Thoreau, and John Burroughs from memory.

He was a neat guy. This was a man who knew every animal track, all the trees, and the plants that animals eat, and yet he could recite poetry at length.

As little kids we didn't appreciate Grandpap's poetry, but we paid attention to his nature lessons. He was a bit of a mystery to us; how did he memorize all those poems? He knew the Bible and could quote it for hours. How did he do that? Grandpap knew Indian history about the areas we hiked. We'd find arrowheads after spring plowing. How did he always know where to look?

We kept Grandpap a secret for a few years, but soon our friends learned about him. One by one, they joined us on Sunday afternoon walks. There might be a snicker or two when Grandpap recited a poem, but a sharp stare from one of us would quickly quiet such rudeness. We may not have understood the poetry, but we sure understood the fun we shared on Grandpap's walks.

No kid, friend or not, would take those away from us. The message was clear: you can come along, but one step out of line and you won't be invited back. Grandpap might tolerate you, but we wouldn't, because it impacted those things we wanted to learn.

My experience of those days in the field was a major step that lead me into hunting. I believe children who share the outdoors with their family will know and understand nature better than those who have not had such guidance. Does sharing the outdoors help one understand hunting or that many wild animals die in nature every day? I think it does.

There is something about a hike in the woods, getting some mud on your shoes, the smell of dead leaves in your nostrils, and a few briar scratches on your arms and legs, that stimulates brain cells. I'll admit that this isn't true for all, but as a general rule, I'd bet it holds.

At the turn of the 20th. Century some nature writers presented animals as thinking, talking human-like creatures. Those writers elevated the lives of animals to a type of romantic existence. The term that describes such humanization of animals is "anthropomorphism."

Such writings disturbed a very famous nature writer - John Burroughs - and he referred to those who humanized animals, yet seemed to know little about them as "nature fakers." (For an excellent essay on John Burroughs and his attacks against "nature fakers" see, (*"Nature Fakers—Then and Now,"* by George Reiger, Field & Stream, Dec. 1998, pages 24, 26.)

The same writers that upset Burroughs also disturbed a famous hunter of that time, President Teddy Roosevelt. Nature fakers created a romanticized-humanized image of wild animals and their lives, and today this makes it hard for people to connect an over-population of deer with problems in the ecosystem or too many muskrats with problems in the marsh.

Today, probably more than at any time in the past, we have more than a fair share of nature fakers. Some are hunters who take uninformed positions without understanding the ecological issues that are involved.

Others are antihunters who might spend a great deal of time, energy and money to abolish deer hunting in suburbs where the majority of citizens want deer numbers lowered. Yet these people know little about the ecology of the problem. Antihunters may say: "so what?" "Really now, what is the difference? So, I'm against killing animals. Do I have to know everything about wildlife to be against killing?"

No, of course not. But the more you know the better and easier it is to help wildlife. Hunters are in duck blinds, not only to hunt, but to see and learn about the surrounding marsh. If a housing developer threatens to fill in a marsh, who would know more about what will be lost? Someone who trapped muskrats there as a boy, or an urban dweller whose only contact with a marsh is an occasional picture or quick look from the seat of a speeding car?

Jose Ortega y Gassett, a Spanish philosopher, stated: "Only the hunter, imitating the perpetual alertness of the wild animal, sees everything." There is much truth to that quote.

Them City Folks.—City folks have a compulsion to get away from the city, into the country. On weekends, city dwellers head for the hills by the thousands; a mad rush to the country. Hunters also dash from the cities to the woods.

Nonhunters and hunters buy farms for the solitude that cities do not provide. Farms, once the hunters favorite hunting spot, have been subdivided into large lots with huge summer homes that encroach on wildlife habitat. Not only does this trend lead to a loss of habitat, it brings many nonhunters into direct contact with something they know nothing about - hunters and hunting seasons.

Unless the nonhunter has a friend who hunts (and fewer and fewer urbanites do), then they don't know that the horror stories, the accidental shooting stories, the poaching stories, and the trophy hunting stories are tremendously exaggerated. They have no idea that hunters love animals. They don't know that hunters are concerned about wounding, about pain, and about unethical hunters.

They have no conception about the very real place of death in nature and little knowledge about their role in the indirect killing of animals. They drive on roads built on and across wildlife habitat. They eat vegetables grown in fields that was wildlife habitat before being plowed under. Those same vegetables have been sprayed with chemicals that cause damage to wildlife.

Most animal activists have little conception of these activities, and some do not seem to care. As Stephen Budiansky stated in his very interesting book entitled "The Covenant of the Wild," "For two million years we were hunters; for ten thousand years we were farmers; for the last one hundred years we have been trying to deny it all."

Animal Rights Or Animal Welfare?—Studies now show that many young people believe in animal rights. However, it is doubtful that most young people, and adults, fully understand what this term means. Many who say they believe in animal rights, probably mean they believe in animal welfare. And "animal rights" is not animal welfare.

Animal welfare is a social movement that goes back in American history almost 100 years. It is a movement concerned with the humane treatment of animals - use animals but minimize any suffering. Animal welfare means better (more humane) treatment of animals in dog pounds, better treatment of animals used in medical research; better treatment of circus animals; of animals raised for food; of animals used in wildlife research studies; of hunted animals; of fish caught on rods and reels; and of animals in pet stores, of pets, of rodeo animals, of work dogs and horses, of seeing eye dogs, etc.

Animal rights also has roots that go back many years, but it has gained popularity in relatively recent times. For extremists, animal rights philosophy, simply put, states that *all animals have the same legal standing as humans.* Any exploitation of animals, then, is speciesism (i.e. the exploitation of one species by another) and that is morally wrong.

Animal rights does not just mean antihunting. For some, it also means the whole spectrum of animal uses; it means that animals have a right to a free life with no exploitation by humans. All uses of animals are taboo.

The difference between animal rights and animal welfare is getting attention within animal rights ranks. In an article in the January, 1992 issue of Animals' Agenda magazine (*"A Movement's Means Create Its Ends"*) Drs. Regan and Francione stated there were "profound differences between the philosophy of animal welfare and animal rights." I agree.

They pointed out that one philosophy wants to minimize suffering while the other wants to eliminate suffering. The article states that pursuing animal welfare reforms will not advance the cause of "animal rights." They noted that "welfare reforms, by their very nature, can only serve to retard the pace at which animal rights goals are achieved."

I agree with them on that point as well. If the goal is to give all animals the same rights as people, then just giving them more humane treatment won't get you these. Keeping medical research animals in cleaner cages won't eliminate having animals in cages. And that is exactly where animal rightists want society to go.

"The goal of the animal rights movement is nothing less than the *total* (emphasis added) liberation of nonhuman animals from human tyranny." Drs. Regan and Francione later stated, Animal rightists "seek to *abolish* all such exploitation in practice."

Why is the distinction between animal welfare and animal rights so important? I think the distinction is one hope for the future of hunting. For extreme animal rightists, the very definition of the terms means *no use of animals for any purpose.*

No matter what the cause or particular issue that is being argued, they want no animal use to occur. People who own and ride horses for pleasure would be out. People who own cats and dogs for pleasure or for work would end as well. Medical researchers who use animals for scientific studies that will lead to cure for human diseases would stop.

There are those who do not like a certain type of hunting, but support other uses of animals. That is not the real problem facing huntings future. No, the real problem for the future of hunting, and one that hunters must recognize, is that in situations where this extreme animal rights value system is in play, there will be no compromise.

Some people might say: "But I am an animal rightist, and I think there is some uses for animals, such as seeing eye dogs or owning a pet cat or dog, that are OK." The answer to that is simple: those people are not animal rightists, they just think that they are. In reality they are animal welfarists. True animal rightists believe that *no use of animals is good.* Wait a minute, surely that is wrong.

"I can be an animal rightist and still believe that some use of animals for medical reasons is OK, can't I?" or "I know that the leaders of the animal rights groups support some use of animals, don't they?" You decide.

The American Animal Welfare Foundation has provided a list of quotes from animal rights leaders. Here is a quote attributed to Ingrid Newkirk, Founder of the People for the Ethical Treatment of Animals (PETA), the largest, most influential animal rights group in the country. "Animal liberationists do not separate out the human animal, so there is no rational basis for saying that a human being has special rights. A rat is a pig is a dog is a boy. They're all mammals." (Vogue, September 1989).

Consider this quote from the same woman. "Six million Jews died in concentration camps, but six billion broiler chickens will die this year in slaughterhouses." (Washington Post, 1983). Does this sound like humans and chickens are being equated? In fact, doesn't this sound like Jews are even less valuable than chickens?

It is doubtful that most nonhunters will buy this value system. But it is important that the non-committed middle-of-the-road nonhunters know the implications of implementing the value system of these animal rightists.

At one point I thought the only way nonhunters would learn about this was if hunters told them. However, PETA and other animal rights groups are gaining so much press (i.e., stop all fishing, stop all uses of animals in medical research, stop all people from eating meat, stop eating lobsters, etc.) that nonhunters are getting the message.

Still not convinced about what animal rights means? How about another quote from Newkirk: "Even if animal research resulted in a cure for AIDS, we'd be against it." (Vogue, September 1989). How about this from Tom Regan, a philosophy professor at North Carolina State University when asked if he would save a baby or a dog if they were in a boat that capsized in the ocean. According to the American Animal Welfare Foundation he said: "if it were a retarded baby and a bright dog, I'd save the dog." (from question asked at seminar at University of Wisconsin, October 1989).

Assuming these quotes are accurate (many have been published over and over again), they show a disdain for human life over animal life. I submit that the average person won't buy it. The average person supports humane treatment of animals. That makes them an animal welfarist, a value system most of us can understand.

The average hunter supports the humane treatment of animals. That makes them animal welfarists. The average doctor supports the humane treatment of animals. That makes them animal welfarists. Some antihunters support the humane treatment of animals. That makes them animal welfarists.

But animal rightists support *no use of animals*, because that violates the animal's rights. The difference is huge.

Society And Hunting Trends.—Twenty-five years ago, the subject of antihunting was not mentioned very much. Today it is an indication of the further change in society, and a change in values as well. Today around 10 percent of the public are antihunting. For some in that category, their philosophy really isn't about saving wildlife or wildlife habitat, it is about a value system that differs from most Americans. It is a value system that wants to change human behavior.

So far the victories have been small ones, but the legal hassles have consumed considerable money, time, and energy of wildlife biologists; money, time and energy they could be used to help wildlife.

Chapter 1

Since 1971, hunters have lost bait and dog hunting for black bears in Colorado, Oregon, Massachusetts and Washington as well as spot-and-stalk grizzly hunts in Montana. We've lost lion hunting in California and trapping in Arizona and Colorado. We lost, then won back, bear hunting in California. At the local level we've lost some hunting in scattered townships, but because of the growth of deer herds, we've added hunting (especially bowhunting) in hundreds of suburban communities.

We've also seen added hunting opportunities on National Wildlife Refuges. And so our running battle with animal activists is a mixed bag of wins and losses, but what does the future hold?

For a perspective on the future, let's consider the words from a letter written by an antihunter and sent to me by a bowhunting friend. The thoughts expressed are fairly typical of many antihunters. The letter said: "In our effort to bring an end to the insane cruelty of sport hunters, we have embarked on a series of small incursions based on the timeless principle of divide and conquer. Our first step has been to isolate and end trapping. Our experience with trapping illustrates fatal flaws in the hunters' psyche. You must understand these to be successful. First, although they kill and eat wild animals, hunters do care about animals, but their concern is for the species and not, like ours, for individual animals. Because they actually care for animals, they are quick to condemn someone else's actions as detrimental to wildlife. So, given hunter's sentimental approach to wildlife and their tendency to vote against each other because of different techniques, what should our next target be? Hunting with hounds obviously."

From these words it's easy to see that some antihunters have focused on hunters who judge the motivations of other hunters. As a case in point, the letter writer noted that many hunters voted to abolish bait and hound hunting for bears in Colorado. He/she was right in this assertion.

And since some hunters oppose hound hunting, he/she felt the antihunting groups should target the use of dogs in hunting. It is an interesting and simple approach. Find something on which hunters disagree; focus on it, knowing that with this approach the antihunters will be joined by some hunters.

Once that facet of hunting is curbed, the antihunters simply move on to another facet, chipping away, bit by bit. Hunters should be aware of this strategy before they decide how they feel about a form of hunting in which they do not participate. For people (hunters and nonhunters) who have not been around it, hound hunting for bears and mountain lions is rather easy to portray as being cruel. Even though opposed to all hunting, some antihunters would not challenge all dog hunting because that would lead to failure.

They understand that nonhunters are not ready to vote against the use of retrievers and pointers for bird hunting. If you feel safe as a bird hunter who uses dogs, beware. The antihunter's letter pointed out that once hound hunting was stopped, they'd move on to other uses of dogs in hunting.

Why have antihunters attacked bear and mountain lion hunting? The letter suggests that since most hunters do not hunt these species, the hunters themselves may help by casting a negative vote. Their strategy will be to tell nonhunters that bears and lions are in trouble, low populations, and protection is needed. Of course, this is not true. But our letter added the kicker. Once antihunters have taken away bait and hound hunting for bears and lions, they will focus on bowhunting.

"Our next logical step is bowhunting," the antihunter wrote. "Again we have a natural chink in their armor. Many rifle hunters resent bowhunters because of our claims that a higher percentage of animals are wounded and lost with arrows than with bullets."

The writer is probably correct. Even though a recent study done by the Minnesota Department of Natural Resources showed that bow wounding losses are minimal, some gun hunters may not listen or care.

Finally the author of this letter stated that bowhunters will split their ranks over equipment and this will lead to an easy antihunter victory. The letter concluded that the way to success was simple; just take away hunting rights a little at a time. There is the chance that the letter was fictitious, but even if so, the words and thoughts are very likely what many antihunters think and feel. Certainly the issues raised should concern today's hunters.

Value Conflicts in the Antihunting Movement; An Example.—What follows is a discussion of a recent issue led by some animal activists, but probably supported by very few. I add this preface so readers can understand that not all antihunters should be judged by the extreme actions of a few.

This example occurred in 1996 relative to the Make-A-Wish Foundation, and though it generated some support it also generated much more negative media comments. The foundation granted a wish to a terminally ill Minnesota boy who wanted to hunt brown bear in Alaska with his father. Several animal rights groups, including the Humane Society of the United States, the Fund For Animals, and Ark Trust, began a major publicity campaign against Make-A-Wish.

They used the Internet and other media to attack the Foundation. The 17-year-old had a terminal brain tumor. As one newspaper noted: "had Erik wanted to go to Disney World, there would have been no reaction to the story. But Erik wanted to go hunting."

Gretchen Wyler, President of Ark Trust, said: "The foundation will never be able to sustain the damage this will do to their image, especially in the Hollywood community."

A group based in Minnesota claimed that "Make-A-Wish is out of business in Minnesota."

Jessica Glatzer, working for the Fund For Animals in Maryland, wrote: "This young man's wish, which calls for the death of an innocent bear, has the strong potential to dissuade many of your donors from continuing to give money."

Ms. Glatzer wrongly assumes that hunting is killing. (For the record, Erik did not kill a bear on this hunt. In fact 1994 success rates for Kodiak brown bear hunters were only 12.6 percent, so the hunt was pretty much guaranteed to be unsuccessful, if measured by the kill, before it began).

Few hunters measure hunt success based on the kill, and it is doubtful if a dying teenager would do so. Safari Club International (SCI) set up the hunt for Erik. A Minnesota chapter of Safari Club held a fund-raising dinner and provided all the clothing and equipment for the hunt. They also negotiated discount guide fees.

This early-May 1996 incident led to death threats and bomb threats to the Make-A-Wish Foundation. A Minnesota radio station that supported the wish of Erik received a letter stating "maybe with a little luck, the sick little bastard will croak before he kills the bear." SCI received this voice message: "Wouldn't it be poetic justice if he shot himself instead of the bear?" Some media representatives chastised animal activists for using a dying boy to advance their cause, no matter their feelings about hunting.

In late May another terminal boy asked the Pittsburgh Chapter of Make-A-Wish to hunt moose in Alaska. At this writing the Make-A-Wish Foundation is nervous. Heidi Prescott, director of the Fund For Animals, said: "we don't want to see the organization harmed, but people find it very ironic that someone so ill would want to take a life."

Two totally different perspectives on what hunting is. Prescott thinks it is killing; the young boy thinks it is hunting.

The experience these two terminally-ill boys were seeking was the same father-son experiences I had as a boy in Pennsylvania. My dad walked my brothers and me into the woods to hunt, not to kill. Our experience was in seeing wildlife, the smell of the woods, the sounds of the dawn, and yes, once in awhile there was a kill. But even if the two ill boys did kill a bear or a moose, it would be part of the Alaska wildlife department management plan that is in place for those two species.

Such management plans are designed and exist to optimize the health and well-being of the remaining populations of each of those two species. The kill is very much a part of those management plans, plans written and implemented by trained wildlife biologists who are interested in preserving and protecting moose and bears for all perpetuity. *

But if we eliminate everything that might lead to the death of animals in this country, then we'd eliminate just about everything we humans do. It seems important that we recognize that the Make-A-Wish controversy is one example of some peoples definition of what is right and wrong. And it appears that those same folks want to impose that definition on everyone.

It also appears that many animal activists give the impression at

*The Iditarod sled dog race in Alaska has been severely attacked by animal activists from the "lower forty-eight" states. They contend the dogs are suffering. Anyone who knows these dogs or have seen them, understand that they love to run. The 1996 winner was Jeff King. A terminally ill teenager (C. J. Kolbe from upstate New York) asked Make-A-Wish to ride in the Iditarod and it was granted. He rode the first seven miles of the race with Jeff King. Interesting that animal rightists did not object to this.

times that they don't care about ecosystems or wildlife. There is example after example where animal activists have taken stands that make little sense for the wildlife involved.

Example...stray cats on the campus of Florida Atlantic University killed 38 of 42 chicks of a rare species, the Burrowing Owl, that nested on the campus. When the idea of capturing and removing the cats was offered as a way to save this species, animal activists threatened to protest.

Example....black-footed ferrets were thought to be extinct in the wild. About 15 years ago a few were discovered in Wyoming, and bred in captivity so the population could reach viable levels for later release. This is a true success story for a species once thought to be extinct. The captive breeding program was very successful and several hundred ferrets were raised for release. These ferrets eat prairie dogs, their preferred diet in the wild. But when a release was planned near a prairie dog town in Wyoming, a group called Prairie Dog Rescue from Denver, Colorado sought an injunction to prevent the release.

Note, at this time there were no black-footed ferrets left in the wild. This animal is (or was) almost totally extinct. But since they eat prairie dogs, the animal rights folks thought it was not humane to release these predators into the wild. Fortunately they were released and are thriving.

Example....coyotes feeding on mice and voles in the grass beside the runways at the Kansas City

International Airport. Pilots were very concerned that a coyote might be sucked into an engine, possibly crashing 300-400 people into the ground and they pleaded for a coyote trapping program. The airport manager agreed, but animal activists protested. They suggested an alternative whereby all areas in and around the entire airport would be paved so that no mice could live there. Very unrealistic.

Around 10 percent of the population hunts and 10 percent are antihunters. Those numbers haven't changed much in recent years, but society is changing. As we will discover later, there are increasing trends towards animal rights and this means an increase in antihunting. Thirty years ago few would question a dying boy's wish to go hunting. Recently it was front-page news.

Some Hunters Values; An Example—Just as there are extremists on the antihunting side, so to are there extremists on the hunting side. Consider that in 1994, 1995 and 1996, the citizens of Minnetonka, Minnesota were involved in a major controversy involving too many deer in their urban environment. Many wanted the deer killed, but a few did not. Legal battles ensued. The city decided to conduct a trap and shoot program to reduce deer numbers.

Antihunters attempted to stop this program via legal maneuvers. During this process an unsigned letter was sent by a bowhunter to the president of the local citizens group opposed to the trapping and shooting of deer. It showed the intolerance of some hunters to anyone with opposing views.

The letter was filled with obscenities and personal attacks. Here are two quotes from the more publishable phrases: "If I ever cross paths with you while I'm legally hunting, your dead! And I'm not above taking someone out—especially a B_____ like you!"

Does this person represent most bowhunters in Minnesota? Of course not. My guess is that most would be extremely disturbed by any link with such a hunter. It does reflect the extreme polarization that can erupt in such instances and obviously made compromise all the more difficult for the parties trying to resolve the deer problem.

The Future.—During the next 25 years there will be further attacks on hunting. Whitetailed deer will continue to cause problems as suburban sprawl continues. Hunting will, continue as an accepted way to control deer populations. Bear hunting will be stopped in more states (my guess is that more western states will be attacked next). In those states where bear hunting is stopped, watch for more and more bear/human encounters followed by a backlash which will lead to a reinstatement of bear hunting as a form of population control.

Of course, mountain lion hunting will also be attacked. But here again, as more people get mauled and killed as the lions lose their fear of man, states will probably vote to open up permit hunting for lions as a form of population control and management. There is no guarantee that will happen because a vote of this nature was held in June 1996 in California (i.e. to allow mountain lion hunting to be opened up again after being stopped), and it was defeated.

There will be a continued appeal by antihunting groups to convince nonhunters that contraception is a viable way to control deer herds. Twenty-five years from now, there may be drugs to control very small, local deer herds, but the technology is very expensive, it's legality is questionable, and its impracticability will prevent the use of contraception as a form of deer control in most wild situations.

A growing number of people will focus on pain and suffering of individual animals as opposed to focusing on the needs of wildlife populations, ecosystems, and species. As more people with no real dirt under their fingernails see wildlife on television or visit a wildlife area near home, they will develop an ethical system that relates to individual animals, not to populations.

Indeed, more people will place the value of wildlife above that of people, regardless of whether such a position leads to a loss of jobs or human life. The perception by young people of life on the farm is that animals there live forever. because they want that to happen.

But that isn't what real farms are like; animals are raised on farms for human use. The perception of young people is that wild animals live forever because they want that to happen. However, wild nature is not Disney World.

Animals die in the wild and nature is very brutal at times. Beautiful, but brutal. The antihunters can file lawsuits to attain goals, they can confront hunters to attain goals and they can make headway with that approach. But at whose expense?

Are they saving individual animals while populations suffer? Absolutely the case because it happens every day.

I believe urbanization is a major factor in these philosophical differences. My state of West Virginia is very rural with only 1.7 million people. Last fall I was in Charleston, our state capital, on the first day of the rifle deer season.

Deer hunting was a major item on the evening television news broadcast. The commentator did a story on deer hunting, and indicated that the previous year he hunted from the very tree-stand shown on the broadcast. He was matter-of-fact about the presentation, no apologies, no problem because hunting was still considered the norm.

Later that night, on major network television, there was a show that discussed urban deer problems and showed people feeding the animals. Each deer was named, and they opposed killing them for any reason even though area humans were suffering and the deer population was totally out of balance with its carrying capacity.

It is a contrast in how we look at wildlife. In one situation people understood the benefits of hunting to the state and to the deer herd. In the other situation people only looked at the individual animal and were not open to any discussion that might improve the condition of the deer herd.

There is change in the wind, and it will impact not only hunting, but the wildlife agencies that have come to rely on revenues gained via hunting. These agencies evolved within a system where hunters paid the bills. Now some nonhunters want to stop hunting, and this activity causes much stress within the agency.*

City folks are calling the shots by passing referendums restricting hunting, and the agencies approach is "we'll just have to educate them about the way we have always done things."

Such education isn't happening, and it may never happen. Urban people, as all people, are part of a predator-prey system, and many don't want to recognize that. Many people are part of a million-year-old system where some animals die because of what we humans do, and they do not like being a part of that system. No amount of education will change minds here. Public knowledge of wildlife issues is pitifully lacking, and it may never improve. It makes for a very difficult job for the wildlife agencies in the future.

One key is to help citizens discover the outdoors, and learn the value of being in the woods. Many hunters have used a relatively subtle approach to bring nonhunting neighbors to the dinner table where they might learn about the hunting ways of the past.

These hunters host wild game dinners, and in so doing, nonhunters may come to understand the values of hunting and the nutritional and sociological values of perpetuating the hunting tradition. There are other programs that encourage people to go to the woods. The "Becoming-An-Outdoors-Woman" program is growing, in heavy demand, and brings more women to some forms of outdoor recreation.

Hunters are interested in their future, but for them to maintain

---

*For a great essay on how wildlife agencies should change, see *"The Wildlife Professional Subculture: The Case of the Crazy Aunt."* R. Bruce Gill. 1996. Human Dimensions of Wildlife 1   (1):60-69.

their present level of recreational hunting several things must happen. First, young wildlife biologists working for state and federal agencies must be educated about the values of hunting. More and more of these biologists do not hunt or fish. In fact, some are against hunting and fishing.

Dr. Robert Muth and his colleagues just published a most interesting paper (cited above in "Things Will Never Be The Same") and found that 18 percent of fish and wildlife biologists, professors and administrators disagreed with the statement that "the traditional North American Conservation Model (based on regulated harvest, intensive management, and sportsmanship) is still highly relevant to achieve wildlife conservation objectives in the future. In addition only 52.5 percent agreed with this statement; "Humans can harvest surplus production of wildlife and fish populations without harming their long-term population viability."

Whoa. Something is happening here that is not good for wildlife. The wildlife management system that worked so well for many years, that brought us the wildlife and fish populations we now have today, are being questioned or deleted by some of the field managers working for our state and federal wildlife agencies. More than ever it is important that these biologists understand our history.

Second, we need to be more tolerant of the beliefs of others. I want hunters and nonhunters to understand that there is another side to some arguments. Antihunters came to their attitudes honestly and believe in them as much as hunters believe in their right to hunt. Although it is sometimes hard for wildlife biologists and hunters to understand the antihunters value system, simply because it often leads to the deaths of many wild animals, we need to try to keep a dialogue open and to communicate as much as possible.

However, even thought the ideas that antihunters support make little sense to many, do not be misled. Most antihunters and animal rightists came to their attitudes against hunting the same way hunters came to their attitudes in favor of hunting. Older hunters were raised in rural environments, with hunting as part of family values and traditions.

New, younger hunters were raised in urban environments, but were given exposure to nature and hunting. It was logical for these people to hunt. Many antihunters were raised in urban environments, with no exposure to hunting or to farming where death of animals is the norm. It was, and is, logical for them to be against hunting.

Third, we need to see a continued improvement of the ethical behavior of hunters. This is critical to the future of hunting. To quote my bowhunting friend Steve Fausel, "it is through actions that integrity and professionalism become visible to the world and promote a specific point of view."

Hunters are constantly asking what they can do to fight antihunting. One way is to join the Wildlife Legislative Fund of America. They are a strong lobby for the hunter rights. Hunters also must realize that they can take the offensive position in other ways.

Host a wild game dinner for your nonhunting neighbors (for information on how to do this, get a brochure from Orion, The Hunters Institute, PO Box 5088, Helena MT 59604). Make it a community tradition. Nonhunters will relate to healthy food taken by an ethical sportsman. Take the offensive position by being sensitive to other points of view, and most important, by being totally ethical when you hunt. Practice these few simple strategies and hunting will still be a part of our culture in the years to come.

"A man may not care for golf and still be human, but the man who does not like to see, hunt, photograph, or otherwise outwit birds or animals is hardly normal. He is supercivilized, and I for one do not know how to deal with him. Babes do not tremble when they are shown a golf ball, but I should not like to own the boy whose hair does not lift his hat when he sees his first deer."

Aldo Leopold

SECTION II

HUNTERS AND HUNTING

Chapter 2. Who Are Hunters?*

With so much press coverage on endangered species, it seems that the general public is given the impression that there is no wildlife left in the country. That is a myth. The truth is that wildlife numbers today are, for the most part, at an all-time high. The main reason is that the United States has the most progressive system of wildlife management in the world. Not only is it progressive, but it is well funded. And the roots of our wildlife management system come from the work of recreational hunters who, over 100 years ago, began protecting and managing habitat and got laws passed to conserve wildlife.

The system they created through legislation—hunters having to buy licenses and also paying federal excise taxes on all hunting equipment—brings in hundreds of millions of dollars a year and it all goes to wildlife management. More hunters means more revenues for state wildlife agencies, and although hunter numbers are relatively stable, the potential for decline in coming years is real. As hunting declines, the license and excise tax revenues also decline, and this will lead to major losses in wildlife and the protection of habitat.

Today, more and more hunters are starting to hunt later in life. Parents are not teaching them to hunt at a young age and studies show that hunters who start younger and learn the outdoors from parents are more prone to be hunting later in life. The trend of starting older and learning from friends may well lead to higher rates of hunter desertion.

History of Conservation.—-I find it interesting to listen to newscasters

*portions adapted (with permission) from Aug. 1989, and Apr. 1992 "On Your Side" column, Bowhunting News; "Know Hunting" Bowhunter Magazine, Aug. 1997, Aug 1998; *"Bowhunting Big Game Records of North America."* Pope & Young Club, 5th edition 1999, Big Game Record Book.

address movie stars who espouse antihunting beliefs as "conservationists" when they barely know a deer from a cow. Actually, to do that is not only misleading, but erroneous.

Relative to wildlife and wildlife habitat, a conservationist would be a person who shows interest, devotes time and energy, and may even provide financial resources to protect, enhance, and conserve that wildlife and habitat. Truth is that the very roots of this country's conservation movement were groups composed of recreational hunters.

In the 18th and early 19th century's wildlife was in trouble. Habitat was being hammered, and market gunners were literally wiping out species. Birds were shot by the thousands for plumes to be used on women's hats. There were few game laws.

Wildlife was vanishing and in trouble.

Recreational hunters came to the rescue. Yes, recreational hunters...men and women who liked to hunt purely for recreation. In 1844, a group of very influential sportsmen formed the New York Sportsmen's Club, and they fought hard to eliminate indiscriminate shooting of birds, and to get strong game laws passed.

They led the battle to get hunting seasons established, thus creating periods during the year when no hunting was allowed. This group of recreational hunters used the term "game-killers" to describe the market shooters.

Soon there were sportsmen's clubs in other New England states and the crusade to save wildlife had its beginning...*legal recreational hunters* were the roots of conservation. Antihunters did not start the conservation movement, nor did nonhunters (though some were involved). For the most part, hunters did it. Consider what recreational hunters have accomplished.

President Teddy Roosevelt, through an interest in recreational hunting, led a charge to create legislation that saved Yellowstone National Park. The Boone and Crockett Club was formed, and members supported various pieces of legislation to save timber habitat, Yellowstone, and Sequoia National Park. The Boone and Crockett Club, and Teddy Roosevelt, also supported protection of our forests and, along with the Sierra Club, they fought to establish a national forest protection program. More parks were created at Mount Rainier and Grand Canyon (1896).

During most of the 19th century there were no game wardens, no game laws, no wildlife training programs, and no wildlife management. Some states passed laws to protect certain birds, and a few limited fish management programs were started (first federal fish hatchery was in established 1872).

In the mid-1850's, Maine hired America's first game wardens. Bag limits and hunting seasons were established on a very limited basis in a few states around 1870. If all of these activities were occurring today, one would call those involved "conservationists" and also "environmentalists." Interesting, but true...hunters were really our first large group of environmentalists.

In the late 1800's, there was a lack of good information available on the status of wildlife populations. Conservationists knew the game taken had to be replenished from the resident populations, but often they had no way other than trial and error to determine what the season length and bag limits should be.

As early wildlife managers learned more, seasons and bag limits changed. Harvest levels were lowered by new game laws. In those early days the seasons were too long and the bag limits too high. But biologists restricted the numbers of animals taken, yet allowed hunting. This led to the situation today where hunting provides the economic incentive for wildlife management.

Recreational hunters played a major role in getting conservation laws passed. During the late 1800's, many states established some form of a wildlife agency to protect game animals and birds. Some agencies evolved from sportsmen's groups. Funds for these agencies came from the general treasury.

The first hunting license law was passed in 1895 in North Dakota, and most states followed suit over the next 30 years. In 1903, President Roosevelt created the first National Wildlife Refuge in Florida. He used his executive power to protect many scenic areas such as the Natural Bridge in Utah, the Petrified Forest in Arizona and many other wildlife refuges. Roosevelt also led the fight to pass the Lacey Act of 1900, and this helped curb illegal traffic in wildlife products.

The Lacey Act was designed to stop market hunting, which it did, and to prevent the shipping of illegally taken wildlife or wildlife products from one state to another. John Reiger, in his excellent book ("*American Sportsmen and the Origins of Conservation,*" Winchester Press, 1975), notes that John F. Lacey and other "nature-lovers," "scientists" and "ornithologists" who supported passage of this act, were indeed recreational hunters.

There was great interest in the protection of birds in the early 1900's, and this was financially supported by recreational hunters. Recreational hunters wanted to see an end to market shooting, and they donated large sums of money to fight for wildlife management. Various state Audubon societies helped pass state game laws. Interestingly, hunters were major players in these bird watching societies. The roots of the National Audubon Society are tied to recreational hunters and hunting.

Commercial hunting decimated waterfowl species during this same period. Wood ducks, trumpeter swans, Labrador duck (shot to extinction), and other waterfowl species were being gunned down by market shooters. Note: these were market hunters, not recreational hunters. At that time wildlife was plentiful and groups of people killed animals and sold the meat. It was a way of life, but as wildlife populations decreased, recreational hunting took the lead in the passage of laws that led to the elimination of market hunting.

Recreational hunters led the battle to eliminate spring hunting of ducks and geese, and helped pass waterfowl bag limits and hunting seasons. During the early 1900's recreational hunters, bird lovers, and gun companies led the fight to form the state and federal agencies that manage wildlife today. Groups such as the U. S. Fish and Wildlife Service were formed at this time.

States soon were taking the hunter license monies and putting them toward wildlife management. For example, in 1917, Pennsylvania passed a hunting license bill that called for the $1 license to go to wildlife management, and that bill raised over $300,000 for wildlife management during the first year. This was a very important step in the evolution of our system of wildlife management. Wouldn't it be something if we could talk to those early Pennsylvania conservation leaders and tell them that today deer licenses alone bring in more than $12 million a year in Pennsylvania with the proceeds going to wildlife management? It's a true success story.

And so it began. Conservation became the in-thing to do. Recreational hunting provided the financial support needed to create and implement game laws. Hunters supported the imposed bag limits, and these activities began the restoration of America's wildlife.

Deer, antelope, elk, wood ducks, swans, geese, grouse, turkey, quail, etc...all species thrived under controlled recreational hunting, and recreational hunting paid for it. Recreational hunting created the need for it. Recreational hunting created the economic incentive for it. Slowly things began to improve.

We passed the Federal Aid to Wildlife Restoration Act of 1937 (more commonly known as the "Pittman Robertson Act") that placed an excise tax on firearms and ammunition. Recreational hunters encouraged passage of the bill as did the firearms industry. The monies raised are used for wildlife management, and today those monies total $155 million dollars yearly.

Aldo Leopold, the father of the wildlife management profession and the very first professor of wildlife management in 1941 at the University of Wisconsin, came on the scene, and was a major player in the evolution of conservation and wildlife management.*

As money from the Pittman Robertson excise tax rolled in, animal populations began to flourish. In the early years those funds were used mostly for law enforcement, and then for wildlife management.

Law enforcement and management led to more wildlife and a growing interest in it. This, in turn, led to a need for trained wildlife biologists and wildlife managers.

In the 1940's and 1950's, wildlife and fisheries training programs sprang up across the country. (Today there are 43 such programs in major Universities—and others in smaller schools—teaching thousands of future wildlife biologists and managers. Masters degree and doctoral degree graduate students in wildlife are conducting hundreds of research projects—much of it funded by Pittman Robertson excise tax dollars.)

Once we had trained wildlife biologists and managers, we then had the beginnings of a professional field. The field of "*wildlife management*" had to develop its own information and experience in how to manage wildlife. In so doing there were mistakes made.

Some states started "put and take" programs for pheasants and

---

*even though Aldo Leopold is quoted by antihunters as being antihunting, he was an avid gun and bow hunter. In fact Aldo Leopold hand-crafted and shot his own long bows.

turkeys. In these situations the birds were raised in captivity and then released for the hunters bag. They began under the belief this would bring back the birds. It did not...habitat was the answer. There is no put and take hunting for wild turkeys today, and most pheasant programs have been eliminated as well.

We also began massive predator control programs, thinking that predators were the main reason that wildlife populations were depressed. Wrong again, though in certain situations predators can be a problem (and there is a need for some predator control today).

The put and take and predator control programs are two examples of activities with good motivation that were changed by the experience and knowledge gained by wildlife managers and hunters.

In the mid 30's and 40's no one was concerned when hawks and owls were trapped to "protect" wildlife. Today, we realize that such trapping was not good wildlife management.

There is a superb paperback book that presents details of the growth of the conservation movement. *"An American Crusade For Wildlife"* by James Trefethen (Winchester Press) is an excellent history of the growth of conservation in the United States. Many interesting facts are found in this book. For example, in Indiana the last deer was killed in 1893, but with money from recreational hunting deer were stocked in the 1930's and, by 1951, there were over 5,000 animals. Today that Indiana herd numbers over 200,000.

When I was a kid, every few months or so, we'd spend Sunday afternoon visiting my great grandfather. He was an outdoorsman and even at age 90, would take us for long walks along trails near Markleysburg, PA. Great grandpa Brumbaugh could spin stories that would spell-bind an audience, especially green-horned kids who loved the woods. One story that is vivid in my mind relates to the paucity of deer found in central Pennsylvania in the 1800's. There were literally no deer at that time, probably due to over shooting and habitat changes during the settling of the area. Anyway, great grandpa Brumbaugh told us that his father once took him on an all-day buggy ride, just to see the track of a white tailed deer! That was really hard for us to imagine at that time. Today with a deer in everyones back yard, it seems almost impossible.

The National Shooting Sports Foundation reported that in 1900 there were less than 500,000 white-tailed deer in the United States.

Today there are more than 20 million. In 1898, only 12,000 antelope survived in the entire country, but now there are over 1 million. At the turn of the century there were about 40,000 elk, but today we have 800,000. In the 1940's we had about 1.1 million waterfowl; today...4 million. The bottom line...game species have increased under a managed program that includes legal recreational hunting.

The federal excise tax monies also are used to help states purchase and protect lands for all citizens. For example, over 1.3 million acres of state game lands (i.e. public lands) have been bought in Pennsylvania.

These lands were purchased with hunter dollars, and at least two recent studies show that nonhunters use these game lands more than hunters do. Again, recreational hunters pay their way, and the way of nonhunters as well...and do so gladly. Hundreds of other projects are paid for by hunters that lead to benefits for nonhunters. Consider the comeback of the peregrine falcon, otters, fishers, and others. Though various antihunting groups down-play the hunters' role in wildlife management, the following information, taken from a speech by Matthew Connolly, Vice President of Ducks Unlimited, is a small sample of what hunters do.

Since 1937 Ducks Unlimited has protected, enhanced or restored over 6 million acres of wetlands and associated habitats. Pheasants Forever has impacted 545,000 acres since 1987. Quail Unlimited has affected 500,000 linear miles of habitat since 1985, and the Rocky Mountain Elk Foundation has conserved over 367,000 acres since 1984. Impressive? Absolutely.

Hunter Numbers and License Sales.—-Obviously, hunter numbers are important in creating the license and tax dollars that support wildlife management. In 1955 there were about 12 million hunters, but numbers increased and peaked in 1978 at about 16.4 million .*

In 1990 there were 15.8 million licensed hunters in the United

*Most reported hunting license sale figures are below the actual number for several reasons. The U. S. Fish and Wildlife Service only reports the number of licenses sold to those 16 years and older. There are many hunters who are younger than 16 years of age. There aren't figures for hunting, but 25 percent of all fishermen are under 16.

Also, not everyone is required to buy a hunting license. It varies from state to state, but farmers and their immediate family members do not have to buy a hunting license in many states. Senior citizens are sometimes exempt as well.

On the other side, some figures are based on the number of hunting licenses sold, and not the number of hunters (though the figures reported above are individuals who bought a license, not the numbers of various licenses sold). I buy hunting licenses in at least 3 states every year, thus, I would be counted more than once in the hunting and license statistics. Even so, hunter numbers are probably higher than published figures would indicate.

States, but from 1990 to the present, numbers have shown a slight but steady decline. There were 15.34 million paid license holders in 1994, 15.23 million in 1995, 15.22 in 1996 and 14.91 in 1997. Even with this drop, it is still higher than hunter numbers in the 1960's.

For 1997, the National Shooting Sports Foundation reported that 32 states had decreases and 18 had increases in license sales. Texas, Wisconsin, Utah, and Idaho reported declines in the 7-9% range, but there is an explanation for this decline. These states either had a license fee increase (which always leads to a decline for a year or two, then a rebound), or went to an electronic point of sale system to replace manual record keeping.

Getting this electronic system installed at each retail store that sells hunting licenses led to problems that caused decreased license sales. Again, it was a short term problem and license sales will rebound.

Texas believes that its point of sale license system will lead to an increase in hunting licenses sold. With this computerized system, they will know more about the purchaser and thus be able to market their license sales programs better. Massachusetts had increased license sales in 1997, and they attribute it to an increase in turkey and deer population.

Although gun hunter numbers have declined slightly, bowhunter numbers have jumped dramatically over the past 10 years. The National Shooting Sports Foundation surveyed gun hunters in 1986 and found that 19 percent also bowhunted.

In 1991 that figure jumped to 33 percent and in 1995 it was 45 percent. The recent growth in bowhunting is rather dramatic. In 1970 there were 1.25 million bowhunters in the United States. This jumped to 2 million in the mid 1980's, and 3.3 million by 1997. Bowhunter numbers in 1993 showed Michigan with 350,000, Pennsylvania 314,000, Wisconsin 210,000, New York 170,000, and West Virginia 125,000.

What is it about bowhunting that has such an appeal? A major reason is challenge. But being able to hunt more is also important, and hunters like the bow season because it is less crowded in the woods, and more peaceful...a pleasant time to be out.

In 1980 hunters made up 9.87 percent of the United States population. In 1985 that figure dropped to 9.09 percent and by 1990 it was 8.89 percent. A 1996 publication by Tom Heberlein and Elisabeth Thomson of the University of Wisconsin (*"Changes in U. S. Hunting Participation, 1980-1990"*, in Human Dimensions of Wildlife, Vol. 1, pages 85-86, 1996) showed that male participation in hunting was: 19.5 percent of all males in 1980, 17.7 percent in 1985, and 16.4 percent in 1990. But this 3 percent drop in male hunting was offset by an increase in female participation; 1.5 percent of all hunters were female in 1980, 1.3 in 1985, 2.7 in 1990 and 13 in 1997.

Why a noticeable decrease in male participation? The authors suggest that 0.92 percent of the drop was caused by fewer people growing up in rural areas; 0.75 caused by an aging population, and 0.24 by a reduction in percent of the population that is Caucasian.

Hunter numbers by state shows Pennsylvania at No. 1 with 1,091,568. Michigan is second with 952,584 and Texas is a close third with 942,359. Then comes Wisconsin 739,345, New York 709,054, Tennessee 600,117, Minnesota 555,630, Ohio 528,703, and Missouri with 515,379 hunters.

A look at the top hunting states by listing hunters as a proportion of the total population, shows the top states to be: 1. Montana (21.3 percent), 2. Idaho (20.8), 3. South Dakota (20.3), 4. Wyoming (19.1), 5. West Virginia (17.5). The bottom states are Florida (almost 0 percent), New Jersey (1.5), Massachusetts (1.9), California (2.5), and Connecticut (2.7).

When states lose hunters, they also lose revenues, (hunting equipment, excise taxes and hunting license monies) and they lose some of the wildlife management goals they had formerly accomplished. For example: there were 184,079 big game licenses sold in New York in 1994, but it dropped to 176,870 in 1996. California hunting license sales dropped 31 percent (134,000) since 1987.

True, hunter numbers are stable or increasing in some states. But decreases are becoming more common and these drops, combined with added wildlife management responsibilities (e.g. nongame programs, endangered species work, etc.) and little or no funding to state wildlife agencies from general revenues (i.e. all taxpayers, rather than just sportsmen), have led to budget crises in some states.

In 1998 it was estimated that the Washington Department of Fish and Wildlife would have a shortfall of 19 million dollars. This means less wildlife and fish management will be accomplished, and all wildlife programs will be impacted. The Oregon wildlife agency will trim 100 jobs over the next six years to prepare for future fishing and hunting license sales decreases. In 1996-97 Idaho Fish and Game made 6 million in budget cuts and eliminated 29 jobs. When license sales drop, revenues also drop. What is most important is that wildlife and fisheries management is lost and our wildlife loses.

In recent years, females who hunt have jumped to 13 percent of all hunters. That's around 3 million women hunters, and double what we had in 1986. Why the influx of women into hunting? Heberlein and Thomson know that it was *not* caused by income, residence, or education...the cause was other personal factors.

What used to be "appropriate" behavior for women has thankfully changed. Along with this new-found freedom has come many programs aimed at making women more comfortable in the outdoors. (Interestingly, animal rights groups have tried to stop such activities).

Over 3.4 million women now participate in outdoor shooting sports, including archery, sporting clays, and trap/skeet shooting. Women are flocking to the shooting sports and to hunting, fishing and other outdoor activities.

Hunting is big business and hunters are willing to spend the money necessary to buy licenses. These state hunting licenses bring in around 440 million dollars per year (and it all goes to the state wildlife agency to be used for wildlife management).

Every spring I hunt black bear in Alberta or Saskatchewan. In May, motels near major airports are filled with hunters. Bear hunting means air tickets, motels rented, restaurants filled, and hunting clothes sold. It means the sale of groceries, gasoline, vehicle rentals, etc.

In 1999 the spring bear season was canceled in Ontario. That cancellation led to a total loss of an estimated $40 million dollars to the economy of the province. That is a ton of jobs.

Last fall my bowhunting partner, Dick Krynicki, and I decided to try for woodland caribou in Newfoundland. Not ten years ago cod fishing was the major employer in Newfoundland. Today that is all but gone. The loss of cod fishing has caused hard times in that region and replacing those lost commercial fishing jobs has top priority. While commercial cod fishing is down, wildlife populations are very healthy. Thus in recent years the Department of Tourism has been promoting hunting in a big way.

Newfoundland has some unique and abundant big game species that appeal to many hunters. Of special note are the woodland caribou, moose, and black bear. The woodland caribou is especially unique because it is found in few places in North America. With great hunting and fishing opportunities, lodges are springing up all over the country.

For our woodland caribou hunt, Dick and I flew from Pittsburgh to Newark, to Halifax, Nova Scotia, and then on to Gander, Newfoundland. Our hosts from Pine Ridge Lodge picked us up in a float plane for a short thirty-minute flight to Deer Pond. The camp was totally remote, beautiful, and the caribou were there. It was mid-October, the peak of rutting (mating) activity for the caribou. We saw moose, bear, and lots of woodland caribou. Because of the rut, we got to see bulls fighting over harems. This obviously made our time in the field exciting.

On the second day Dick and his guide got close to a dandy bull and just after it had lost a fight with a larger bull, Dick made a good shot and harvested that animal. Two days later I also got a beautiful bull. We saw no other hunters and the bush experience was memorable. Fog prevented us from leaving the lodge for three days. Socked in...not atypical weather for that time of the year in Newfoundland. Again, just part of the outdoor experience.

Dick and I observed first hand how these lodges create much-needed jobs. Our camp had three guides, plus the cook, and Pine Ridge had two other such lodges in other locations. This spring I hunted bear in Newfoundland at Owls Nest Lodge. They have 12 such lodges throughout the country. Again, jobs there, but also airline tickets, motels in and out, rental cars, gift shops, meat packing and shipping....a major boost to the economy of Newfoundland....and since management is being done properly, the wildlife resource is renewable every year.

Chapter 2

When Dick and I got back to Gander, all flights to the states were packed with hunters who had also been fogged in. We stayed in the Comfort Inn and it was filled with hunters. In fact all Gander motels were filled with hunters. The staff at the front desk indicated that hunters were their major clients in the fall months. Hunting provides a major economic boost in Newfoundland.

Hunting and fishing creates many jobs, generates plenty of tax revenues, and has a huge trickle-down economic impact in your home state. But politicians and others often ignore these facts.

Melinda Gable, Deputy Director of the Congressional Sportsmen's Foundation, gave a paper at the 1998 Governor's Symposium on North America's Hunting Heritage in Pennsylvania that put a new spin on the economic impacts of hunting, fishing and trapping.

For example, we know the U. S. Fish and Wildlife Service is a big federal agency. So is the Bureau of Land Management, the National Biological Survey and the National Park Service. But if you took all the federal tax revenues generated by sportsmen, you could pay the budgets of all those federal agencies combined...for two years.

WalMart is the largest Fortune 500 employer in the United States, but sportsmen support more than twice as many jobs as WalMart. In Texas sportsmen support more jobs than Exxon, the largest state employer. Sales tax revenues generated by West Virginia sportsmen could pay the state's entire parks and recreation budget.

Retail sales generated in Idaho by sportsmen is equal to the value of their potato production. The retail sales generated in Utah by sportsmen is 1.5 times greater than that's states beef production. Sales of hunting and fishing equipment, motels, gas, vehicles, etc. in Alabama is double the value of that states cotton crop.

If hunting and fishing were a corporation, it would rank 10th on the Fortune 500 list. Whoa...look at these facts. The economic values of hunting and fishing are staggering.

It is interesting to compare hunter participation to the amount of participation in other sports. The National Sporting Goods Association reported the following figures in the March 1994 issue of Outdoor Life. When comparing number of participants of all outdoor sports, hunting ranks ninth. In fact, with around *16 million hunters* the ranking

54

is right behind *tennis with 17 million;* way ahead of *skiing with 11 million;* and ahead of *cross country skiing with 3.5 million.* There are 24 million golfers and 22 million joggers. More people hunt than ski, and hunter numbers are not far behind golfers and joggers.

So, considering all available data, the conclusions for hunter numbers are that total numbers are currently declining slightly, but are higher than in the 1960's. However, these numbers are destined to decline unless recruitment takes place.

Hunters, as a percent of the total population, are down; male hunters, as a percent of the total male population are down, female hunters are up; and bowhunter numbers are increasing. License revenues used for wildlife management are at an all time high.

Hunters and Hunter Attitudes.—-Hunters, on an average, are 43-years-old, and as with the general population, their average age is growing older. As many as 40 percent have college degrees, and that percentage is rising. Their average income is $43,120 and that too is rising. One 1997 study showed that over 20 percent of all hunters earned over $50,000 a year (see Floyd, M. F., and J. H. Gramann. 1997. *Implications For Market Segmentation of Hunters.* Leisure Sciences 19:113-127).

Ten years ago the majority of hunters were rural, blue-collar workers, but today there are just as many white-collar and urban-based hunters. Eighty-three percent were introduced to hunting by family members; 59 percent by their fathers.

Bowhunters average 36 years of age, they earn an average of $42,000, have some college education and 35 percent come from small cities/towns, 38 percent from rural areas. They began bowhunting at an average age of 21.7 years. Only 32.9 percent were introduced to bowhunting by family members; and only 16.5 percent of those were fathers (1997 study by Southwick Associates, Alexandria, Virginia).

In 1979, Dr. Stephen Kellert at Yale University did a massive study to learn more about what all people think about animals. He surveyed people in every state, and categorized our beliefs into many different attitude types. Dr. Kellert learned that *hunters have three different attitudes.* This means that our view of hunting and our perspective of hunting, is centered around these three attitudes.

In essence, these attitudes best describe why hunters hunt. Now understand that no one hunter has a makeup that is completely of one attitude type. Most hunters have a mixture of all three. Let's consider these three hunting attitudes.

First, there is the *utilitarian* attitude (more commonly referred to as "meat" hunters), which means that animals are to be utilized, or used, by man...i.e, they have "utility" to man. This doesn't mean that wild animals were put here for us to abuse, but it does mean that we use the meat for food, use the fur for clothes, leather, etc.

This attitude led to the settling of the west through the trapping of beaver. It led to domestication of wild animals too. It led to the use of wild animals for meat as well. In colonial days, and for many years thereafter, this attitude was literally the only attitude toward animals that existed. Our grandparents almost all had a utilitarian attitude toward animals. They came from the farm, and farmers are utilitarians. Christians are too, for the Bible teaches that man is above animals, that they are not equals, and that animals were put here for man to use. The utilitarian attitude toward hunting is the most common attitude type among hunters, but it is much more common in older hunters, and this attitude type is decreasing rapidly.

Second, there is the *dominionistic* hunter attitude (more commonly referred to as "recreational hunters"), which means that Man has dominion over animals. The recreation hunter as well as the trophy hunter, fit under this heading. Note that this attitude does not mean that man is cruel to animals just because he/she has dominion over them (though some would suggest this is the case).

The third hunter attitude type is the *naturalistic* attitude (more commonly referred to as the "nature" hunter). This attitude means that the hunter is interested in all nature, not just the animal being hunted. This hunter attitude is definitely the least understood.

The nature hunter hunts to "get back to nature." This person wants to become part of nature, and to get within nature to observe it. Killing is a minimal part of the hunt for the nature hunter.

Don't misunderstand: the kill is the goal for hunting, even for the nature hunter, but the nature hunter doesn't require a kill to have a quality day in the field. Nature hunters are different than meat or recreation hunters. They are younger, tend to be white collar workers rather than blue collar, and they tend to come from cities rather than rural environments.

Causes For Hunter Desertion.—-Dr. Dan Decker is one of the top wildlife research professors in the world. His human dimensions research is second to none, and he is widely recognized and honored in the wildlife profession. Dr. Decker and his cohorts at Cornell University recently published a paper about the recruitment and retention of hunters ("*Factors Affecting The Recruitment And Retention Of Hunters*: *Insights From New York*," 2 th Congress of the International Union of Game Biologists, 1991). They classified two types of hunters; traditional hunters who come from families and environments where hunting has always been a way of life, and experimental hunters who do not have a strong cultural tie to hunting.

Decker found problems with experimental hunters, and all of the problems stem from one main factor...many experimental hunters do not come from hunting families. There is very little hunting tradition in these hunters' lineage. The family tree of the experimental hunter is devoid of hunting tradition and therein lies the problem.

Experimental hunters come from cities while many hunters come from rural backgrounds. Then who teaches these people how to hunt? Many learn from friends...not fathers or other relatives. This means that they enter the sport without any of the benefits that traditional hunters received. And without those benefits, desertion rates could be higher than for traditional hunters.

As a child whose first hunting with my father was for squirrels there were rules, and my brothers and I paid attention. To violate any ethical or legal rule, meant no squirrel hunting the next weekend. At 13, such a threat was more than enough to guarantee that we paid attention. When you learn from a friend, there is no such penalty. Instead of an ethics lesson, each hunt is more like a social gathering. Two very different environments.

Equally important, peer-recruited hunters lack a strong family support system or mentoring system. There is no one—family or peers—available on a stable continuing basis to teach and reinforce their activity so they drop out of the sport. However, if they do have a good nonfamily mentor with appropriate ethics, they are probably just as likely to learn as if their father had introduced them to hunting. Finding such a mentor is the critical missing link.

Another disadvantage for experimental hunters is the age when they start to hunt. Experimental hunters who learn from friends, usually start hunting at an older age, while most hunters who learn from parents begin at age 12 or less.

A hunter who starts at age 25 or so (instead of 12), learns to hunt from friends (rather than father), and there is no family hunting tradition to lead them in the proper direction. Thus, they are not as successful as other hunters.

When we consider that many young boys and girls want to go into the woods to hunt (but do not have family to take them); when we consider that many people who now live in large cities want to escape to the woods and go hunting (but do not have family to take them); we quickly realize that there is a whole new group of hunters out there who need nurturing, help and education so that they remain in hunting. They make mistakes and some sportsman might judge them as unethical. I think that is a hasty decision.

I believe they are well-meaning, interested hunters who just need some help; the kind of hunting education many of us received from our parents. As time passes there will be many more new and different "types" of hunters, and active hunters must be prepared to work with them.

Dr. James Applegate at Rutgers University also has looked at hunter desertion ("*Patterns Of Early Desertion Among New Jersey Hunters*", Wildlife Society Bulletin 17:476-481, 1989). Hunters, in one year, who did not purchase a license the next year were presented a series of reasons for dropping out of the sport. The following table shows the top reason selected was the former hunters found other forms of recreation they would rather pursue.

The second reason was there were too many other hunters, and the third related to finding a good place to hunt. Sixty-three percent wrote in their own answers and indicated they quit because they did not have enough time or did not have the interest. Note that economics ("I don't have equipment") and philosophy ("people disapprove of hunting") were the least important reasons for quitting. Age was also a factor. Sixty-eight percent of hunters who started before age 14 were still hunting five years later. For those who started after age 14, only 38 percent were still hunting. There was no relationship to desertion by gender, education, or population density of the former hunters current residence. Nor was there a relationship with desertion and available hunting lands, which is a most interesting find.

Reasons Former Hunters From New Jersey Did Not Purchase A Hunting License

(sampled 296 hunters)

Reason	Very	& Not Important
Other things I like better than hunting	55 %	45 %
Too many other hunters	66	33
No good hunting places	34	66
Hunting is more expensive than I thought	26	84
Don't like to kill animals	21	79
Hunting not as much fun as I thought	20	80
Can't get anything while hunting	18	82
No one to hunt with	16	84
Don't have equipment to hunt	12	88
Some people I know disapprove of hunting	11	89

The above: copyright permission was granted by the The Wildlife Society.

There also were cultural relationships to desertion. If the hunters family hunted, then they tended not to desert the sport. If the hunter hunted with his/her father during their first hunting season, they did not desert (62 percent of those who did not desert hunted with father the first season, 45 percent of those who did not desert did not hunt with fathers during first season). If you hunted with a friend during your first hunting season, the tendency was to desert.

And this is a most interesting finding from this study. Hunters who killed game early in their hunting careers often stayed in hunting. For example, 78 of 95 hunters (82 percent) who killed a deer during their first five years of hunting, continued in the sport while only 46 percent of those who were unsuccessful for five years continued with the sport.

Hunters who started out when they were older tended to stay in the sport if they were successful during their first five years of hunting. Dr. Applegate concluded that new hunters with a strong family hunting heritage, and who started when young, stayed in the sport longer. Those who began hunting later in life, without a strong family hunting heritage, dropped out unless they had some early hunting success.

Causes For The Trends In Hunter Numbers.—-Hunter numbers are fairly stable, but the future trend will be down, even though women hunter numbers are increasing. Utilitarian hunters are decreasing. Nature hunters are increasing.

Demographics in this country do not bode well for hunter numbers to be maintained from traditional sources. The male population in ages 13-23, the pool from which two-thirds of hunters would be drawn, is decreasing. In 1987 the number of males in this group was 88 percent of what it was in 1981. In 1993 it was 75 percent.

The National Shooting Sports Foundation reported that in 1986 over 17 percent of all hunters were between the ages of 18-24, but in 1995 only 8 percent were in that age bracket. Hunters aged 25-34 also dropped from 31 to 17 percent. And a new, unpublished bowhunting study to be released soon shows that only 15 percent of bowhunters from a midwestern state were taught by their fathers; 30 percent were self-taught and 33 percent were taught by friends. So, there are high school and college-aged boys, girls, men, and women who want to hunt but have no mentors.

Other data confirms that at present, new hunters are coming from older age categories. In New York in 1978, 30 percent of new hunters were 20-years-old or older. In 1983, 43 percent were 20-plus. Since we know that hunters who start when older often drop out of the sport at a higher rate, this too does not bode well for hunting's future. In 1978 one-third of the new hunters came from cities; in 1983 it was up to one-half. Again, the city hunter has a higher drop out rate.

Steve Bissell, Mark Duda, and Kira Young published a paper in 1998 (*"Recent Studies on Hunting and Fishing Participation in the United States,"* Human Dimensions of Wildlife 3 (1): 75- 80) that showed hunter dissatisfaction was caused by poor access to hunting lands, loss of habitat, work obligations, poor behavior of other hunters, and too many hunters in the field.

Hunters became inactive because of less free time, lost interest, too much work to do, family activities, and the perception of causing pain to animals. They also concluded that antihunting activities did not seem to impact participation by hunters.

Though hunter numbers are stable, they will begin to drop unless new recruiting takes place. We are moving from a rural traditional hunter to a modern-day situation. The pressures of living in today's society—and there are many—are still being resolved and soothed by going to the woods.

But the realities of living in an urban environment means that people have less access to the woods. The 1996 *"National Survey of Fishing, Hunting, and Wildlife-Related Recreation"* done by the U. S. Fish and Wildlife Service showed that the number of bird watchers and wildlife photographers has dropped by 17 percent over the past five years (76 million participants to 63 million).

Indeed, times have changed and they will never be the same again. But, relative to hunting, the new days will only be as good as the old days IF we understand the society we live in; and, if hunters meet the challenge of introducing nonhunters and potential hunters to the outdoors and nature.

We have a situation where women have become more involved in the shooting sports, and many have moved from shooting to hunting. This trend should continue.

Society is starting to show a concern with the loss of rural values, and there is a desire to "return to nature." Hunting is a part of our human spirit and heritage that many are finding useful in dealing with the uncertainties of today's urban environment.

Developmental Stages and the Specialization of Hunters.—-The late Dr. Robert Jackson was the leading researcher of our time on hunter education. He was on the faculty at the University or Wisconsin at LaCrosse, and his work was superb. He and I worked together on bowhunter education projects. We worked together to plan the Western Bowhunting Conference following the successful Midwestern Bowhunting Conference that he organized in 1983. He died of cancer in 1994, but his work lives on.

In a classic study Bob proposed that hunters go through developmental stages; these stages are not cast in cement (Jackson, R. Norton, and R. Anderson. 1979. *"Improving Ethical Behavior in Hunters."* Trans North Am. Wildlife Nat. Resource Conf. 44: 306-318). There may be discrepancies; every hunter may not fit the developmental sequences that Dr. Jackson proposed. And although he matched the stages to age of the hunter, that too can vary. There is a tendency for these stages to occur, but they are not inviolate. But, for many of us, it is easy to relate our personal experience to the stages that Dr. Jackson proposed.

These stages were: *Shooter Stage, Limiting-Out Stage, Trophy Stage, Methods Stage, and Mellowing-Out Stage.* The shooter stage is typical of young, beginning hunters.

They plink away with B-B guns or .22 rifles and enjoy using the equipment. Then, a few years into hunting, they become concerned about getting their limits.

I remember that well about squirrel hunting when I was in high school. Many of my classmates hunted, and the very first two questions asked on a fall Monday morning were: "Did you go squirrel hunting Saturday?, Did you get your limit?"

It was obvious we had passed through the Shooter Stage to the Limiting-Out Stage. It is during these early stages of hunting that young hunters need guidance and education from older friends and mentors to help them maintain a proper balance between ethical hunting behavior and filling the bag at all costs.

(Interesting too, it is this same time of life when young people need guidance from older friends and mentors in all aspects of their growing lives.) Without proper education and guidance during these early stages, ethics and legal violations can occur as peer pressure leads beginners into doing things they should not do.

Once limits are obtained, then there is the quest for larger animals...the Trophy Stage. As a hunter ages, he/she becomes involved with various aspects of the hunt, i. e., the various methods to call turkeys, stalk game or use tree stands. Finally, somewhere around the age of 37-40, hunters mellows out. The kill becomes less important, enjoying the outdoors is the focus.*

Note, these shooting stages were really just Dr. Jackson's theories, and he did not have time to nail them down before he died. There is a tendency for these stages to occur, but there are also exceptions.

Some hunters might skip earlier stages with proper mentoring. It is easy for me to envision the nature hunter, who starts hunting later in life, skipping the shooter and limiting-out stages of hunting and not trying various forms of hunting (e.g. squirrel hunting, rabbit hunting, deer hunting with gun, bowhunting).

Instead, they may well have a close friend who bowhunts for

---

*It is also at this time that some hunters "burn out" and stop hunting; similar to behavior found in most forms of outdoor recreation.

deer, and it is there they start hunting - - - right in the Methods Stage. We won't know if this occurs until we do some research in this area.

Dr. Jackson emphasized that hunter education can be used to get hunters through the early stages faster, bringing them to the mature stages where fewer violations occur. He also noted that fines do not improve hunter ethics, but that peer pressure is the key. (Probably no different than other human activities). He also suggested that hunters set examples, refuse to hunt with those, even if they are friends, who violate laws. Such conduct will change other hunter behaviors better than any other approach.

Beginning hunters will benefit from a mentor who is in the "mellowing-out" stage. Mature, ethical teachings help hunters pass through the Shooter Stage and Limiting-Out Stage. In fact, mature, ethical teachings will probably shorten or eliminate those stages for some hunters.

Dr. Jackson noted that Aldo Leopold stressed that responsible hunters impose restrictions upon themselves. Individual value systems dictate most aspects of our lives, including how we hunt. Research shows that to raise an individual from one level of ethical behavior to a higher plateau involves being around a person who is at that higher level. So, who you hang out with, and who you hunt with is critical to development of a strong ethical value system while hunting or doing anything else for that matter.

Peer pressure from a higher level is what leads individuals to act more ethically. Dr. Jackson stated: "it's time hunters become activists in demanding ethical behaviors of their peers, and in recognizing and reinforcing quality of behavior rather than quantity of bag." Well said.

"In a civilized and cultivated country, will animals only continue to exist at all when preserved by sportsmen. The excellent people who protest against all hunting and consider sportsmen as enemies of wildlife are ignorant of the fact that in reality the genuine sportsman is, by all odds, the most important factor in keeping the larger and more valuable wild creatures from total extermination."

Theodore Roosevelt

Chapter 3

Why People Hunt*

For one million years man has hunted, both for protein and for pleasure. Today people hunt for the challenge and to escape to the outdoors. These are the same reasons people hike, ski, mountain bike, or take nature photos. All of these outdoor recreational activities have a goal. But because the goal of hunting is a kill, should we then stop that activity?

An easy answer to that question is "yes," but then we ignore the one million years of human evolution as a hunter. We ignore the spirituality of hunting long felt by early man and more recently by Native Americans as they evolved. Just as nonhunters do not appreciate that spirituality, some modern-day hunters do not appreciate the spirituality of the hunt. Such hunters provide fuel for antihunting fires. If hunting is to survive, hunters and nonhunters will have to understand our evolutionary roots, and hunters will have to exhibit ethical behavior at all times when in the field.

Motivations To Hunt.—At least 16 studies report why people hunt. Most show the same major factors. The top three reasons—not in order—are nature, escapism and companionship.

Nature; being close to nature, smelling the woods, hearing the sounds of the woods, these are major factors in hunting. Escapism; getting away from everyday problems, from civilization the escape is important for man. Companionship; being with friends and family, your companions also are important.

Challenge is another top reason listed in many studies. Bagging game is also a factor, but few studies show it to be important. However,

*portions adapted (with permission) from "On Your Side" columns, Bowhunting News, Aug. 1989, Nov. 1991, May 1993, and from *The Spirit of Hunting*, Pennsylvania Sportsman Nov. 1993 and *The Spirituality of Hunting*, Pennsylvania Sportsman Dec. 1993.

bagging game must be present, or at least possible, otherwise we are talking about an armed hike rather than hunting.

A recent phone survey conducted by Responsive Management of Harrisonburg, Virginia showed that 43 percent of hunters hunted for recreation, 25 percent for meat, 21 percent to be close to nature, and 12 percent to be with friends and/or family. (Understand that if not given just one choice, most hunters would select all of these reasons, to one degree or another, for why they hunt).

Again we turn to Dan Decker and his excellent human dimensions research group at Cornell University for more answers. They asked hunters: "What satisfied you most about hunting?" The answers were:

1. Getting outdoors and relaxing.
2. Seeing deer.
3. Hunting with family and friends (companionship).
4. Bagging game.
5. Experiencing family/friends bagging game.

Drs. Jodi Enek and Dan Decker determined that there were three major *motivations to hunt,* and the motivations varied between seasons. (Enek, J.W. and D.J. Decker, *"Differing Perceptions of Deer Hunting Satisfaction Among Participants and Experts."* Northeast Wildlife 51: 35-46, 1994). These motivations were achievement, affiliative and appreciative.

Achievement motivated hunters set their own standard for performance and are very motivated, i.e., they want to achieve things, and do things, before, during and after the hunting season.

The affiliative motivation for hunting is based on the camaraderie with family and friends to strengthen relationships i.e., they want to affiliate with friends and family.

The appreciative hunter wants to relax, enjoy nature, escape, get away from the details and problems of everyday life. They want to take time to appreciate nature and wildlife.

The reasons hunters hunt are really no different than the reasons people engage in other forms of outdoor recreation. Nature, companionship, escapism, and challenge are why people hike, white-water raft, mountain bike, ski, take pictures of wildlife, mountain climb, backpack, camp, and hunt.

Thus, when looking at all these studies we can see there are many reasons why hunters hunt. It doesn't take long to realize that killing an animal, harvesting game if you will, is not the major satisfaction. It bothers some hunter friends of mine that they, as hunters, are criticized for "killing animals for the sport." They do not do that. They hunt for recreation, they do not kill for recreation. Killing animals is not hunting.

True, when they shoot an animal, it is dead. The hunter takes it home, cleans it, butchers it, freezes it and later consumes it, but there are many more days when they are not successful. It is easy for most hunters to understand that although the kill must be a part of the hunt, at least sometimes, there are many other factors that are more important than a kill. It is not so easy for nonhunters to see that the kill is not important.

Some suggest that if nature, companionship and escapism are reasons hunters enjoy hunting, why not take pictures of wildlife instead? Wildlife photography gets you into the woods and nature, and can help you "escape" from the day-to-day drudgery of life.

Indeed, nature photography has some of the same drives and motivations common to recreational hunting. Both hunters and photographers must scout an area for animal sign. Both must be able to stalk and get close to an animal. Both are "hunters" and have roots in "hunting" that go back a million years. One does not eat a photo, but one does display a trophy photo. A Michigan State University study shows that experienced members of the National Audubon Society were utilitarian—they wanted state game areas to be managed so people could have access to habitat and "bag their sightings" via a photograph. Not really unlike the hunter....almost.

Though hunting and wildlife photography are similar, there is one huge difference. Once the animal is found, and once you are close, the photographer shoots his/her picture and the animal walks, runs or flies away, while the hunter shoots the animal, and ends its life. The equipment is different, as are the results.

The fact that one part of hunting is the kill, is why hunting differs from hiking, photography and all other outdoor sports. The kill is a goal, an uncertainty only attainable in certain instances. The hiker or photographer also has that uncertain goal; i.e., a mountain peak, or a picture of a large elk walking into a sunset.

There's uncertainty there. You may hike along an unfamiliar trail

Chapter 3

Motivations To hunt during the preseason, the season, and the post season.

(From Enek and Decker 1994.)

MOTIVATION	PRESEASON	DURING SEASON	POST SEASON
Achievement	Buying hunting equipment Sighting in rifle	Seeing deer Shooting at deer Bagging a deer	Butchering deer Eating venison Tanning deer hides
Affiliative	Sharing stories before the hunt Talking over deer hunting strategies with family and friends	Hunting with family members Hunting with friends Helping others in the woods	Sharing venison with others Reminiscing about the hunt with friends
Appreciative	Seeing other wildlife while scouting for deer Gaining a feeling of relaxation while scouting for deer Gaining a sense of belonging to the environment	Taking advantage of early season opportunities that offer less crowded Seeing other wildlife while hunting deer	Hiking or skiing to favorite deer stand in the off-season Personal reflection

to that peak; the sun may set before the elk is in the proper position for a good picture; that big buck you watched in early fall may never again show up in the same general area you scouted.

Remove the goal, or remove the uncertainty of the goal, and you lose the experience. Guarantee a hunter a deer every time he/she hunts, and most would not hunt again. Remove all chances for success always, and again the hunter would quit.

Guarantee a photographer a prize winning photo on every shot on every roll of film and he/she would get bored very quickly with photography. It is like a gambler using a slot machine. The "romance of Las Vegas" is the uncertainty that attracts thousands of people to the casinos. So it is with hunting and other outdoor recreational activities.

I have shot bows since I was 10 years old, and bowhunted since

I was 13. Gun hunters like the challenge, same as bowhunters. But they also hunt for companionship, while bowhunters tend to be loners. Seeing wildlife, being in the woods alone, and escape to nature are also top reasons for bowhunters to hunt. The kill and being with other bowhunters (i.e. companionship) rank at the bottom of the many reasons for bowhunting.

Appreciating The Wild.—-The rustling sound in the leaves caught my attention, but oddly enough, the sound was coming from above me in the trees. I slowly twisted in my treestand and scanned the skies. I finally located the creature making the noise - an owl. No, it was more than that, it was that serene, silent, majestic bird of the far north, the great gray owl. What a sight. I watched him flutter from tree to tree for thirty minutes as he searched for the many small mammals that scurried about on the forest floor. Slowly he moved out of my line of sight and when no longer in view, I felt a bit disappointed. Seeing the owl was an exhilarating experience for me, as it would be for many.

I saw that owl on a black bear hunt in northern Alberta. Bear hunting means many long hours in a tree stand near a bait site. Nonhunters often wonder how hunters can spend so much time on a stand without getting bored.

My wife has questioned me on this point more than once: "David, how can you stay in one spot for hours without seeing game, with nothing to do?"

My answer is simple. Even when the hunted species are not around, when you are in the woods, there is always something to see and to appreciate. Hunters value aesthetics.

And if there are no creatures visible then I think about what I might see the next instant, what I might *expect to see*, what surprise may be in store as I sit in my stand. My hunt is full of questions.

What trail will the deer or bear walk down? Will it be a big animal? What time will it appear? Will the same buck I saw last week in this area, reappear again? It is these expectancies that make hunting so exciting for many of us (and something nonhunters and antihunters do not recognize).

I love to see wildlife when I hunt, but I enjoy the sounds of the wind in the leaves, hearing the acorns fall and the distant call of a crow as well. Hunters love wildlife and all nature. In that regard we are no different than nonhunters (though some believe the knowledge of wildlife gained while spending so much time in the woods may give hunters a greater understanding for wild creatures).

People in general like wildlife. Go to the main intersection of the city where you live and stop the next 100 people that pass by. Show them a photo of a wild animal (any mammal or bird) and then show them a photo of a tree, and ask which one they like best. Most will pick the animal.

I know I would, but why? Why do we have more appreciation for wild animals than trees (even though we love trees)? Dr. Holmes Rolston, a philosophy professor at Colorado State University, wrote a paper on our aesthetic relationship to wildlife ("*Beauty and the Beast: Aesthetic Experience of Wildlife*", from the book, Social and Economic Values, 1987).

Dr. Rolston pointed out one reason we get so excited about seeing wild animals is because *animals move*. Rolston discussed this animal movement relative to feeding behavior.

He pointed out that predators move, and when the prey moves just as fast as the predator, there is more excitement. Anyone who has watched a film of a leopard chasing an impala, senses a feeling of excitement.

Somehow it is less exciting to watch a deer feed on plants. We want more wildlife, more movement, more excitement. Another factor that makes wildlife watching so enjoyable is the *potential* for movement. That big old aspen in the lower meadow is always there. Even when an owl is perched on a limb, it is more exciting than the tree, because we *know* it will move. Every time you return to the lower meadow that aspen is there. That great gray owl may never be there again.

Hunters don't remember the aspen because it is there. They remember it because a six-point buck walked beside it last year, or 10 years ago. They didn't expect to see a buck that evening but he showed, and walked beneath the tree, and they were excited; they will always remember it.

Dr. Rolston believes that television and nature photography, and even wildlife art, are not good substitutes for seeing the real wild creature. My inner soul has always felt that way, but I could not put those feelings into words. Rolston says that art and photos remove the surprise, and the same with zoos, or pet animals. "The motion has been tamed," is the way Rolston phrased it. I agree with him; the taming of what once was a wild animal definitely takes something away from the excitement of seeing that animal. There is no way a domesticated cow is as exciting as seeing a wild bighorn sheep. As Ted Nugent would say, the "spirit of the wild" has been removed.

Zoos have always bothered me, even the good ones. Now mind you, I'm not anti zoo, for I know there is a value there, even if just for a family of urban dwellers to see an animal they might never get a chance to see. But to watch a bear rub continually on a tree or pole in his/her cage and, as a bear hunter who has observed many bruins in the wild, to know that such continual rubbing is abnormal. It makes watching them difficult.

There is something very sad about the sight of a majestic wild creature in a cage, pacing or rubbing. It contrasts with the feelings of imagining the same creature, somewhere in the wild, every hair on end, nostrils in the wind, sniffing for signs of intruders; eyes moving, ears twisting and turning; huge body flowing with the grace of a dancer. Hunters who watch animals in the wild combine their real nature experience with observed behavior, and when that is accomplished, there is learning. Seems a far cry from what we see in zoos. Again, some "spirit of the wild" has been removed.

Hunters have always learned while spending time in the woods. For thousands of years it meant survival, but today hunters still learn about the species they hunt. It might be something simple, such as, "here's a new deer trail I didn't know was in this area."

Regardless, my guess is that hunters always learn something when in the woods. If you are a hunter, how often do you find yourself asking the question "what scat is that or what made that track or what species of bird is that?"

Now we'll tie all this in to what Rolston discussed in his article. He noted that behind all this ability that animals have to move, to call and see and react, is a wild animal's struggle for survival. Animals are free to move about, but there is a life and death struggle involved with that movement.

Survival of the fittest is coupled with aesthetics. And hunters, as they sit in treestands or ground blinds, observe this activity and learn from it. In so doing they build up immense reservoirs of memories.

I love to see deer, but love to see big bucks even more. Recall all the deer you've seen.

It's hard isn't it? Now recount the three biggest bucks you've seen. It's much easier to remember and what vivid memories they are.

Those big bucks pass on traits to their offspring that will lead to higher survival. Hunters observe those behaviors, and not only do they watch them, but they write them down in a diary and review them. They'll mentally study what they saw before the next hunt, and in so doing they increase their knowledge of, and appreciation for, that animal. And hunters have been studying and appreciating and gaining knowledge about wildlife for over one million years.

Hunters do not appreciate wildlife any more than some of the antihunters or nonhunters who walks in the woods, study the animals and are knowledgeable about them. But hunters do see and think of wildlife differently and that is one reason they hunt and support wildlife management.

Man, The Hunting Animal.—-Hunters have always had trouble expressing exactly why they hunt. For years I've heard hunters comment that hunting was "something they had to do,"...that they couldn't explain why, but it was just "in their blood." I would be totally skeptical of such comments except that deep down inside of me I too have a constant gnawing and questioning...at times I had that same "in the blood" feeling as well. There was no compulsion to kill, but there certainly was a desire to hunt.

These feelings recently reached a peak for me. I've come to realize there is something to this "in the blood" feeling. It started in May, 1991 at a hunter education workshop in New Hampshire. I was one of four members of a hunter education panel; the star of the panel was George Butler.

You don't recognize the name? I didn't either. George is President of White Mountain Films, and in 1990 he released the film, "*In The Blood.*" Still don't recognize the name? Well, lets try this. One of George Butlers first films was "*Pumping Iron*" and he followed that very successful venture with "*Pumping Iron II.*"

Now you know the name, but the man is not your average

Hollywood film director and writer. George Butler is a hunter and his film, *"In The Blood"* is about Man The Hunter. This film is about man's roots; man's roots as a hunting animal.

Everyone knows that for over 95 percent of the thousands of years that humans have evolved, they did so as hunting animals. (Of course there are some people who would like to forget that their forefathers were hunters, but it is a fact nonetheless). There are hundreds of articles and books that detail our evolution as hunting animals.

Butler's film is about Man The Hunter, but it is also about African safaris. Being raised in Kenya helped George's perspective, but history provided the backdrop. This film is actually about two safaris.

The first was in 1909 and was taken by President Teddy Roosevelt. Butler uses black and white footage from the Smithsonian Institute that was taken on that safari to help tell his story.

The second safari features exceptional footage of a modern-day safari under the tutelage of Robin Hurt, professional hunter extraordinaire. The 13-year-old great-grandson of President Roosevelt goes on safari with Robin Hurt, and carries the same Holland and Holland rifle used by the President.

There is hunting in the film. But it is the dialogue around the camp fires that make this a special film. I know dialogue around a campfire doesn't sound like much, but trust me, this is one exciting film with a strong pro-hunting message.

The film is about why people hunt. It also is about why *hunting is the main reason there is wildlife left in Africa.* Butler ties together the safari, the need for hunting, modern-day hunting, and hunting of the past. It is beautiful, it is real, and it is about Man The Hunter. The film ends with the dramatic harvest of a huge Cape buffalo by this young Roosevelt heir, using his great grandfather's rifle. As the natives fulfill a tribal ritual by smearing blood on the new hunter's face, it mixes with tears and a realization that indeed, hunting is something that is *"In The Blood."*

The African sounds, the story of a boy taking a step toward manhood via the hunt, a story about man's roots as a hunter, will make you love this film. I'm sure some who read this last sentence will be upset about a boy killing a Cape buffalo and taking a step toward manhood.

But the reality is that an amazing number of kids would love to try a similar hunting experience, would love to take such a step into manhood as did their forefathers, but never will get the chance because their parents either don't hunt or don't want their children to hunt.

A red squirrel scolded from a nearby branch as the sun began its descent. Four turkeys fed through the corner of a nearby field and soon there were several deer feeding. A wood thrush sang its evening song and a bat whizzed by, headed for some far off spot thousands of miles away in a tropical rain forest.

It was the fall hunting season and the woods were alive. For me (and most hunters), this is the very best time of the year. A time for rejuvenation, a time when we can get totally immersed in nature. There are feelings we have about hunting that are very different from those for golf, tennis, bowling and other sports? Ever wonder why?

Maybe it is because hunting is so deeply rooted in the distant human past. Maybe the urge to hunt is in all of us, waiting for the exposure to "release" the need. Hunting is not a recent invention. It developed simultaneously with the human species and had a tremendous influence on our physical and mental abilities.

A relatively recent scientific paper by Dr. Ann Causey ("*On The Morality of Hunting*," found in the winter 1989 issue of Environmental Ethics) takes a most refreshing look at hunting and our roots as hunting animals. Dr. Causey pointed out that two writers, Roger Caras (who leans toward antihunting) and philosopher Jose Ortega y Gassett (whose book "*Meditations On Hunting*" is a classic look at humans, the hunting animals) feel that our desire to hunt is a "modern vestige of an evolutionary trait." They point out that our agriculture tie is relatively recent in our history and thus what really shaped our evolution and our heritage, our being, was hunting.

Caras concluded that hunting is inherent in man, that the desire to hunt is very entrenched in our being (see his book, "*Death As A Way Of Life*"). Dr. Causey pointed out that early man had to kill to survive. She also noted there had to be pleasure gained from the hunt, and from the kill; to reinforce the urge to hunt, to make sure that man learned from each hunt, to guarantee success in future hunts. Early man had to be successful, or he/she died. It was that simple.

Successful hunts meant survival. We don't need to hunt today to survive, but our forefathers did. Thus, the entire evolution of early man centered around successful hunting and killing. Does this mean that hunting became instinctive? Some say yes, others say no.

To consider that early hunters who lived thousands of years ago may have gained pleasure from the hunt may upset modern antihunters. They argue that hunting today is different from hunting in the past because in the past it was done only for survival. However some scholars question that by stating that hunting was done for survival in the past, but that hunters enjoyed it, had pleasure doing it, got more than just meat from the hunt and this helped to reinforce the behavior making it more successful.

It's tempting to speculate that hunting has even influenced the "spiritual" side of humans, and that hunting, at least for some, is nothing short of a "spiritual" experience. Some argue that the hunter, who has participated in the life and death struggles on the land, develops a strong, intimate connection to nature.

Many hunters are participants; they get immersed in nature, physically and mentally. Is there more to it than that? Is it a spiritual immersion? I have a bowhunting friend, Len Cardinale, who runs an archery shop in downtown Newark, New Jersey. Len is a unique and wonderful person; his skills include teaching archery to some of our top Olympic shooters as well as movie stars. He loves to bowhunt, but his store is in the middle of an urban environment.

Several years ago we were discussing how much we love to bowhunt; how important it is to our lives. During the bow season, Len would get up at 3:00 AM, drive two hours to get out of the city, and on some mornings, he was so excited to just be there, in that spot, that he would literally run into the woods.

Trapped in a city environment, Len found total release by escaping to the woods. Total spiritual immersion for Len. Many of us feel that way. I'm sure that some hikers and campers also feel trapped in the city, and develop a similar spiritual immersion from the woods.

At the same time there are many hunters who seem to be missing the very essence of hunting. I know some hunters who haven't taken time to think about any connection between the land and the animals they hunt.

Too bad. There is much to be missed when hunters and nonhunters simply pass through nature, skimming her surface as a tourist on a casual walk. Some hunters feel it is impossible for nonhunters to experience the same "feelings" that hunters have for the woods?

I think they are wrong. Though some of our best naturalists were hunters, others were not. I know some very serious, nonhunting, bird watchers who have spiritual feelings about nature. I have a friend who does not believe in hunting yet has strong spiritual connections to the land. No person I know has stronger ethical feelings about our environmental problems than this person.

Let's look at the physical and mental legacy hunting has imprinted on the human species to see if that helps answer questions about the spiritual significance of the hunting experience. Various anthropologists believe that humans are skilled runners today because of thousands of years of evolution where man hunted fleet, plains game like antelope and bison.

Gassett believed our hands and legs evolved as those of a hunting animal; that running was conducive to being a successful hunter. He went further to suggest that our minds evolved as a hunter too.

By the same logic, the ability of a professional football quarterback to throw a football with pinpoint precision to a receiver 50 yards down field is no accident. Nor is it solely the result of diligent training by coaches.

The inner ability for such hand-eye coordination is a result of thousands of years of hunting, during which humans threw rocks, spears, lances and other missiles at game they had to kill in order to survive. Scientists also theorize that human intelligence and the human trademark of effective communication grew out of our hunting past.

Physically, early humans were no match for their prey or their predator. Group cooperation and communication was essential to survive by consistently killing larger, stronger, and faster game. That cooperation and communication helped the human species develop its extensive mental powers.

An essay by Robert Ardrey on *"The Evolution of Hunting"* (published in 1968) stated: "In a very real sense our intellect, interests, emotions, and basic social life—all are evolutionary products of the success of the hunting adaptation." In essence, over thousands of years of evolution, where man survived by being a successful hunter and killer of animals, everything centered around the hunt. Life centered around a successful hunt.

That suggests that over thousands of years, people who hunted were successful and evolved into a certain way of life. Later on Ardrey stated: "The entire evolution of man took place during the period in which man was a hunter." In other words, today's humans are what they are because their ancestors were hunters.

Did this lead to an "urge" to hunt? Did this lead to an "instinct" to hunt? I don't know. But anthropologists have made it quite clear that man evolved as a hunter. What we are today is a result of man being a successful hunter.

Dr. Causey pointed out that our modern hunting instinct is tempered by reason, and suggests that it is our modern intellect mixed with thousands of years of evolution that causes hunters who kill an animal to have a mixture of elation and remorse.

She then quotes Gassett: "reason can be described more appropriately as the greatest danger to the existence of hunting." Why is man's ability to reason considered a threat to hunting?

I believe when Gassett wrote that he meant that it is difficult for modern man to understand our roots. That if modern-day humans try to "reason" the existence of hunting, their "reasoning" will come up short because it is based on our short life span and not the millions of years that man has existed as a hunter.

Look at society today. Urbanism (a term coined in 1997 by Dr. Larry Marchinton, wildlife professor at the University of Georgia, which means "a way of looking at life from an urbanized perspective") is prevalent. We look at things from a legally suspect, politically correct, urbanized, and isolated from nature, point of view. From that perspective it is rather easy to say that modern man does not need to hunt.

We don't need wild game for food. We should treat all animals the same way we treat all people. I've even heard some people suggest that in the past 30 years or so, man has changed. And in that changed state, there is no reason"to hunt.

Thirty years compared to one million years!!! Sorry. Individuals might change, but humans can't change their evolution that quickly.

It's more difficult to pin down the spiritual connection to hunting, but some hunters feel it strongly. When a hunter stands on a high ridge at dawn with the forest coming awake, and the eastern sky brightening, is there then a direct connection to a bigger world? As they wipe camo paint across their cheeks and feel the weight of their bow or gun balanced in their hand, is there a kinship to earlier hunters who stalked the same ground? I believe there is.

That Spiritual Feeling.**—-If we look at human history, or even the few groups of people around the world that still live by hunting today, we might get some answers as to why modern hunters have such strong feelings for hunting and how hunting fits into our spiritual view of the world. Consider our Native Americans.

Indians have always felt the need to hunt; for food, for cultural traditions, and for ceremonial purposes. The last two reasons are obviously tied to some "urge" and to the honor and status that was accorded a hunter who was successful. In fact, Indians believe the best hunters are closer to the spirit of wild animals and that their kinship helps them to be great leaders. It is said that Sitting Bull, leader of the Sioux once said: "When there are no buffalo we will hunt mice for we are hunters and want our freedom." Obviously the Sioux had a spiritual feeling toward hunting that represented their freedom.

Those who oppose hunting often note a perceived difference in modern hunters from early man. They say early man hunted for food, while we hunt for pleasure. From this quote from Sitting Bull and other records of primitive hunters, it is obvious they hunted for food, *and pleasure* just as we do today. The relationship between primitive man (the predator) and his prey is best written by Richard Nelson, anthropologist and nature writer.

His essay on *"Stalking the Sacred Game"* (Published in the Governor's Symposium on North America's Hunting Heritage, 1992 and reprinted there with permission of Susan Bergholz Literary Services, New York) is a classic description of the way Native American hunters viewed nature and the predator.

That relationship is filled with the spirituality of hunting. In Nelson's study of the Inupiaq ("enupiak") Eskimos, he learned the

*2 excellent references on this topic are: a book *"Wisdom of the Elders: Honoring Sacred Native Visions of Nature"* by David Suzuki and Peter Knudtson (Bantam Books) and an article *"Stalking the Sacred Game"* by Richard Nelson, in proceedings of the Governor's Conference on North America's Hunting Heritage, available from North American Hunting Club, 12301 Whitewater Dr., P. O. Box 3401, Minnetonka, MN 55343.

greatest hunters were those that studied and knew animals better than others. Those hunters were held in highest esteem by others and served as models for other hunters.

Primitive peoples all over the world studied animals, learned about nature, learned about the environment so they could be better hunters. They were not simply tourists walking around in the woods. Hunting was serious business then, as it is for many of us today. Those early hunters were fanatical about it, to the point where their relationship with animals became religious and spiritual. Many modern-day hunters would argue that they experience a similar relationship between hunting and the hunted.

As Nelson pointed out, hunting and religion were inseparable for many native peoples. As you might imagine with any religion, there were many ethical and moral principles that were followed while fulfilling the desire to kill prey for food and clothing. It was this morality and respect for animals that guided primitive hunters and their relationship to the animal.

Primitive hunters took great steps to avoid offending the spirit of the animals they wanted to kill. The animal willingly gave its life to the hunter, but only if the hunter was ethical. If the hunter offended the spirit of the animal then his hunting luck would rapidly deteriorate.

This respect was shown in many ethical rules that governed the hunt. The animals could only be hunted in a certain way. Once killed, they had to be used in a certain way. Nothing could be wasted. The hunter had to practice humility, because the bragging hunter would offend the spirit of the dead animal, and the spirit of the animal was very important.

Offend that spirit and your future hunting fortunes would suffer. Prey are there for predators to eat, and humans are predators. But there are rules and ethics to obey.

There is a moral system that must be followed. When that happens the prey will lay down its life for the hunter, for the predator. It is the moral hunter that is successful. The immoral hunter will lose the ability to harvest animals. There is a symbiotic relationship between predator and prey and the hunter must have a love, a genuine love, for the hunted. The more respect shown for the animal, the more success the hunter will have.

Chapter 3

Some native people felt that certain animals could give power to men. The Tzeltal people of Mexico believed that all humans had an animal soul as a companion. They believed the most powerful humans had a jaguar as their soul companion. Less powerful humans had lesser animal soul companions.

Certain primitive peoples avoided grave sites because they believed that evil spirits (of strong predatory animals) lived there. The Koyukon Indians slice the eyes of the bear so that its spirit cannot see the hunter if he makes a mistake and does not treat the animal with total respect during the process of butchering.

It is obvious that hunting has been an important part of human life for thousands of years, and that hunting has provided a framework through which many of the world's peoples still view the universe. For many hunters, hunting is much more than a diversion, but for others it is not.

For some of us, hunting is a way of life. For others, it is simply an excuse to get into the woods and away from the office.

Those who oppose hunting ask that modern man throw off the cloak of the past, that we should be more compassionate and rational, and not kill anything. On the other hand, many anthropologists feel that to turn our back on hunting's evolutionary past is irrational. Maybe, just maybe, it is the hunting human with spiritual ties to our forefathers who is rational. Man the predator is the natural man and not the outcast ridiculed by some.

Thus, almost certainly some of how we feel about modern-day hunting is tied to millions of years of evolution. But is that special feeling hunters get when they enter the woods the result of instincts passed down across countless generations? Can we inherit our spirituality through instinctive mechanisms?

I don't have an answer, but I do know that for me the feelings I have for hunting in the woods are very strong. So strong that it is a spiritual happening, a compulsion to which I am somehow driven. I'm not driven to kill, just to hunt. Many hunters understand these feelings, but my hunting world would be much better served if *all* hunters and nonhunters understood them as well.

Our Past Is Our Future.—*"In an eagle there is all the wisdom of the world "* (quote by Lame Deer, a Minnicoujou Sioux). To the Sioux

Indians the eagle was sacred and central to many of their medicine ceremonies. They allowed only the most brave to wear feathers from the eagle.

The Sioux believed that the spirit of the eagle gave the best hunters and fighters their courage. Because of this almost religious feeling for the eagle, no Sioux would kill that bird either in thought or in deed. That same feeling of love and respect for animals was carried by many Native American hunters and even went far beyond the eagle to those species that were hunted. Their relationship to animals—predator-prey relationship—was mystical, magical, spiritual, and religious.

What about the hunter of today? How does he/she relate to the animal? Do they have a spiritual relationship to wild prey similar to that of former native hunters? Many modern-day hunters do have a relationship with nature and animals that is also very special. For some, entering the woods to hunt is a spiritual happening. But the sad truth is that as with any human activity, there is a continuum of hunters, from slobs to dedicated, purist hunters.

On the bad end of the stick are some hunters who are not good role models. They have a poor hunting attitude, do not practice good hunting ethics and do not respect animals. Not much spirituality for those hunters.

That's too bad, because today's modern-day hunter need the "I am ethical and respect animals" image more than ever. Today's hunter is under fire from the general public because of poor behavior, and poor ethics.

Hunters today live under a microscope and every instance of unethical or illegal behavior is held up for public scrutiny. The fact that slobs hunt should not incriminate all hunters; slobs also drive cars, but we don't get rid of the automobile to control their behavior.

Antihunters tout unethical hunting as typical but such is not the case. Hunters will state that bad hunting behavior is the exception, and it may be, but it still is all too common.

Rand Johnson, in an article in Trilogy (Winter, 1993), discussed what he called the "ugly hunter." He noted that the goal of those people is to kill rather than to hunt. The ugly hunter has no respect for the hunted animal, nor for people in general.

Chapter 3

The ugly hunter is loud, boisterous, brash, and pays no respect to private property. He doesn't take the time, nor understand the reason, to be quiet and thankful after the kill. As Mr. Johnson pointed out slob hunters are an embarrassment to us all. Antihunters also despise these individuals.

The hunters defense to the nonhunters often takes the position that even though we have some ugly hunters, the activity of hunting is still good, and it is good for the animals. Telling nonhunters that killing animals is good for them is a hard sell, but I believe the general public understands the ecological need to control populations.

It is a much easier story to tell when hunters are ethical and law abiding. However, there is an aspect to hunting that nonhunters can relate to; the same aspect that Native American hunters show toward animals; a part of that spirituality of hunting that is so important to our future.

The aspect of hunting that is needed and nonhunters will understand is *respect for the animal.* Consider what would happen if *all* modern-day hunters believed as our early Native Americans did that you must treat the hunted animals with total respect. That you would be a successful hunter only if you treated animals with respect, that the spirit of the animal controlled your hunting success.

If all hunters so believed, then there would be *no* hunting violations. There would be *no* ethical violations. No ducks would be shot on the water because that would violate the spirit of the animal. No hunter would laugh or brag at the site of a deer kill as that would offend the deer's spirit. No hunter would shoot more than the bag limit, for such behavior would mean poor hunting for years to come.*

---

* A friend of mine read this section and suggested that there had to be instances where Native Americans got prey any way they could, in order to keep from starving to death. In those times they shot ducks on the water, and built pit traps that killed more animals than they could use, etc. The suggestion was that we should not make Native Americans and other primitive hunters more noble than they were. My friend also suggested that when modern hunters are following game regulations they are not necessarily showing respect for the animals, they are more likely showing respect for rules of society; they are being ethical toward other people.

I agree with those points. I'm simply saying that early Native Hunters were tied to animals, they identified themselves as being on the same basic level as wild animals, yet they had to hunt and kill animals to survive.

Through the hunt they evolved and developed a kinship for cultural and subsistence reasons and their culture evolved within this framework. It is probably true that some hunters follow the game regulations because of their respect for the rules of society, but I would suggest that many hunters also do it because they respect the animal they hunt.

In short, if modern-day hunters had more spirituality in their hunting motives and thoughts, antihunters would have less added fuel for their emotional fires. Hunters would be much more acceptable to the general public because of their display of feelings for the hunted animals. Nonhunters understand that early man had a need to hunt. They understand that early primitive peoples hunted for food. At the same time nonhunters have some feeling of respect for living animals and they can relate to the fact that Native American hunters also felt a respect for living animals, even though they killed them. However, most nonhunters do not understand why we choose to haul dead animals around on the roof of our cars. They don't understand the loud boasting after the kill, especially in public places. They don't understand the compulsion for a few hunters to kill more and more animals.

I'm not saying that the majority of hunters are not ethical, I'm simply stating that any amount of poor behavior makes all hunters look bad.

I'm also saying that if hunters showed more reverence for the live and dead animal, nonhunters might well accept hunting more than they presently do. Each hunter must have his/her own set of unwritten ethical rules. Each hunter must decide what is right and wrong in the field.

In hunting, most of the time we are alone, and so it is *you* that must make the right ethical decisions that show respect for nature, animals, and the land. In essence, hunters must develop an attitude about hunting. Place more value on the right to hunt by placing more value on hunting laws, the land you hunt, and on the animals you hunt.

My bowhunting friend, Judy Kovar, is a Northern Cheyenne Indian who goes into the public schools of Illinois and Missouri, and gives talks about her hunting heritage and her native predatory instincts.

"From the time I was a little girl, I've been taught that Mother Nature provides everything; it's up to us to use it wisely," she said.

Chapter 3

"Without this outlook my people, the Northern Cheyenne would have perished. We need our animals, and they need us."

"We need to get back to basics; the high people get from drugs and alcohol does not compare to the high archery gives a person, from the first glimpse of a fawn nursing its mother to the call of the wild turkey. The Good Lord put the woods out there for you to use, no matter how bad things get on this earth, I'd like to think you can always go out in the woods and find a little peace."

The beauty of this letter I received from Judy Kovar is that it shows the great respect her people show for wild animals. When this female Indian bowhunter walks into a public school classroom, wearing her grandmother's white elk wedding robe, and carrying her bow, students and teachers get a different image of hunters.

They hear that hunting really isn't bad. They learn that having predatory feelings is something that Native Americans have had for hundreds of years. They hear that human predators love the animals they hunt.

Those public school kids have never been exposed to a native American before, much less a hunter. When Judy Kovar talks to those kids, not only do they learn, but the teachers probably do too.

Most Native Americans hold animals—the animals they hunt—in the highest regard. It is a spiritual love that nonhunters can relate to. It is that same spiritual feeling that all hunters must have and display today.

The Izaak Walton League of America has run a hunter ethics program for many years. Recently they hosted a meeting with the objective of writing a code of conduct for hunters. The code they wrote is a pledge that all hunters should take. *Here it is:

I PLEDGE TO:

Respect the environment and wildlife;
Respect property and landowners;
Show consideration for nonhunters;

---

*you can get copies of the brochure or wallet cards with this pledge are available from: IWLA Outdoor Ethics Program, 1401 Wilson Blvd., Level B., Arlington, VA 22209. Include a donation for postage.

Hunt safely;
Know and obey the law;
Support wildlife and habitat conservation;
Pass on an ethical hunting tradition;
Strive to improve my outdoor skills and understanding of wildlife;
Hunt only with ethical hunters.

Things die so that we might live. That is a harsh fact; it is reality. Things that die might be garden carrots, cauliflower from an agrifarm in California, a cow from the country farm, or a doe from a hunt. Removing these living things from the outdoors can be done callously or it can be done with respect. It is your choice, but hunters need to know that self respect, the respect of other hunters and, yes, even respect from nonhunters, will come from hunting in a manner that demonstrates responsibility to the animal and to hunters and nonhunters.

There are many potential critics looking over the hunter's shoulder. The spirit of the animal might well be there too.

"Golf is sophisticated exercise, but the love of hunting is almost a psychological characteristic."

Aldo Leopold

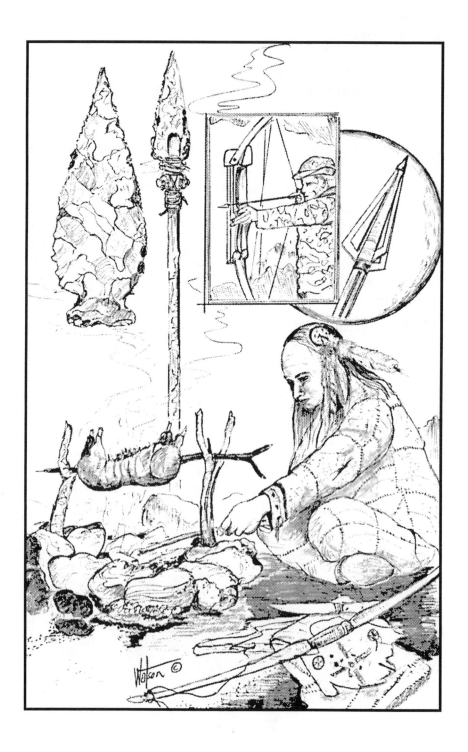

Chapter 4

The Values of Hunting*

Hunting has many values. One obvious value of hunting is from the meat. Those opposed to hunting state that we don't need to eat wild game any more. However, researchers have shown that the Paleolithic diet of wild game, fruit, and vegetables is very healthy. Wild game is low in fat, high in omega-3 fatty acids, and has other positive qualities recognized by doctors throughout the country.

There are also many "hidden" values of hunting, values not often discussed or noted in the printed word. Hunting teaches us to share, builds character, teaches self esteem, and gives certainty to our lives. Hunters have always been stewards of wildlife. Modern hunters must not back away from that stewardship responsibility. That must continue if citizens are to support hunters and hunting today.

We Do Need To Hunt.—-In the last chapter we discussed some of the values of hunting, and the evolutionary history of man-the-hunter. We learned that for hundreds of thousands of years humans were immersed in the woods and wild nature.

Now, some people are questioning the motives of hunters. If one takes a superficial view of hunting, just skimming the surface, they might reach the opinion that hunting is not needed today, but let's dig around a bit; let's consider some of the deeper values humans obtain from hunting. We'll first consider the values gained from eating wild game, and then move to other values that a hunting way of life has always provided.

Healthy Food—-The seminar was interesting...no, it was downright fascinating. Dr. Mark Smith, medical doctor, nutritionist, sport scientist, nonhunter, was discussing his diet of wild game.

*portions adapted (with permission) from "*We Do Need To Hunt*", Bowhunter Magazine, February - Mar 1996, and "*The Values of Hunting*", Pennsylvania Sportsman, November 1995.

Chapter 4

Dr. Smith eats stone age, Pleistocene, foods. A new fad? I don't think so because this diet has been eaten by humans for 99.5 percent of our time on earth. According to this nutritionist, our bodies evolved eating a wild game diet.

A wild game diet lowers fat and decreases heart disease and cancer. It is a diet that erect walking "humans" have eaten for one million years and it is simple. Yep, Dr. Smith is one of a growing number of nutritionists who believe that humans today would be much healthier if they consumed the original hunters diet of wild game, fruit and vegetables.

Through his publications and speaking engagements, this nutrition expert from Colorado State University was telling the world, telling vegetarians, telling all the fast junk-food eaters, that wild game is the basis for human health. He was not the only doctor telling the Paleolithic diet story.

In 1985 Dr. Boyd Eaton from the School or Medicine at Emory University stated "the nutritional quality of such meat (deer, bison, mammoths) differs considerably from that of meat available in modern American supermarkets: the latter has much more fat. Not only is there more fat in domesticated animals, its composition is different; wild game contains over five times more polyunsaturated fat per gram than is found in domestic livestock."

Dr. Smith offered us more nutritional facts about eating wild game. He noted that the fat in wild game meat contains one polyunsaturated fatty acid that helps reduce arteriosclerosis (i.e. heart attacks). Whoa, this is important and heady stuff. Wild game helps reduce clogged arteries. Now there is a value to hunting that hasn't been expressed very much; eating wild game can reduce heart disease.

In an article in the New England Journal of Medicine, Dr. Eaton showed that the Paleolithic diet differed significantly from what humans eat today (see Table 1). Wild game, fruits, and vegetables provided early hunters with lots of protein, very low fats, more polyunsaturated fats, lots of fiber, much less sodium and plenty of calcium (without eating dairy products that didn't evolve until 5,000 years ago). Current Americans have diets with less protein, a ton of fat, less fiber, and lots more sodium. Our diets today are obviously not healthy. But if modern-day humans ate wild game, they would get the same benefits such meats brought to prehistoric hunters.

The amount of cholesterol is high in the Paleolithic diet, but that is because Paleolithic human beings consumed large amounts of meat. But Dr. Eaton pointed out that this was offset by the low fat in their diet.

"They ate much less fat than we do, and the fat they ate was substantially different from ours," he said. "Whether subsistence was based predominantly on meat (wild game) or on vegetables, the Paleolithic diet had less total fat, more essential fatty acids, and a much higher ratio of polyunsaturated to saturated fats than ours does."

Table 1. Comparison of Paleolithic diet and current American diet.* Also listed are nutrition suggestions recommended by the U. S. Senate Select Committee.

	Paleolithic	*Today USA*	*Recommended*
Percent dietary energy			
protein	34	12	12
carbohydrate	45	46	58
fat	21	42	30
P:S ratio**	1.41	0.44	1.00
cholesterol	591	600	300
fiber	45.7	19.7	30-60
sodium	690	2300-6900	1100-3300
calcium	1580	740	800-1200
ascorbic acid	392.3	87.7	45

The point I'm trying to make (as were Drs. Eaton and Smith) is that humans evolved eating the Paleolithic diet. Our bodies evolved eating wild game, fruits and vegetables and it is this fact that makes such a diet important for man *today*. Dr. Eaton, Dr. Smith and many others believe that our nutritional diet requirements were established in prehistoric times when much of it was wild game.

Man evolved eating wild game and genetically we have changed only 1.6 percent over 6-7 million years. So, at a time when antihunters

* adapted with permission from "*Paleolithic Nutrition, A Consideration of Its Nature and Current Implications*" by S. Boyd Eaton and Melvin Konner, New England Journal of Medicine, vol. 312, pages 283-289, 1985. Copyright © 1985 Massachusetts Medical Society. All rights reserved.

**P:S denotes polyunsaturated: saturated fats. The higher the ratio, the better it is for humans.

are stating that "modern man" has changed in the past 50 years and that we do not *need* to hunt for meat, a growing group of nutritionists are saying wild game should be part of our diet.

Consider that a 3.5 ounce portion of lean roast beef contains 14.3 grams of fat and 5.7 grams of saturated fat while the same portion of deer has 3.2 grams of fat and 1.2 grams of saturated fat. Elk has 1.9 grams of fat and 0.7 grams of saturated fat. Make no question about it, wild game is healthy food.

This "flintstone diet" idea creates a problem for those who say that humans can get meat in our diets without hunting, or that we should all be vegetarians. But if it is wild game that provides good nutrition, then hunting may be the politically correct thing to do.

Hunting, politically correct? Is modern society ready for this? (Actually, modern society can't be ready for this. Realistically we could not feed the world with wild game. Suffice is to say though, that wild game is good for the diet. In fact, some doctors ask heart patients to eat wild game as part of their medical treatment.)

Values Beyond The Meat.—-Let's consider some of these values, things that go beyond the nutrition and the meat. James Swan, in his must-read book, *"In Defense of Hunting,"* * discussed the many values we get from hunting; the fact that there are hidden benefits from hunting that modern society, especially our children, need today. Indeed, Dr. Swan feels strongly that modern man does *need* to hunt.

To make his point Swan noted that modern man does many things even though he/she does not "need" to do them. Humans marry, when they could live together and bear children without marriage. They share with each other when they are not forced to do so. They are polite to neighbors, generous, cooperate, and help people. Humans aren't forced to do these things, but we do them anyway. They are done because they benefit our human spirit. It makes us feel good to do them.

Swan contends that being in the woods is something that, through evolution, we "need" to do. Humans get something valuable by being in the woods, and by hunting. It has always been that way.

---

* *"In Defense of Hunting"* was written by Dr. James Swan and published in 1995 by Harper, San Francisco, a Division of Harper-Collins Publishers. It is available in hard cover or paper back and is the finest book I've ever read on this subject.

Sharing Wild Game.—-For example, man has always improved family and community bonds by hunting. One way is by bringing home wild game and *sharing* it with your family and friends. Some people criticize hunters for providing meat for the homeless and hungry. They say that sharing meat is a gimmick just to justify hunting.

Actually, the opposite is true. This is not a new or novel idea; humans have shared wild game for millions of years. Today most Native Americans still share wild game with family and friends, as do most hunters.

Last fall I gave a deer roast to our neighbors, Carol and Tom Brown. Carol is a gourmet cook, but said she wasn't fond of venison. I said perhaps the game she had tried had not been properly cared for before coming to her kitchen.

She volunteered to give it another try. She invited other neighbors, and the results were fantastic. They loved it, and in thanks, Carol sent a dessert to our home.

The other neighbor then got involved by sharing food with the Browns. Every fall I make sure the Brown's get some venison, and they share with us, and sharing wild game has enriched our relationship.

It probably has done the same for millions of people for thousands of years. I also share wild game with my in-laws and they look forward to receiving it each year. My mother-in-law prepares the meat and invites the family to dinner.

These sharing activities are especially common during the holidays. And it is at this time that families develop traditions. Is sharing wild game good for the neighborhood and the family? You bet. Do we need more family bonding, family traditions, community sharing, and community involvement? I think so.

A 1995 study completed at West Virginia University showed that in one West Virginia county 29 percent of the households of nonhunters, received wild game. Hunters of today are obviously still sharing wild game with nonhunters. I wonder how many hundreds of thousands of times wild game is shared around the country each year? Some sportsmen will remember the wild game dinners of the past. Most were held in churches, and that spiritual connection to the wild was no accident.

Chapter 4

Why do we have "wild game dinners"? Are they new to man? Of course not. My guess is that wild game dinners go back to the days of *Homo erectus*, over 1.8 million years ago. Sharing wild meat was, and is, a great activity for kinship bonding, a great family activity, a great community activity—yes, even a great cultural activity.

I recently suggested that if individual hunters want to do something to honor their hunting passion, they should host a wild game dinner for family and neighbors.* If only 10 percent of all hunters hosted one wild game feast each year, there would be about two million dinners; two million exposures of wild game to nonhunters; two million sharings of wild game with families, and community. Is this good for society today? Definitely.

Character Building.—-Hunting also is a way to *teach character*? Humans have always gone to the woods to develop character. Church camps, Boy Scouts, Girl Scouts, urban youth camps, antidrug camps. Guess where we hold these activities? In the woods.

There is something special about being in the woods that builds character. Something *spiritual* occurs in the woods that builds character. Today's kids seem lost and bored at times. This is especially true in the cities. They are looking for ways to "fit in" to the world around them. They are searching for satisfying experiences that help them understand their own worth and the skills and talents they bring to the world.

Such experiences have become harder to come by in today's highly technical, commercially driven world. Young people, especially those in urban areas, find few opportunities that are simple enough to invite their participation yet yield deeply satisfying personal rewards.

In a rural economy, these experiences were always close at hand in the simple chores that had a real value to family and community well being. Today, such experiences are elusive, difficult even to imagine. So more youngsters turn to drugs, gangs and violence to fill that personal void.

There are ways to build *self-esteem* and *self-worth*. Athletics is one, and many children take that route. Doing well in school and working hard also helps. But based on my experience and that of

*Orion—The Hunter's Institute has a pamphlet that tells you exactly what to do to hold a game food dinner. Contact them at P. O.Box 5088, Helena MT 59604.

many friends, there are few activities that hold the potential for intense, positive, personal experience that ethical, properly instructed hunting can offer.

A kid who is a successful hunter feels good about him/herself and his/her being. Dr. Swan suggested that hunting also teaches kids about the realities of life and death, and this translates into a more meaningful consideration of the value of human life (something that does seem to be disappearing in our society).

With the recent high school shootings has come the charge that hunting has made children more callous toward life and living creatures and been the cause of these shootings. I don't think so, and hundreds of hunters I've talked to about this subject don't think so either. In fact, they agree with Dr. Swan; exposing kids to hunting is a positive rather than a negative. It gives positive meaning to a young life. Hunting teaches cooperation, patience, and it lets kids understand the realities of life and death.

If hunting turned kids into monsters, then hundreds of thousands of hunters would be shooting and killing our fellow citizens. But, the opposite occurs. Hunters are the leaders of the conservation movement. They clean up the streams, buy habitat to protect it, join groups that protect wildlife. Sure, there is the occasional nut who commits violent crimes on fellow citizens, and who also has hunted at some time in the past. But in general, hunters are good citizens.

In fact, it would be interesting to get some statistics on drug use, or alcohol use, or violent crimes, comparing kids that grew up in hunting families as opposed to those that did not. My guess is that kids who spend time in the woods with families have much lower negative statistics than those who do not.

James Swan has another book —"*Nature as Teacher and Healer*"— that discusses the idea that "high risk" outdoor activities build self esteem. And, in fact, some of the country's most successful drug treatment programs use challenging outdoor experiences as part of their treatment methods. Most hunting can't be viewed as "high risk" but to a twelve-year-old sitting in the early morning dawn on his first hunt, hunting is definitely a new challenge, one in which his or her own personal resources can be brought to task in the pursuit of "success," whether that success is perceived merely as the taking of game or as the personal enjoyment of participating in a hunt.

Chapter 4

Does hunting make kids feel high? Yes it does. Rock star and hunter, Ted Nugent has delivered the message of getting high on the woods and not on drugs, for many years. The message makes sense.

In fact, it has made sense for millions of years. If you attempt to do something that is interesting for kids, provide programs that have good messages, the woods is a great environment to make it happen. In those situations most kids do not find the woods boring. Most youngsters find the woods mystical and exciting, and find hunting exciting and mystical.

Find Certainty In The Woods.—-For some of us, hunting puts balance in our lives and the woods gives our life meaning. Though foreign to many people today, the woods are not foreign to hunters. We feel good and feel secure there.

Life is certain in the woods. Even though many things are uncertain, you can still find certainty in the woods. Bucks always rut in November. Squirrels always store nuts in the fall. The leaves always turn color in the fall. There are no exceptions. Come to the woods and your life will have certainties that society cannot begin to give you. The woods have always been that way.

Dr. Holmes Rolston is a philosophy professor at Colorado State University. In one of his many interesting papers ("*Values Deep in the Woods*", in American Forests, May 1988) he noted: "Humans go outdoors for the repair of what happens indoors, but they also go outdoors because they seek something greater than can be found indoors—contact with the natural certainties."

The message is clear and historic. Come to the woods and your life will have certainties that human society cannot provide. It fulfills a need.

James Swan added that without the woods, modern human lives are out of balance. Hunters have always known that the woods are special. They hunt in certain locations because they have special meaning, and they go there year after year, even if wildlife populations have changed.

As I read Dr. Swan's book and his comments about the special places that we go to hunt, I thought of several such spots. From 1968 to 1980 I hunted one such location around twenty miles from home. Late afternoon, after work, I'd rush to that location, climb into my tree stand for an evenings bow hunt. It was a neat spot; only two hundred yards off a dirt road, in big timber along a stream bottom near some impenetrable cover.

Over the years that spot brought me some of my best hunting memories. There was the six-point albino buck that I saw there twice during one bow season. A local farm boy harvested that buck later in the year. At the base of that same tree stand I watched my father shoot his last deer at age 75. His eye sight was waivering due to cataracts, but I sat beside him and pointed out the buck on that cold November morning. The shot was close, and true.

As we left the woods that morning, we both knew that this was his last hunt. It was a special time for me. My father taking me hunting when I was a kid had led me into a life time of wildlife management. It was the hunting experience that led me to become a wildlife biologist and teacher. It also led my twin brother into the same career. Hunting has led most wildlife biologists to their careers.

Time has since changed that hunting spot. The farm became more developed, and more and more people used the area. It wasn't the same, and there were better places to deer hunt. But for several years I continued to go to that location, just because it had special meaning to me. Although I do not hunt there any more, I still think about that spot a lot. I remember the tree, the stream, the rutting scrape made there each year by bucks. Last year I drove to that hollow and walked into the spot I'd hunted for so many years.....just to visit it again. It wasn't hunting season; just a time and place to remember.

Stewardship.—-Hunters may perceive many values from hunting, but today's society may not. Dr. Ben Peyton, wildlife professor specializing in human dimensions at Michigan State University, noted the one special redeeming value of hunting today is *stewardship.*

Hunters must learn and know that, and they must practice it. If hunters are in the woods, if hunters pay for the funds for wildlife management, then those same hunters have the responsibility to be the stewards of wildlife. The moment such stewardship is not practiced, the moment the public comes to distrust those stewards, society will have little reason to value hunting or to tolerate hunters.

The value of hunting in the past has been that it produced good stewards who took responsibility for many environmental matters and led the way in many conservation issues for society. But today, hunters show signs of balking at the need to continue to support conservation efforts that extend beyond their own preferred game species like deer and turkey.

If this trend continues, hunters will lose their hard earned reputation as conservationists and their primary value to society. Nor will hunting have the same value to society. Stewardship must be viewed and continued as an investment not only in hunting, but in a healthy environment that both hunters and our children need for survival.

Up until now, hunters have done a fair job of stewardship. But today their realm of stewardship must extend to nongame species, to species that are not hunted. Thirty years ago such species got very little attention.

Today, they have a lot of attention. Thus, hunters are perceived in a positive light, only if they are good stewards of *all wildlife.* A new federal "Teaming For Wildlife" program is being contemplated by Congress. This program would divert millions of tax dollars to the management of nongame species.

Hunters and hunting groups have taken the lead in promoting this important piece of legislation. They have joined forces with interested nonhunters in support of such legislation.

There are other values of hunting that haven't been covered. Hunting has recreational values. It makes us feel good, and it is a fun time. There are economic values (see chapter 5). There are management values; hunting provides a wildlife management tool (see chapter 5).

Because of the values mentioned, and others not yet covered, I believe more than ever before, that modern man needs to hunt. Many benefits are derived from hunting: healthy food, self worth, family bonding, development of community values, relaxation in knowing that some things are always certain. To turn away from these values is not only foolish, but evolutionarily wrong. Man has always needed to hunt, and modern man more so than ever before.

"True wisdom is not given to man by birthright. Reflections of the Great Spirit's infinite wisdom are given to us through the creation of wild creatures and stars and the moon to guide man's path. They were sent that man's knowledge would remain rooted in love for the natural creation. Most men see the moon, but few can feel it."

Steve Fausel

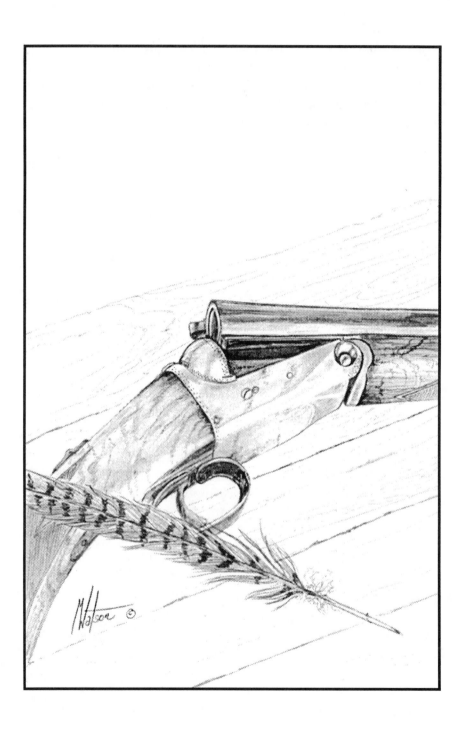

Chapter 5

Hunters And The Science Of Wildlife Management*

We've already addressed the financial issues involved with the millions of dollars raised from license sales and excise taxes on hunting equipment (see chapter 2). I want to devote this chapter to things that hunters do that benefit wildlife, other than spending money to pay for management.

Many hunters join local sportsmen's clubs and those clubs are very active in their communities. Not only do they participate in projects for wildlife, but they also are civic minded. Such hunters commonly hold fund raisers for needy families, blood drives, etc. In addition hundreds of thousands of hunters belong to national wildlife organizations, with activities almost totally devoted to enhancing and protecting wildlife habitat.

Antihunting groups have attempted to initiate the myth that wildlife management is not scientific. Not only is that incorrect, in the United States the science of wildlife management is huge and especially well done. Fortunately, and not surprisingly, the general public has not bought into the myth, and they have great trust in wildlife management agencies.

Another little-known fact is that hunting provides the economic incentive to keep wildlife populations healthy. Abolish hunting and the reason to keep game species populations high will be lost. If hunting is lost, who will care enough (by providing needed monies for management and law enforcement) to keep our great wildlife system in operation?

Hunters Pay For Wildlife Habitat.—-There is no way to cover all

*portions adapted (with permission) from "On Your Side" columns, Bowhunting News, March and June, 1990 and February and March, 1992 and "Know Hunting" columns, Bowhunter Magazine, December 1993 and August 1995.

the pro-management activities accomplished by the thousands of sportsmen clubs, nor the hundreds upon hundreds of activities performed by sportsmen groups such as the Ruffed Grouse Society, National Wild Turkey Federation, Pheasants Forever, Ducks Unlimited, the Isaac Walton League, The Boone and Crockett Club, The Pope and Young Club, Safari Club International, Game Conservation International, the North American Wild Sheep Foundation, Rocky Mountain Elk Foundation, the National Rifle Association, Quail Unlimited, etc. But let's sample the many different activities these groups and clubs do.

The September 1991 issue of *Safari Club International's* Magazine gives some idea of the activities of their various state and local SCI chapters. This is just a small sampling of what the local SCI chapters do for wildlife management.

My list only covers what is mentioned in the September issue of the magazine, not every 1991 activity performed by every SCI chapter in the country. If those were listed, it would require many chapters of typed print to do so. Instead, I'll list the activities of the SCI local chapters in alphabetical order as was printed in the magazine.

The SCI Alabama Chapter renewed a $10,000 grant to fund four wildlife graduate students at Auburn University. As a former wildlife professor, I can tell you that such support is critical to wildlife research. They also donated $2,500 to the state's bald eagle restoration program. (This is just one small example of the projects devoted to nongame species, but funded by hunters. Such projects are commonly funded by hunters).

The Sacramento Chapter carried out an extensive education program for 450 sixth grade school children using mounted animals. Apparently this Education Day was well received by school teachers and administrators, as a great way to reach nonhunters. The California Sierra Chapter built 40 wood duck boxes for placement by a wildlife biologist. The Orlando Chapter has several education programs going on, including the expansion of an outdoor nature study area at West Orange High School.

The Detroit Chapter ran a "Sensory Safari" for blind children. Sensory safaris were created by hunters and use mounted animals as an educational program for blind children (and adults). SCI runs many sensory safaris all over the country every year.

The Mississippi Chapter helped sponsor 100 Project WILD

Hunters And The Science Of Wildlife Management

Teacher Workshops. Project WILD is a wildlife management education program aimed at public school teachers.

The St. Louis Chapter contributed funds to the Missouri Conservation Department for wild turkey research, and otter research. The Pittsburgh Chapter funded a cheetah project in cooperation with local zoo officials. This program involves captive breeding of endangered species.

When one considers that there are hundreds of SCI chapters around the country, and the above is just a sample of what a few chapters did in one year, it's easy to grasp the input that hunters have in conservation activities.

And this is just one group. Hundreds of hunting clubs and organizations around the country contribute to programs like these. When I was a kid, my dad belonged to the Flood City Bowmen in Johnstown, Pennsylvania. That bowhunting club did what most clubs do; they hosted bow shoots, picnics, etc. But, they also had regular conservation projects to help wildlife and habitat. It was common for my brothers and me to trail along on such "work" days.

Almost every year I can remember tree planting days. I'm not sure where the club got the trees, but we planted them by the hundreds. Then there were days when we built fish structures working with the Pennsylvania Fish Commission. Hard work, placing rocks along eroding stream banks, building dams to provide fish habitat. Such activities are commonly done by hunting clubs everywhere.

The September 1991 issue of the Pennsylvania Game News had an article that describing the wildlife management activities of hunting clubs in that state. Examples given are typical of projects done by hunting clubs across the nation. These clubs manage hundreds of thousands of acres of wildlife habitat. The Pennsylvania clubs plant thousands of trees and shrubs for wildlife, hire forestry consultants to assist, create wildlife travel lanes and edge habitat, protect seed trees, seed roads, establish wildlife food species, etc. Many hunting clubs now hire forestry consultants to help plan timber management on club properties. These activities benefit wildlife.

One argument is that hunters do these things so they can kill more animals. It is a shallow argument for many reasons. First: it ignores the many things done by sportsmen groups that are aimed solely at nonhunted species (some of which were mentioned above). Second, it ignores the fact that most wildlife habitat management activities benefit all wildlife, not just game animals. When you manage for whitetail deer you benefit chestnut-sided warblers.* When you manage for waterfowl, short-billed marsh wrens also benefit. Third, it ignores the fact that many modern hunters are conservationists and are most interested in helping to improve wildlife and habitat for no other reason then because it is important.

The *Rocky Mountain Elk Foundation* is a relatively new organization, in comparison to other sportsmen groups. However, in their short life-span, RMEF have become a major contributor to improving wildlife across the United States, but especially in the west. Their September 1990 newsletter reported that they just had purchased 8,500 acres of critical elk habitat.

These purchases involved cooperation with state agencies in Pennsylvania, Washington, Nevada and Idaho. The purchases included a Washington ranch that was extremely important for wintering elk, and another Idaho ranch was also important for several wintering species including moose, deer, elk and eagles. Saving those ranches means that nongame species there also will benefit.

The Foundation also helped buy a Nevada ranch in a key area where elk were being reintroduced. The Pennsylvania purchase was aimed at protecting a nonhunted elk herd that has been present for many years. The motto of the North American Elk Foundation is "working for wildlife," and they live up to it. In 1988-89 alone, they funded 90 projects that totaled over $1.9 million. In recent years this funding has increased dramatically. They indeed live up to their motto.

This may be a bit tedious, but let's list some of those Elk Foundation projects just to give you an idea of what one organization does. In western states, in one year, they; reconstructed three 20,000-gallon water tanks on the Kaibab National Forest; provided materials for 300 fence modifications; built a livestock exclusion fence protecting 160 acres of wet meadows and springs important for all wildlife; reseeded a 2,000-acre burn on the Coconino National Forest; modified many existing water devices, reseeded an area on the Apache-Sitgreaves National Forest; installed two large wildlife guzzler watering devices on the Apache Forest; rehabilitated 2.5 miles

*In essence, the economic incentive of having deer for hunters means that warbler habitat also is improved. No one else is doing warbler habitat management.

of riparian habitat in the White River National Forest (cooperative with the Colorado Division of Wildlife and Trout Unlimited); and other beneficial projects.

The list goes on and on. There was a funded study on the behavior of elk in response to expanding a ski area (in cooperation with the Colorado State University, Colorado Division of Wildlife, U. S. Forest Service). They also purchased a radio telemetry receiver for an Idaho study, paid for a prescribed burn to rejuvenate habitat (most fires are good for wildlife and habitat), fenced a tract of native grasslands, and sponsored campers to the Montana Natural Resources Youth Camp. There's more. They scarified and reseeded defunct roadbeds, funded various ecological elk studies, controlled the spread of noxious weeds, and assisted in an elk transplant in Saskatchewan.

Are these projects working? I think so. Elk herds have doubled since 1975 with populations now found in 24 states and five Canadian provinces.

The *Foundation For North American Wild Sheep* is a very philanthropic group of sheep hunters who annually donate millions for the conservation of wild sheep and sheep habitat. For example, in 1996 they committed $10 million to a long-term project in Hells Canyon Idaho. Hells Canyon is one of the prime sheep habitats in the United States. Last year many sheep died there from pasteurella, a bacterial disease that is common in wild sheep. The hope for the herd comes from the sheep hunter dollars.

Other hunter-based groups do their share to protect habitat. *Ducks Unlimited* has raised almost $1 billion since 1937 and they've conserved over seven million acres of wetlands in the process. When ducks migrate south, many will owe their lives to the habitat protected by Ducks Unlimited.

How are ducks doing? In recent years many of our waterfowl species have reached an all-time high in populations, thanks in part to the work of duck hunters and Ducks Unlimited.

Pheasants Forever has planted over 10 million trees and 300,000 acres of warm season grasses for nesting cover. Habitat loss led to a great decrease in ringneck pheasants in the 1960's-80's, but thanks to federal legislation and the work of pheasant hunters and farmers, the birds are back, over four million pheasants in South Dakota alone.

Chapter 5

The *National Wild Turkey Federation* has been part of one of the greatest wildlife management success stories of all time...the recovery of the wild turkey. There were only 1.3 million turkeys in the United States in 1973, but there are 4.2 million today.

For each of these hunting organizations I could write a chapter on their conservation activities alone, but the previous paragraphs gives some idea of what they accomplish for wildlife.

It is so easy to pass off what hunters do for wildlife with glib comments such as: "They do it so they can kill more animals."

Is that why hunters are the major contributors to volunteer nongame programs via checkoffs on state income taxes in many states? Is that why hunters spend thousands of hours doing habitat work that benefit nongame species during the off-hunting season? Is that why they support programs to save otters, eagles, and other nongame species? I don't think so.

Hunters support such programs via the above organizations and hundreds of others because they care. They truly do care about wildlife of all kinds. They spend many hours observing wildlife, they know wildlife, they understand ecosystems, and they are concerned about wildlife and nongame species.

Hunting groups are the major contributors of time and money in such activities. Antihunting groups are not in the field doing things for wildlife. They are not building water devices, protecting wetlands, reseeding overgrazed areas, or planting wildlife shrubs.

Someone recently suggested that if the antihunting groups began to support pro-wildlife activities it might enhance their credibility so that the nonhunting public might pay them some attention and ignore the advice of hunters and pro-wildlife management groups. While this suggestion may be true, it won't happen. Over the coming years, antihunting groups will probably start to dabble in the above activities mentioned, those things that hunting clubs do as a normal matter of course.

But they will never get involved to the extent that hunting clubs and sportsmens groups do and the reason is simple. It takes an intimate knowledge of how nature really works to create that aura of involvement. It takes hours of observation of wild things and wild environments to create the inner need and desire to do things for wild animals.

There is one other important aspect of the role that hunters play in supporting wildlife management. Hunters are a part of the massive network of conservationists that link county, state, and federal agencies, their lands, and the hunting industries. In order for antihunters to be effective wildlife advocates, and become involved in programs that support wildlife and their habitat, they would have to become a part of this huge network, this partnership.

And though antihunting groups do attend occasional wildlife meetings and the meetings of wildlife organizations, it is rarely their purpose to work with those agencies and organizations. Rather they are there to see what the organizations and agencies are doing, to learn more about their agendas or programs, so that they might better organize their antihunting activities.

Where The Money Comes From.—-The Friends of Animals, a large antihunting organization, has a nice poster available that lists myths about hunting. Myth No. 5 states that hunters contribute only a "minuscule" amount of the funds used for wildlife management. The People for the Ethical Treatment of Animals (PETA) has a pamphlet on hunting that states that "taxpayers pay for most hunting programs. Hunting licenses and other small fees and taxes pay for only a fraction of the millions of dollars spent by state and federal agencies to accommodate the hunting minority." These statements are incorrect.

First, each year about $155 million dollars are apportioned to the states from excise taxes * on hunting equipment. These monies have been going to states for 61 years, and they are commonly known as Pittman Robertson taxes. They are used solely for wildlife management programs in the states. (Over the years these funds have totaled $3.2 billion).

While we are on the subject of excise taxes, note that taxes on fishing equipment (Dingell Johnson or Wallop Breaux funds...this bill was originally passed by Dingell and Johnson, but the latest

---

*the bill that created this tax on hunting equipment is the 1937 Federal Aid in Wildlife Restoration Act. It was passed after hunters and the hunting industry lobbied for the tax. The purpose at passage was to fund state wildlife conservation projects. Since passage 37 states have received over $50 million and 5 have received over $100 million for such projects. Most biologists call this the most successful wildlife conservation program in history.

amended version was led by Wallop and Breaux) brings in about $240 million dollars each year. These monies are apportioned to states for various fisheries management programs. That means that a yearly total of $395 million dollars is used for fish and wildlife management and it came from equipment purchased by men and women who hunt and fish.*

Each year the sale of hunting licenses brings in an additional $450 million and fish licenses totaled $375 million. Thus, from sportsmen and women, and through equipment excise taxes and license sales, over $1.2 billion dollars a year are raised for fish and wildlife management. This is a staggering figure.

These funds *must* (by law) be used for wildlife and fisheries management. The words "minuscule" and "fraction" do not accurately fit the real world situation.

After a removal of six percent for administrative purposes, every penny goes to the states for management activities. The federal law is so written that state politicians cannot touch the revenues for any nonwildlife/fisheries purpose. The money is "ear-marked" for fish and wildlife. This is a great idea....and it works so well.

So how can anyone suggest that hunters pay only a small percentage of the total costs? The "logic" presented in the Friends of Animals "hunting myths" poster is that sources other than excise taxes and licenses pay for most of wildlife management.

Those other sources - about $750 million - are the entire budget of the U. S. Fish and Wildlife Service. They also point out that some of what other federal agencies do is good for wildlife. Thus, part of the budget for the Soil Conservation Service (now called the Natural Resource Conservation Service) and the U. S. Forest Service goes to wildlife and fisheries management programs.

There is no doubt that certain federal agencies are doing things for wildlife and fisheries management that go beyond what sportsman monies do. These activities are paid for by all taxpayers, including hunters, nonhunters and antihunters too.

But how much of those funds go directly to specific, in-the-field work that benefit wildlife and fish? The budget for the U. S. Fish and Wildlife Service (USFWS) will exceed $1 billion dollars sometime

* the total for 1997 was $426 million.

in the next few years. What do they do with those funds? The USFWS receives its mandates by federal laws. Thus, they must review environmental permits.

The most important aspect of that program is to review Corps of Engineers' 404 wetland permits. These permits are given to people who needs to dredge or fill a wetland and thousands are filed each year, a very time consuming task. And there are many other types of environmental permits that they also must review.

The USFWS is also responsible for protecting wildlife habitat, and to categorize and inventory our wetlands. They also must enforce federal environmental and wildlife laws. Again, this is a huge, costly job that does much more than protect fish and wildlife.

They also manage the National Wildlife Refuge system which consists of over 500 refuges, 149 waterfowl production areas and 58 wildlife management areas. They manage over 800 migratory bird species (most of which are not hunted), manage some marine mammals, conduct wildlife and fish research (especially on migratory birds and marine mammals), operate around 70 fish hatcheries (stock fish for fishermen and for mitigation from environmental damage such as might be caused by dam construction), and provide technical assistance to other federal agencies.

They also identify, list, protect, and manage all endangered species, and conduct numerous international activities and research all over the globe. As one example let's consider the 1985 USFWS budget of $592 million dollars. Endangered species got $27 million (states do endangered species work with hunter and fishermen funds too), $63 million went to land acquisition (but $16.4 million of that was paid from the Duck Stamp account. Ducks Stamps must be purchased by all duck hunters every year and the proceeds go toward the purchase of wetlands. Stamp collectors purchase some stamps, but most are bought by duck hunters), $38 million came from Dingell Johnson contribution from excise taxes paid by fishers for angling equipment (this fund has since jumped up to over $240 million a year with the passage of the Wallop Breaux amendments to the DJ funding. Wallop Breaux implemented new taxes on new fishing equipment), Pittman Robertson was $85 million (the excise tax paid by hunters when they buy hunting equipment. This fund has jumped to $155 million a year since 1985), $12 million went to the refuges, and $37 million went to migratory birds, (but a big chunk is paid for by Duck Stamps sales.) Law Enforcement got $19.5 million.

Thus, claims that hunters and fishers do not pay for all wildlife/ fish/habitat/ environmental work in the country is true. Some funds that help wildlife and fish come directly from tax dollars that fund the USFWS. But a big portion of the USFWS budget comes from the excise taxes on hunting and fishing equipment.

For example, in 1991, $322 million of an approximate $750 million dollar budget for the USFWS came from PR and DJ funds. That's over 40 percent of the USFWS budget paid for by anglers and hunters. The USFWS activities that are paid for by hunters and fishers benefit all citizens.

As you read the above, it's easy to discover that endangered species, law enforcement, protecting the environment, are very important activities that benefit everyone. Land purchased by USFWS budget and Duck Stamp funds benefit everyone. Everyone can use these lands, and everyone uses them.

Endangered species work benefits everyone. Law enforcement benefits everyone. Environmental protection benefits everyone. Even deer management, turkey management and trout management benefits everyone. It's a fact that hunters and fishers pay for most of these latter activities.

Another interesting fact. It is obvious that federal agencies utilize some of their budgets (i.e., funds from all tax payers) to benefit wildlife and fish. That is correct. However, consider how those budgets are generated.

Who lobbies Congress to get federal agencies to increase their budgets for fish and wildlife? Who fights for the wildlife and fisheries budget in the U. S. Fish and Wildlife Service, or the Forest Service or the Bureau of Land Management? Do antihunting groups do that? Does Friends of Animals do that? Not really.

Here's who goes to bat for fish and wildlife. Hunters, fishermen, hunter organizations, fishing clubs and organizations whose historical roots are firmly entrenched with hunters and fishers (such as National Wildlife Federation, National Audubon Society, Isaac Walton League). This is not to say that nonhunters do not go after such funds for wildlife and fish because they do. But the antihunting organizations appear to do very little.

Hunters And The Science Of Wildlife Management

Consider the U. S. Forest Service's 1992 budget in Congress. The President's budget asked for $93 million which was almost $14 million less than in 1991. The Wildlife Management Institute believed that the U. S. Forest Service needed $144 million to implement fish and wildlife plans on the national forests. So groups like The Wildlife Society, National Wildlife Federation, Wildlife Management Institute recommended a much higher budget than the President recommended.

The same was true for the Bureau of Land Management budget. (By the way, the fish and wildlife portions of the budgets for the U. S. Forest Service and BLM are only a very small part of those agencies budgets but they are increasing every year and that is good for fish and wildlife.) But, leadership in lobbying for fish and wildlife funding in federal agency budgets comes from the hunting and fishing (i.e. conservation) constituency, not from the antihunting and antifishing constituency.

So the antihunting literature is right to a point. General tax payers do contribute large amounts of monies that benefit fish and wildlife via federal agencies like the USFWS and the U. S. Forest Service, etc. Having said that, it is still obvious that *most* funds for fish and wildlife work, especially work done directly in each state comes from hunters and fishermen.

Count the number of USFWS employees and other federal employees who work in wildlife and fisheries management in each state, and then count the number of state Department of Natural Resource wildlife and fisheries biologists, managers, law enforcement officers, information specialists, etc. working in each state.

There is no comparison in manpower, especially in the eastern and midwestern portions of the country. Consider that every state wildlife agency has many wildlife and fisheries managers, many conservation officers (wildlife and fisheries law enforcement officers), wildlife and fisheries biologists, wildlife and fisheries planners, some information and education specialists, some computer experts, and other staff, technicians and clerks. Most state agencies have over 200 employees plus another 100 or more working in law enforcement.

My home state of West Virginia is small, yet we employ over 180 people in the wildlife and fisheries agency and 125 wildlife and fisheries law enforcement officers for a total of over 300 people. All work to manage fish and wildlife and conserve habitat. Within this

West Virginia group are 42 hands-on wildlife and fisheries managers who have 10 conservation aides who directly assist them in the field.

Federal agencies employ relatively few wildlife and fisheries managers, some conservation law enforcement officers, and some wildlife and fisheries biologists (this number varies depending on the number of federal refuges, national forests, or research laboratories in the state). They may also have a few planners, computer staff, policy experts and others working for them in each state.

If you count the federal folks working as wildlife and fisheries biologists and managers for the U. S. Fish and Wildlife Service, the U. S. Forest Service, the Natural Resources Conservation Service, and the Army Corps of Engineers, in West Virginia, the total would probably not reach 50. The ratio of the number of federal wildlife and fisheries employees to state employees varies depending on its size and on the amount of federal land in the state (more federal land, more federal fish and wildlife employees). For most states, the state agency funded by hunters and fishers carries the majority of the load for wildlife and fisheries management.

In recent years hunters have claimed that only their monies buy lands that are put into our National Wildlife Refuge System. The Friends of Animals claim that nonhunters pay for "refuges." The truth for both sides is somewhere in between. The Migratory Bird Conservation Fund was started in 1934 and is used to buy refuge land. Most of these funds come from the Duck Stamp that waterfowl hunters must buy. In 1976, around $11 million a year from this fund was used to buy wetlands and refuge lands.

The Land and Water Conservation Fund also buys refuge lands. It was established in 1964, and all citizens contribute via offshore oil and gas royalties, the sale of federal surplus property, and motorboat fuel taxes. In 1976, $10 million came from this fund to purchase refuge land. Thus, in 1976, hunters and nonhunters contributed about 50-50 for the purchase of refuge lands.

However, in 1992 only 15 percent of the total $135 million used to buy refuge lands came from the Duck Stamp under the Migratory Bird Conservation Fund. Most came from the Land and Water Conservation Fund.

Conclusion? In the early years a great deal of refuge lands were purchased from hunter dollars. In recent years, the major dollar input comes from all taxpayers.

The Economic Incentive.—-Economic incentive is the most important reason that we have more wildlife in the United States (and Canada too) than anywhere in the world. As a wildlife professor, I had the opportunity to meet biologists from all over the world. They were always amazed to discover how much money was raised each year from hunting license sales and federal excise taxes on hunting and fishing equipment. They were astounded to learn that we harvested so many animals, yet we had so much wildlife.

They love our system of wildlife management. Why it works is really quite simple. We provide an economic incentive to keep animals alive.

It was a cold, chilly morning as the Land Rover headed from the base camp. I knew that soon the sun would send temperatures to sweltering levels. I was bowhunting at Humani Safaris in southeastern Zimbabwe; impala, kudu, and other plains game.

Mush Nichols, my guide, dropped me off at a small pond over thirty miles from camp. We quickly constructed a crude blind, and with just a tinge of daylight peaking over the mountain, I knelt and began to sharpen my broadheads.

Immediately behind me was a hilly jungle of vines, briars, and rocks. As I worked on my broadheads, a growl came from the rocks. It was a sound I'd not ever heard, but it didn't alarm me. In Africa, a newcomer is surrounded by strange bird calls, sounds of the jungle never heard before.

But when I heard it a second time, I slowly turned and there, not thirty yards away, and closing, was the first leopard I'd ever seen. He was a gorgeous animal. The colors were bright, he seemed awfully big. Maybe all leopards were big? The situation though, did not allow me to gawk at this great animal, for he was stalking me. In hind sight, my guess is that this leopard was returning to his day bed from a nights hunt, and stopped at the pond for a drink of water. Seeing me crouched down probably was a signal that I was a prey animal.

Leopards were not legal with a bow in Zimbabwe at that time, so I never thought about shooting this great animal. But I did think about protecting myself, so I quickly nocked an arrow and came to full draw. I talked to the leopard and at 10 yards he stopped still, twitching his long tail. Just as quickly as he appeared, he disappeared up and over the rocks.

Up until that moment I had remained fairly calm. But after he was gone, I sat down, rather shaken....and I remained such for almost 30 minutes. The sight of that great cat was one of the great thrills of my many years of bowhunting.

In the classic African adventure, *"Death In The Long Grass,"* the late Peter Capstick discussed what it takes to keep African leopard populations healthy. The answer is economic incentive.

If no market existed for leopards, then the very healthy populations now living in Africa would not exist. He made an eloquent and logical sales pitch for the hunting of leopards and their use for furs and trophies.

The argument is rather simple. Hunters will pay extremely large amounts of money to hunt leopards. Much of that money goes into the economy of the country from which the leopard comes. Jobs associated with each professional hunter (cooks, skinners, trackers, construction workers, taxidermists, taxidermist assistants, etc.) exist only when there is an abundance or an overabundance of a species. In this example, it's the leopard. If the government allows poachers to wipe out the species, then all those jobs, all that economic incentive, is lost for most of the citizens in that country.

If you abolish leopard hunting, in the interest of tourism, will tourists then provide the economic incentive needed to maintain large numbers of wildlife? Kenya has done just that, but it appears that this approach does not work as well as our system. Apparently, not enough funds are made available via tourism to maintain and protect large numbers of wildlife.

Hunting leopards, and the tremendous spending that comes with it, provides a reason for African countries to maintain good populations of leopards. The fact that leopards are alive, in large numbers (large enough to allow some to be harvested), provides money that then can be used to manage the cats and other wildlife as well.

Over the past few decades African species like rhinos and elephants were totally protected yet their numbers spiraled downward at a rapid rate. Tourism was the only value source to keep the animals alive, but it wasn't enough. Today things are changing.

Many African countries are again moving toward a sustainable-use policy that includes hunting, even for rare species. Hunting creates a huge value and incentive to natives to keep the animals alive, and to thwart poaching. Trophy fees for elephants in Zimbabwe (where there are approximately 25,000 more elephants than the habitat can sustain) are around $17,000. Add to that safari camp fees of $300 a day per person, travel and tourist visits done by hunters when in Zimbabwe, and the economic benefit is huge. It would not be unusual for an elephant hunt to bring over $25,000 into Zimbabwe's economy.

At the November, 1994 Convention on International Trade in Endangered Species (CITES) (CITES is an international meeting held every two years where most countries gather to discuss endangered species problems), Namibia proposed safari hunting resolutions for species formerly protected. Other countries that formerly opposed these resolutions, like Kenya and India, voted strongly in their support.

Safari Club International led the way, lobbied hard, and helped form a coalition of African countries to change the way we look at safari hunting. Importing trophies, even some listed as endangered, is now more possible than before.

The late Mollie Beattie, then U. S. Fish and Wildlife Service Director, spoke in favor of safari hunting as a conservation tool. Was this an important step for African wildlife? Yes!

Total protection with no hunting was not working. Certain species (such as elephants and rhinos) were being eliminated by poachers in some African countries. Without safari hunting , without an economic incentive, they might be lost forever.

Hunting such species, along with programs like Operation Campfire in Zimbabwe, that place some of the profits from those hunts back into local villages (thus creating an incentive for local villagers to thwart poachers), will lead to huge revenues. Those revenues go to local villagers and to federal wildlife agencies to manage all wildlife species, including those species that are hunted.

This value will create an incentive to protect these animal populations and cause their numbers to increase. That system, where hunting creates the value that keeps animal populations growing, has worked in America and is now understood by most countries around the world. Controlled hunting is the only hope for African wildlife.

Thus, in our country (and in parts of Africa that support safari hunting), there is an economic incentive to keep animals alive. The value is on the live animal. Sure, hunters do kill animals, but once they are dead there is little or no value to anyone except the hunter.

In America, when a hunter kills a deer, that animal has no value to anyone but the hunter. They keep the meat and that provides value to them and their family, but to no one else. What if deer meat could be sold to restaurants? Then you create value for a dead animal.

In America, there is pressure to *privatize* wild animals, to convert wild animals to a value in the private market or converting what was public value into private value. Elk and deer meat is very tasty. Some biologists fear if it becomes legal to sell such meat to restaurants, then criminals will realize that there is value in a dead elk or deer. *These criminals will hit the woods, kill the animals and sell the meat.

Creating an economic incentive for dead animals is exactly the opposite of the philosophy and management practices that have led to the large populations of many species America now enjoys. Here, the value is on the live animal. The more live animals, the more the value via hunting. If tourism or photography led to large economic values for wildlife, then those activities would also create an economic incentive to keep the animals alive. In most places around the world, values generated from these nonconsumptive practices do not approach those generated via legal hunting.

While browsing the internet recently a story on an animal rights group web page caught my eye. They were hammering a state wildlife agency pointing out that when whitetail deer were reestablished it was for the purpose of recreational hunting. No doubt that is true, and that reestablishment took place 57 years ago. They went on to state that the organization (the state wildlife agency) that should be protecting deer is killing them. Again, yes and no.

From the above you know that the money to manage deer comes from recreational hunters. Definitely true. We also know that deer have done very well over the past 50 years, and that many citizens like to see deer. Hunters definitely benefit too. The state wildlife

*The venison you see on restaurant menus is Fallow deer raised on private farms, and not whitetail deer.

114

agency has the responsibility to manage the deer herd for all citizens, so they authorize hunting seasons to curb deer numbers in areas where citizen complaints are high, and where hunting is needed (which is most everywhere today).

If there is an area in a state with low deer numbers, hunting pressure is reduced or not allowed.

The next logical question is whether the state wildlife agency is managing the herd for more deer to keep the hunters happy, or for all citizens. The state wildlife agency has a tough job; they need hunter dollars to manage *all* wildlife yet they also need to keep deer numbers down to satisfy other nonhunting citizens.

It is impossible for these state agencies to satisfy everyone. Hunters complain that there aren't enough deer; farmers complain that there are too many; gardeners in local areas want deer shot. Families where Lyme disease has occurred want deer killed. Animal activists want no deer killed. This makes for a tough row to hoe for a state wildlife agency.

But the economics are fairly straight forward. When legal recreational hunting is stopped, even just by a small amount, the license monies and the excise tax monies are reduced. This means potential lay-offs for employees of state wildlife agencies. It means cuts for law enforcement, research biologists, managers, etc. When this happens, *all* wildlife suffers.

Wildlife Management Is Scientific.—-Earlier I referred to The Friends of Animals poster that lists "10 Myths About Hunting." Since my value system is obviously different than theirs, it should be no surprise that I have a different perspective on their myths. However, one myth in particular bothers me more than the rest because it attacks my scientific community.

For 30 years I was a Professor of Wildlife Biology at West Virginia University. Myth No. 9 says that wildlife management is not scientific. It attacks the integrity of all 43 universities that offer wildlife management training programs. Let me quote directly from the poster: "A number of universities in our nation operate as trade schools offering "wildlife management" courses. The chief requisite is that the candidates repeat three times, 'Deer don't climb trees.'

When they offer the solution, "burn and cut down the tree so low-growing browse will erupt to explode the deer population," they are given a Bachelor of Science after their names."

I know that many readers feel that this description of our wildlife students and our wildlife universities is so ridiculous that it does not deserve comment. I agree.

So rather than attack the Friends of Animals, let me run through exactly what occurs in wildlife curricula across the country. Let's find out whether such programs are nothing more than "trade schools," and exactly what the students must learn before given a Bachelor of Science degree.

Wildlife management is a full undergraduate curriculum in 43 major universities in the United States. No country comes close to the training our students receive, and many foreign students take advantage of the great educational opportunities offered here in wildlife and fisheries management. The programs are fairly similar from school to school, though differences are found. Incoming freshman usually take two semesters of chemistry, two semesters of mathematics, two semesters of English and two semesters of general biology. They then move on to most of the following courses; organic chemistry, calculus, scientific writing (because biologists do a lot of writing), statistics (because data analysis is very important), computer science (modern science requires a knowledge of computers), a soils course (because vegetation and habitat grow on soils), silviculture (because timber management is a very important tool to manage wildlife), dendrology (because tree identification is necessary for proper management), genetics and physiology (because wildlife management students are biologists, thus they need some basic biology), political science (decisions are not made in a vacuum in our society), economics (same reason), sociology (same reason) and public speaking (because biologists give lectures or talk to the public as part of their job).

On top of these courses, wildlife majors also take approximately six wildlife courses. Most have laboratories. Most students take the following: Animal and plant ecology (discussion of ecosystems and the ecological relationships of animals, plants, and ecosystems), population ecology (discussion of reproduction, mortality, and factors that affect populations), wildlife and fisheries policy and administration (a discussion about wildlife laws that create policy, financing management, how wildlife agencies are organized), wildlife principles (basic theory and principles that allow the management of wildlife), rural and urban wildlife management (management of songbirds, nongame mammals, etc.), waterfowl management, wetland management, and others.

Is the wildlife curriculum a tough one? Absolutely. Almost all the above courses have labs, so wildlife/fisheries majors have one of the most rigorous scientific curricula offered in major universities.

Wildlife curricula are not for the faint-hearted. Those that make it through have done so after hard, diligent, scientific, work. And once the students finish their B.S. degrees, many move on for masters degrees or doctorate degrees in wildlife and fisheries management.

Any science usually has a professional society. Wildlife management is no different. Our practitioners belong to The Wildlife Society. Space does not permit us to discuss all the activities of The Wildlife Society. One important part of their programs are certification of students as wildlife biologists. When the students have completed a minimum number and type of college courses, they can be certified by The Wildlife Society.

This international organization has many state and university chapters and it plays a major role in determining wildlife management policies all over the world. Science is a major factor in dictating the policies set by The Wildlife Society. Any science usually has professional journals, where researchers publish results so that others in that science may learn.

The two major journals published by The Wildlife Society are the Journal of Wildlife Management and the Wildlife Society Bulletin. These journals are filled with articles aimed at making the science of wildlife management stronger and better each year. (This book has many such references herein).

Wildlife practitioners also publish in many other journals such as the Journal of Mammalogy, Ecology, Auk (a bird journal), The Wilson Bulletin (also a bird journal), American Midland Naturalist, and probably 30 other similar journals.

I note all of the above so readers can better understand that wildlife management does not just happen. It is not an accident that we have more wildlife today than ever before. It has happened because we have dedicated, well-trained, scientists and managers working hard for our great natural resources.

Counting Animals.—I believe one reason some animal activists put down the science of wildlife management is because we cannot tell people exactly how many animals are out there. We have estimates, but for most species we cannot give exact numbers.

Exactly how would you count the number of deer in Pennsylvania, Texas or tiny Rhode Island? Deer move around, live in very dense cover, and are hard to see even with trained eyes. There is no way to make a total count, so wildlife biologists use several techniques to make estimates, and to get an index to the number of deer.

Not only can we not get total deer counts, we have no way to get total counts for most species that live in this world. There isn't enough money and time to conduct a census for any animal in any area. Fortunately, we don't need exact numbers to manage conservatively—estimates about populations or trends work just fine.

I recently read that the last human census done in the United States might have been off by as much as 20 percent. Here are people that pay taxes, have last names, live in houses, get married, have mailing addresses, etc., yet for some reason (probably many reasons) we can't get a total head count. It sounds pretty simple to me; walk down the street, stop at each house, interview the people that live there and make a total count. I'm sure the census people also utilized computers to analyze tax returns. Just read all the tax returns for one year and count the number of people involved including husband, wife, and the number of dependents. That should work, but even with these techniques, city after city complained that the total census was in error and by large amounts.

Counting people is difficult. Apparently exact counts of people even in moderately-sized towns is nearly impossible. Counting animals is difficult. Exact counts of animals in large areas is impossible.

However, the science of wildlife management continues to expand its use of new technology. Each year techniques for counting animals become more sophisticated and estimates become more accurate. Even though wildlife biologists cannot count the expected number of animals, their estimates are very close in most cases.

They've developed techniques that provide yearly indices to animal populations that allow them to set harvest levels. One measure of their ability to do this is the abundance of wildlife, including hunted species, in the United States. Antelope, elk, mule deer, wild turkeys, black bear, mountain lions, bighorn sheep...all are hunted and all are very abundant.

Wildlife Careers.——What do wildlife majors do after they graduate?

Hunters And The Science Of Wildlife Management

They work for county, state, or federal wildlife agencies as managers, biologists, planners, computer data analysts, writers, law enforcement officers, etc. Today, probably 15-20 percent of our undergraduate wildlife majors end up working for state wildlife agencies. Another 20-30 percent go on to graduate school, and those will find good wildlife jobs in the private sector or with state or federal wildlife agencies. What about the rest of our undergraduate students?

Many work for environmental consulting companies on various environmental projects. They work for other natural resource agencies like water resources, solid waste management, surface mining, soils, etc. Many work for federal agencies like the U. S. Forest Service, or Bureau of Land Management, or the Natural Resource Conservation Service. Many work as Rangers on watersheds managed by the Army Corps of Engineers. Some work in the area of endangered species or for nongame management. Many work for private industry, usually in environmental impact and protection.

Indeed, many thousands of our wildlife majors work to protect the environment. Wildlife majors write environmental laws, inventory wetlands, inventory eagles, control toxic wastes, do research on acid rain and global warming, and are major consultants to foreign countries interested in becoming more environmentally sound. It is probable, and almost assured, that more wildlife majors work in environmental protection jobs than any other college curriculum.

Academic wildlife/fisheries programs are the life blood of protecting our environment and managing our wildlife. Bashing such students, professors, and their training programs helps convince nonhunters that the animal rights value system is really something to be feared.

Wildlife management is a proven science conducted by people extremely well educated and trained in natural resource ecology. These students and employees are professionals and they have helped to make the wildlife system in the United States the most successful management system in the world.

"Millions of acres and countless millions of wild animals exist today because of Theodore Roosevelt's foresight and love of nature, which can be clearly traced to his lifelong passion for hunting."

James Swan

Chapter 6

Is Hunting Ethical?

It was a great evening and I could not have been in a more beautiful location. Early June at the headwaters of Roan Creek near DeBeque, Colorado. There was much activity in the stream that ran close to my tree stand. Cutthroat trout were hungrily feeding on a hatch of insects.

There had also been good, recent activity at the bear bait. In fact, earlier in the week I'd seen a huge, blond-colored bear on the mountain as I sat in the tree. That monarch was obviously one of the dominant boars in the area. He harassed sows with cubs, and probably killed several every spring. Several smaller bears visited the bait over the next few days, but I chose to pass, waiting on that great bear. After eleven days in those mountains, I had to quit and return to work. No bear, but that was typical of bowhunting over bait.

For me, there was no question of whether such hunting was ethical or not. My guide was a cattle rancher and a hind quarter from one of his winter-killed cows was the bait. Weeks before John Lamicq and I scouted the area thoroughly before selecting this beautiful spot. Although I'd seen several bears there, I chose not to shoot. Still, I viewed the hunt as successful...a reprieve and escape from the office to the mountains.

Ethical for me, but unethical for others. (At the time you could bait hunt in the spring in Colorado, but it is now illegal). It filled the definition of hunting, and met my own standards for ethics. One myth about bear hunting with bows over bait is that it is like shooting fish in a barrel. Not so on this hunt. In fact, if such hunting were guaranteed, then it would not meet my ethical standards for hunting because the kill would be guaranteed.

The Definition Of Hunting.—Noted anthropologist William Laughlin wrote a chapter (*"Hunting: An Integrating Biobehavior*

System And Its Evolutionary Importance"), in the book Hunting And Human Evolution and therein listed the five components of hunting for primitive man.

They include: (1) training and skill development as a child, (2) scouting (learning to read animal sign, learning what areas to hunt), (3) shooting (learning to shoot, learning where, when, and how to shoot, actually shooting the animal...the kill), (4) recovering the animal (learning to trail and track an animal that has been shot), and (5) preparation of the meat (learning to clean and butcher the animal, storing the meat, cooking the meat).

These five components provide the best definition of hunting today. In fact it is these five components that separate hunting from killing. Killing is just one component of the hunt. If an activity does not include all of the five components, then it is not a true hunt.

But within each of the five components there can be a gradation of behavior. For example, how much learning to trail and track a wounded animal makes a hunter ethical or makes hunting moral? Those decisions must be addressed by each hunter, in each hunting situation, and if the hunting community does not meet the challenge and address such issues, then society will do so. And society may draw the line where hunters don't want it to be drawn.

I recently watched a television expose where a "shooter" killed a tame lion in a shooting preserve. There was another sequence in a shooting preserve where an individual watched a pack of dogs attack a black panther, and he finally shot the animal. The so-called tame lion, black panther "hunts" noted above have only one of these components of hunting. The kill.

Little training was needed, there was no scouting nor any tracking of the animal, and someone else butchered the animal for the shooter (though in these two examples there probably was no meat preparation). In these examples, "hunting" was simply shooting.

By definition, shooting or killing is not hunting — it is shooting or killing. Such canned hunts are morally repugnant to most hunters. Yet, the hunter when interviewed, gave the impression that this pitiful spectacle was what hunting was all about.

In comparison, that would be like an interview with a drunk driver who was depicted as the "norm" on the highway.

The Ethics Of Hunting And Other Manipulations Of Animals.—- Ethics is defined as the discipline which deals with what is good or bad. It also refers to a group of moral principles, a set of values and the character of people. The commitment to right and wrong is deeply personal. In essence, everyone is different and has his/her own set of values, hunters included.

Hunters have laws they must follow. But they also their own values that dictate how they hunt. When I was twelve years old, my father took me squirrel hunting. On those hunts my brothers and I were constantly being taught what I later called "mini-ethics lessons."

There were literally hundreds of such lessons. Here are just a few.

Lesson 1. Never shoot unnecessarily while hunting. If you wanted to plink with your 22 rifle, then you did that on the shooting range. In the woods, you never shot unnecessarily.

Lesson 2. Always keep your gun unloaded except when in a hunting situation. In fact, while walking into the woods, our guns were always empty. Only when we reached that portion of the woods where we would hunt would the guns be loaded.

Lesson 3. Always carry the gun barrel pointed at the ground. Following behind my father as we entered the woods, he would occasionally glance back. There was no mistaking his eye; making sure our guns were not high, even though they were unloaded.

Lesson 4. Never climb over anything with a loaded gun. Unload the gun, climb over the fence or log, receive the gun from your partner. Hold your partners gun while he/she climbed over. Then reload and hunt.

Lesson 5. Never climb a tree stand with your bow. Climb first, then use a tie line to pull up the bow.

Lesson 6. Never brag about your hunt in public in a boastful, rude, disrespectful manner. Sure, we could talk about the hunt and kills with friends. And we could do so with satisfaction. But no disrespect.

Lesson 7. Share game taken with the landowner. It was the polite thing to do. Even if the landowner declined, always make the offer before you leave the land.

Note, none of the above lessons (and I could list many, many more) are laws. These are things that my father thought were the "right" things to do when hunting, and he taught his sons the same. They became part of my hunting value system.

The question of whether man has the right to kill animals is very complex. First there is the tie with guns used in hunting to guns used in violence. Dr. David Klein noted "it (the gun) is seen as the direct agent of death and destruction." (In *"The Ethics of Hunting and the Anti hunting Movement"*, Transactions of the 38th North American Wildlife and Natural Resources Conference, 1973).

There is also the inclination to tie guns used in hunting to guns used in wars. In fact, after all major military conflicts in the 20th century there has been a rise in antihunting sentiment. The Viet Nam war was an especially graphic, demoralizing war that played out on television in front of most Americans every night on the evening news.

Most certainly it made us all a little sick of guns and killing. Victor Scheffer noted, "Sensitive people draw no moral distinction, except in degree, between killing people in political wars and killing wild animals for sport or vanity. They equate body counts with bag limits." (In *"The Future of Wildlife Management"*, an address to the annual meeting of the Humane Society of the United States, September. 18, 1975, Houston TX).

Dr. Klein also brought up another point. Man manipulates animals in many ways (i.e., horse racing, bull fighting, keeping pets, showing dogs, zoos, raising beef, medical research and hunting, just to mention a few), and we do this to improve our own well being, not for the well being of the animal.

Surely, we give our pets a great deal of care and love, and we get some affection in return. But in the end, it is we who choose the relationship and set the rules under which these pets live. We do it to satisfy our needs, and not those of the animal.

Having said this, Klein noted that "any ethical distinctions that exist in the justification of any other uses of animals....must relate to the relative values of these activities, to man....and not to differences in the effects on the animals involved."

In other words, almost all of man's methods of manipulating

animals lead to their death (or an "abnormal" life, i.e., wild horses and wild dogs lack many of the biological faults found in race horses or pet animals), and thus it is the value of the manipulation activities to man that is important. Klein is saying that if hunting is important to man, if it has value to man, it is acceptable even though it leads to the death of animals. In this light, hunting is no different than most of the manipulations we place on animals.

There are other thoughts that relate to what is moral relative to animals. Robert Bidinotto is a journalist who has written about the problems that occur when one gives animals the same rights given to humans. In a panel presentation in Norfolk, Virginia (*Mixed Messages: Who's Really Communicating The Wildlife Story?* Northeast Assn. of Fish and Wildlife Agencies, 1992) Bidinotto argued against the idea that all nature has intrinsic value. Intrinsic value means inherent value, i.e. that animals, or a specific animal, or trees, or a specific species of tree, have value just because they exist. The animal rights idea is that all things have intrinsic value and thus have rights. Bidinotto says that isn't so.

The dictionary defines "value" as the worth of something in money or goods, the estimated worth of something, the exchange worth, to think highly of, etc. Bidinotto pointed out that in order for something to have "value" it must have someone or something to value it.

Nature, deer, and ducks give us pleasure. We value them for many different reasons. Thus, man is the decider of what is good or evil, what has value, and what is moral.

So, a deer does not have inherent value to another deer, or to the woods, but only to man. A large buck that kills another large buck during a late November battle over breeding rights is not a bad deer because of the killing. Fighting is what big bucks do in late November. Man makes the judgments on what is good or evil. It's common sense thinking.

Any discussion of good, evil, morality, ethics, will often lead to religious discussions. The late Dr. Manford Meitzen, former head of the Religion Department, West Virginia University, took a most interesting look at the ethics of hunting from a religious viewpoint.

He noted that biblical ethics "revolve about man, i.e., man's relationship to God and to other men. Animals are involved in ethical considerations only insofar as they might have a bearing on relationships between human beings or between God and man. It is not possible to sin against an animal: one only sins against man or God." (In "*The Ethics of Hunting*; *A Christian Perspective*", J. of Theology, 1976).

Dr. Ann Causey is a college teacher who has written two very interesting papers about the morality of hunting. The first ("*On The Morality of Hunting*") was published in 1989 in the journal Environmental Ethics. The second, "*Is Hunting Moral?*," was published in the proceedings of the Montana's Governors Conference on Our Hunting Heritage, 1992. Both are must reading.

Antihunters feel hunting is unethical and that taking the life of a sentient (living) being is unethical, and taking the life of a wild animal is demeaning to man. Hunters would obviously disagree.

Let's see what Dr. Causey says about whether hunting is ethical or not. In her Montana Conference paper, Dr. Causey made several introductory points. The first was that the ethics of a hunter and the "making of a moral decision is guided by conscience."

I agree.

A second major point was that there is a difference between what is moral and what is legal. There may be some hunting activity that is legal, but immoral to some hunters and some people. Hunting bears over bait is a prime example. It is legal in some areas and enjoyed by many, decried by others.

Dr. Causey goes on to note a very important point, you can't mandate morality by laws. If you could, then America would be crime free. There would be no drug use, because we have laws against it. There would be no gun tragedies in our public schools, because we have laws against that. Simply passing a law doesn't mean that all citizens will be moral and respect the rights of others by not violating that law. How I wish that were the case. A final introductory point was that hunters should not slander antihunters nor attack them for their beliefs, but rather address the issues in the debate. Once again, I agree with Dr. Causey.

She then addressed the question, is hunting morally acceptable? She pointed out that one common way hunters have of trying to make hunting acceptable is to present scientific data, but the morality and ethics of hunting is not about science. Given that hunting generates economic benefit, it raises money for wildlife management and for the purchase of habitat; game animals have increased under modern hunting laws, hunting is good wildlife management, etc. But relative to the question of morality, such information and data really aren't relevant.

As Dr. Causey pointed out, the real question is: Is hunting moral? The hunters answer will be yes, and the antihunters answer will be no, and the reason for the difference is because each person or group has a different value system. As an example of this difference, consider the idea that hunted animals suffer pain.

Hunters think about it and try to avoid it. They do not ignore the fact that animals can suffer if the hunter behaves irresponsibly and sometimes even if they behave responsibly. But hunters consider other complexities as well.

The pain an animal experiences is not the worst that can be experienced in the act of dying by a wild animal (starvation, predation by coyotes, crippling diseases). Hunters look at the pain issue from the broad perspective of an animals struggle to live in the wild. Antihunters focus more on the idea that animals suffer pain caused by hunting. They focus more on this one aspect of hunting. Different value systems yield different views on the ethics of hunting.

Ethical For Some, Unethical For Others.—-Although I agree with much of Dr. Causey's writings, there are a few of her thoughts about hunting with which I disagree. She questions trophy hunting, as do others.

Hunting selectively for certain animals is very misunderstood. When presented as some rich dude who pays an unethical guide to help him take a huge trophy using illegal methods, trophy hunting is obviously bad. But almost no one does that and most hunters would find such activities reprehensible.

But hundreds of thousands of hunters select large quality animals in a responsible, ethical manner. They are just very selective in the animals they shoot — trophy hunting. (More on this in chapter 14).

Dr. Causey also questions shooting animals over bait. In recent years bait hunting for bears was the subject of much controversy in Colorado, and citizens there voted it down by supporting Amendment 10 at the polls. Many who voted against bait hunting for bears were not opposed to all hunting, just to bait hunting for bears because they viewed it as unethical.

Baiting is a deeper subject than meets the eye. If bait hunting simply involved using a 4-wheeler to dump jelly-filled donuts across the landscape where hikers and bikers often travel, then there would be a real problem with how some hunters and others would view the practice.

If the bait hunting situation just becomes an effort for one bait hunter to out-compete another bait hunter at all costs, this would be a problem. In my opinion, sitting on a trash dump, or on a bait site that hasn't been cleaned up for several years is a situation that is undesirable.

If people believe that bait hunting bears means that hunters will see a bruin every time they hunt over bait and that shooting one is easy and unfair to the animal, it is easy to understand why some people are opposed to the practice, regardless if they are hunters or nonhunters. I've bear hunted with my bow over bait for many springs. My image of bait hunting is to scout hard for very remote areas that may hold bears, place limited bait as inconspicuously as possible, be selective in the animal you shoot, and clean up the site when finished.

Sitting in the Saskatchewan bush for days on end, seeing eagles, beaver, hawks, deer, coyotes, and sometimes after many days, seeing a black bear approach the bait site is hunting to me. Bowhunting over bait does not guarantee a bear for the hunter.

I find bait hunting for bears involves all five aspects of hunting. It demands training and skill development, scouting (finding the perfect bait location), shooting, trailing, and taking care of the meat. It is not just killing.

But, if you've never sat on a clean bait for black bears, next to a wild mountain trout stream in the fading evening calm, your impression of bait hunting might be different than mine. Try to explain the hunting aspects of bait hunting for bears to a nonhunters or another hunter who hasn't bait hunted with a bow and you will have your hands full. I've listened to what some bait hunters say about it, and their comments sound foreign to my bait hunting experiences. My point is that even the same form of hunting might be unethical to some, and ethical to others.

What may be unethical to Dr. Causey, might be ethical to Dr. Samuel, and vice-versa.

The question relative to baiting is whether such hunting is "fair chase." Jim Posewitz discussed fair chase in his book, "*Beyond The Fair Chase: The Ethic and Tradition of Hunting*" (Jim is the founder of Orion, The Hunters Institute in Helena, Montana and this superb small paperback can be purchased by calling (800) 582-2665).

Fair chase focuses on the shooting component of hunting. The key to fair chase is whether there is a proper balance between the hunter and the hunted.

If a hunting situation is such that the animal has no chance for escape, that the predator always kills the prey, then that is not a fair chase situation. If the kill is guaranteed, that is not fair chase. As Posewitz points out, today's modern technology has closed the gap between the equality of predators and prey, of man and hunted animals.

Couple that technology with diminished habitat, and increasingly more people, and we have a different set of circumstances about the relationship of hunters and quarry than existed 100 years ago. Determining that relationship often is a personal decision.

As Poseweitz noted, only the hunter can judge what is fair chase. Fair chase involves the five components of hunting, especially shooting, but it also involves the law. However, just because something is legal doesn't make it "fair chase" for some hunters.

Let me offer an example. Grouse hunting is a common activity in West Virginia. As a group, grouse hunters are some of our most ethical hunters. They practice all five components of the hunt. When it comes to actually shooting at a ruffed grouse, although it is legal to shoot a bird on the ground, before they fly, every grouse hunter believes that such behavior is unethical. In fact, I've never known of a grouse hunter to shoot a bird on the ground, even though it is legal.

Grouse hunters draw the line on the shooting part of the hunt, and this is their personal choice. In fact, among grouse hunters it is understood that ground swatting a grouse is unethical and the same thing applies to shooting birds out of a tree.

Society doesn't have to deal with it by making a law, because grouse hunters just don't do it. If they did, sooner or later you would see it on some television expose, citizens would then become upset, and a law would be passed to stop it.

It is the unethical hunter, and the unethical acts of hunters that hurts hunting. Every time a hunter turns his/her back on a hunter's unethical behavior it hurts all hunting. Doing so one time is once too many. Hunters can no longer tolerate unethical or illegal behavior in the woods.

Dr. Causey noted that we've made some improvement in hunter behavior in recent years. We no longer see the "happiness is a warm gut pile" mentality T-shirts that were common 10 years ago. Dead deer on car fenders or tops are not as common as they once were. We are seeing greater efforts to reduce wounding and more hunter education to train hunters to recover their game. More hunters are becoming aware of the feelings of nonhunters and rightfully so.

This returns us back to the question: is hunting ethical? Dr. Causey believes that one person cannot answer that question for another. I see and read about hunting activities that are legal but are undesirable to me. But much of what I know and see about hunting is good.

The hunter appreciates nature, wild things, and ecosystems. He/she is not intruding into the environment. They study it, know it, love it, live it, appreciate it, and respect it. It is a morally good activity.

The ethical, moral hunter lives out "prehistoric urges," and maintains his/her contact with nature. One can make a good case for such activity as being moral. Those values are defensible.

"I believe killing wildlife, as part of hunting, is acceptable only when it is the true and artful climax of the hunting ritual, practiced as the timeless art of self-sustenance, with reconnection to, and participation in, the natural process of "live unto life only through death." Full appreciation of this most fundamental and bittersweet process comes with full participation, and full participation though the hunt cannot occur without experiencing, first-hand, the kill."

Stephen Mealey, Forest Supervisor, Boise National Forest, Keynote Address ("*Ethical Hunting: Updating an Old Heritage for America's Hunting and Wildlife Conservation Future*"), Foundation for North American Wild Sheep Conference, 1994

"A peculiar virtue in wildlife ethics is that the hunter ordinarily has no gallery to applaud or disapprove of his conduct. Whatever his acts, they are dictated by his own conscience, rather than a mob of onlookers. It is difficult to exaggerate the importance of this fact."

Aldo Leopold

SECTION III

ANTIHUNTING

Chapter 7. Peoples Attitudes About Hunting And Antihunting*

It's obvious that hunters have strong attitudes about animals and about hunting, but antihunters also have strong attitudes about animals. They have honest attitudes; they arrived at those attitudes as they grew up, and they strongly believe in those feelings.

Hunters cannot change antihunter's minds on how they feel about hunting, nor can animal activists change the minds of hunters. However, relative to wildlife management and what goes on in nature, animal activists attitudes can create problems for wildlife. In this chapter we will consider the views and attitudes that some of our citizens have about hunting and hunters. We'll examine several myths about hunting. We'll consider the myth that citizens support of deer hunting is on the decline. When bow hunting is urged to lower deer numbers, especially in areas where plenty of people live, antihunters tell us that it is not safe. That is another myth that we will consider.

There are many surveys to consider, so let's get to it.

Antihunting Attitudes.—-Twenty years ago few people ever questioned hunters about their motives. Today it is common for people to ask individual hunters this question....How can you kill animals? If we look at that question in a serious manner, it becomes evident that all people are responsible for the death of animals in one way or another. Vegetarians, school teachers, farmers, hunters, nonhunters, even antihunters are directly responsible for the death of animals. But most folks do not recognize that fact, or if they do, they do not want to face up to that reality.

*portions adapted (with permission) from "On Your Side" columns, Bowhunting News, September. 1989, Oct. 1993, and "Know Hunting" columns, Bowhunter Magazine, and "*The Next Twenty-five Years*", Bowhunter Magazine, October 1996.

However, hunters do face up to the reality of death of animals, and when they respond to the question of how they can take the life of an animal, by explaining that hunting is more than killing, many nonhunters will agree. One common response I get is, "I don't hunt, but I understand the necessity for hunting."

But explaining hunting to antihunters is rather fruitless. No amount of discussion will impact the strong antihunter. What follows may explain that feeling. In chapter two I discussed the extensive study of Dr. Steve Kellert, which categorized how people viewed animals into different attitudes. Dr. Kellaret found two prevalent attitude categories among antihunters, both of which focus concern on the individual animal rather than the overall animal population.

First is the *humanistic* attitude. People with this attitude relate to wild animals through their relationship with individual pet animals. Kellert felt the humanistic attitude was the fastest growing type found in the country (others have questioned that growth and feel they aren't growing, but are simply more evident. The reason being that as we move from a rural to urban environment, humanistic attitudes pervade society more and thus, humanistic attitudes are expressed more as we become less associated with how animals are used for our own purposes and for survival).

Remember, all people have some of many attitude types. Thus, hunters, nonhunters, and antihunters have some humanistic attitudes. Most of us, hunters and nonhunters alike, own a pet dog or cat, and we tend to humanize our feelings about that animal. Having pets affects how we look at other animals. But it affects antihunters much more than hunters.

Antihunters have the highest ratings for humanistic attitudes. Those with this view look at wildlife as individual animals, the same as they see their individual pets. Apparently the greater their relationship with pets, and the less they are related to wild animals (more urban as opposed to living in rural areas and farms), the more humanistic a persons views may be.

The humanistic attitude is common to men and women, but scores are stronger for women. A few studies have also shown high humanistic scores in younger children, especially among those growing up in cities.

It is easy to see how this attitude can create problems for wildlife agencies. If a person relates to wildlife through their pet dog or cat, they then may view wildlife in the same way. Hunters and wildlife biologists look at wildlife as a population.

Whether a person supports or opposes hunting is partly a matter of perspective, tradition, and the attitudes people learned as they grew up. Years ago most hunters grew up learning about wild animals by being in the woods. Most antihunters grew up learning little about wild animals, except what they saw in zoos, on television and from their pet dog or cat. That pet had a name, was cuddly, was fed and kept warm in the winter.

With that perspective, would you want someone to kill your pet dog? Of course not. Then why would a hunter want to kill a deer? After all, it is an individual animal too, and it is beautiful, and if it is cold and hungry in winter, then we should feed and keep it warm. From the perspective of the antihunter, the last question is a good one, and I'll address it below.

Few, if any, wildlife biologists agree that we should feed all wildlife, keep them warm in winter, and protect them from all predators. Biologists understand that we cannot feed, give warmth, and protect all individual wild animals. In most situations, it is not realistic to treat wild animals as individuals.

For most people, the personification of wild animals doesn't make them persons, but for some it does. One situation where these two philosophical views of wild animals are in direct conflict is in urban areas where deer are a problem.

State wildlife agencies try to manage deer by harvesting them in an urban area when they believe removing a certain number from the population will benefit the whole herd. Antihunters only see the individuals killed, and do not relate the harvest to an aggregate view of the entire deer population in the area. (For a discussion on urban deer populations, see chapter 13.)

The humanistic attitude almost certainly is part of the reason for the following report in the Los Angeles Times. Their poll showed that Americans believed "animals are a lot like humans when it comes to emotions and reasoning ability."

Happy, sad, excited, mad? Do animals exhibit such emotion? Apparently many think so.

Chapter 7

Heres a figure that shows how far removed most Americans are from nature. Forty-seven percent said animals "are just like humans in all important ways." As an aside, 54 percent said they oppose hunting for sport and half objected to wearing fur.

The second attitude type typical of antihunters is the *moralistic* attitude, which means they are against all animal cruelty. Though the humanistic attitude is far more prevalent in society, the moralistic attitude is the dominant one among antihunters.

While hunters have some humanistic attitude, they have little moralistic attitude. Apparently from the way they were raised, in hunting families with hunting traditions, hunting is not viewed as being cruel to animals.

Even though this section of the book is about antihunting attitudes, since I brought up the question, let's back up and consider why hunters think it is all right to kill a deer, while others are opposed to killing a wild deer.

I believe attitude scales help answer this question. Antihunters have more humanistic and moralistic attitudes and they view hunting as killing, and as a cruel activity.

Hunters view wild animals as populations, as part of the natural system, as animals to be used to benefit man; they view death as natural, and revere wild animals in an almost spiritual way. With that perspective, hunting to them is not cruel.

People with strong humanistic concerns can be antihunters, but they need not be and many are not. People with strong humanistic concerns can be informed about hunting and other alternatives; their values do not demand that they take a position against hunting.

People with moralistic attitudes have humanistic attitudes, but the reverse is not necessarily true. People with *strong* moralistic attitudes *must* be against hunting, but moralistic attitudes are not prevalent among society, and is not close to the prevalence and strength of the humanistic attitude

Attitudes of strong moralistic antihunters cannot be modified because they have made a decision that is not influenced by new information. No matter what information is shown them, they still feel that killing animals is cruel.

Attitudes of most hunters also would not be modified by new

information. Most hunters would never embrace antihunting or animal rights philosophies, regardless of information presented to them.

There is one other attitude of interest to hunters and antihunters. The *ecologistic* attitude is exhibited by those who are interested in ecosystems, ecology, biodiversity, etc. Obviously, this attitude is common among hunters, but a small percentage of antihunters also have this attitude. We should acknowledge this ecologistic group since they are focused on the same level as many hunters and wildlife managers. They have a concern for ecological systems and populations.

Do You Approve Of Deer Hunting?—-Most towns east of the Mississippi River have a deer problem. Because of this, there has been a lot of press about the need to hunt deer. From all of this coverage, one might get the impression that support for deer hunting is decreasing. That is not true.

In order to learn how the public feels about deer hunting, the best approach would be to do a long term study. In that way, any ups or downs that might occur from year to year would be kept in perspective. Doing such long-term research is difficult, but fortunately, there is one major study on deer hunting.

A survey of citizens of New Jersey is conducted every five years by Dr. James Applegate, wildlife biologist professor at Rutgers University. Dr. Applegate is an outstanding scientist and his reputation for quality research is unchallenged.

His survey began in 1972, and was run biannually until 1982 when it shifted to once every five years. Data was collected by phone interviews as a part of the Eagleton Institute for Politics with only people over 18 years of age surveyed.

Questions asked were: "Have you ever hunted? Have you hunted in the past two years? and most importantly, **Do you approve of deer hunting?**"

If we look at the data for 1972 to 1992 *there is no decline in the support of deer hunting.* One year the percent approval is up and two years later it is down. There is no downward trend in approval of deer hunting in New Jersey. In fact, in 1992 there was a major upswing in the support of deer hunting by New Jersey residents. Interesting. Everyone knows that New Jersey is an urbanized state with more people per square mile than any other. Everyone knows that in such urban situations antihunting sentiment can grow and threaten the future of our present system of hunting and wildlife management. Can anti sentiment really be dropping in New Jersey?

Responses Of New Jersey Citizens On The Question Of Whether They Approve Of Deer Hunting Over A Twenty-year Period.

YEAR	% APPROVING	% DISAPPROVING	UNDECIDED
1972	54	38	8
1974	49	43	8
1976	50	40	10
1978	55	37	8
1980	52	40	8
1982	49	44	7
1987	54	38	8
1992	65	29	6

This table and the next were adapted from "*Attitudes Toward Deer Hunting In New Jersey: 1972- 1982*" James Applegate, 1984 Wildlife Society Bulletin 12(1), pages 19-21. Copyright permission from The Wildlife Society.

No data exists since 1992, so it's important to be cautious since 30 percent of the population is still opposed to deer hunting, and that is a high percentage. But based on available data, approval rates for deer hunting in New Jersey are up. During the period of 1982 to 1992 support for deer hunting has increased by 16 percent.

Even if we take the 1972-1982 average of 51 percent approval of deer hunting as a comparison, there is an increase of 14 percent over the past 10 years. The study shows an 11 percent increase in support of deer hunting over the past five years (from 1987 to 1992).

There is another interesting thing that can be gleaned from this data. From 1972 to 1987 there was no increase or decrease in antihunting sentiment in New Jersey. Over a 15-year span, when antihunting and antihunters were getting all kinds of publicity, antihunting sentiment did not increase.

Dr. Applegate has no ready answer for the big increase in support of hunting in New Jersey in 1992. There is some speculation that Lyme disease has been a major factor. The first case in New Jersey was not reported until 1978 but today there are over 1,000 cases reported each year.

There obviously has been a concurrent major increase in publicity about the disease. If we couple Lyme with a major increase in pest complaints due to deer damage this could lead to an increase in support of deer hunting.

Being highly urbanized, and having a large deer herd leads to many encounters between people and deer. Deer/car collisions are common. Deer munching gardens and yard shrubs is a common occurrence.

All of these factors may have led to increased support of deer hunting. The basis for this support lies with high deer numbers that lead to those problems noted above. When people's tolerance for damage, health concerns, etc. are exceeded, they turn to hunters as the only viable friend they have to prevent negative deer encounters.

This increase is all the more surprising considering the decreasing percentage of active hunters in New Jersey. Just over nine percent of the people surveyed were active hunters in 1972 but this decreased to 4.8 percent by 1992.

When will nonhunters support hunting? Dr. Applegate has shown that nonhunters have a better chance of supporting hunting if they know the hunter. A decrease in the percentage of people who hunt in New Jersey means that over the coming years there will be a decreased chance for nonhunters to know a hunter.

The last line in the table below shows that the percent of nonhunters who have no friends or family members who hunt is increasing. This factor makes the increased support of hunting all the more interesting.

Relationship, Hunting Participation & Approval (A) or Disapproval (D) of Deer Hunting in New Jersey.

	1972	1982	1987	1972 A	1972 D	1982 A	1982 D
Active Hunter	9.3%	4.9%	7.3%	84	15	93	7
Past Hunter	16.2%	12.6%	12.7%	71	25	81	12
Nonhunter with friends or family who hunt	31.9%	29.7%	27.8%	57	34	54	41
Nonhunter-no friends or family who hunt	42.6%	52.4%	51.9%	39	50	35	56

Nonhunter association with hunters is also related to their approval or disapproval of deer hunting. Obviously, active hunters approve of deer hunting. Ninety-three percent of hunters approved of deer hunting in New Jersey in 1982. Nonhunters with friends or family who hunt approve of deer hunting while those without such friends or family tend to disapprove of hunting. And their disapproval rates were higher (56 %) in 1982 than in 1972 (50 %).

The New Jersey deer management program is one of the most successful in the country. It is headed up by noted wildlife biologist Robert McDowell, and that agency has been on the cutting edge of progressive deer management in urban settings. Their bowhunter education program has been mandatory for many years.

They had one of the first trapper education programs in the country. Their wildlife agency has been a prime developer of the philosophy that increasing hunter recreation days is important. Thus, New Jersey bowhunting has been on the increase for many years.

They have many special deer hunts because of localized deer problems that cannot be solved on a county-wide basis. New Jersey has led the way on offering special permits for bows and guns to help increase deer harvest in problem areas. Perhaps there is more support for deer hunting today in New Jersey because their citizens recognize this quality management of wildlife.

Perhaps the great safety record of bow and gun hunters in New Jersey has been recognized by the nonhunting public. And maybe hunts that have been held have been viewed as successful by nonhunters.

It will be most interesting to follow New Jersey over the next 10 years to see how things change or don't change. Meanwhile, it appears that state's antihunting sentiment has reached a 25-year low, and in the past we have seen that as New Jersey goes, so goes other eastern coastal states.

Will we see similar increased support for deer hunting in New York, Pennsylvania, Virginia, or Maryland? Only time will tell.

Other Studies.—-Other recent surveys show public support for hunting. A 1993 survey in West Virginia showed 79 percent approval of hunting, and 17 percent disapproved. Sixty-seven percent believed more deer should be killed to control problems, and 52 percent reported that they, or a member of their household, hunted. Hunting is a major activity in West Virginia.

The Gettysburg (Pennsylvania) Civil War National Park has 1,200 deer and should have about 120 animals. One proposal was to have sharpshooters kill deer.

Chris DeRose is an animal rights activists who worked for the TV show, "Hard Copy." In a 1995 Hard Copy show they used a 1-900 number to solicit public response to the idea of returning the park "to being a bloody killing field."

Covered in camouflage, and hidden under a netted blind, DeRose said, "I watched a doe be shot by a hunter and then saw its fawn running wildly bawling." Scenes of deer being shot and dragged away were mixed with his words. Obviously "Hard Copy" expected this biased presentation to convince the public to buy into animal rights values that would continue to see the deer and the park's vegetation suffer.

Results of the poll on whether the deer should be shot? Eighty-eight percent voted yes, and 12 percent voted no. Another Pennsylvania study showed that 83 percent of it's residents approve of public hunting.

A 1993 survey in Vermont showed that only 4 percent objected to hunting under any circumstance. Sixty-eight percent found hunting acceptable under "some circumstances," and the circumstances were: 72 percent against trophy hunting, but 100 percent accepted hunting to reduce overpopulation. Twenty-seven percent found hunting fully acceptable while 67 percent found trapping acceptable under certain circumstances.

In Connecticut, 76 percent approved of hunting, 19 percent disapproved. In New Hampshire, 69 percent approved, and 25 percent disapproved. In Arkansas, 82 percent approved.

In Minnesota, 72 percent agree that "hunting is a natural activity for people." In Colorado the animal activist movement is very strong. Twenty-seven percent believe in animal rights, 32 percent believe in moderate use of animals (animal welfare) and 31 percent are strong utilitarians.

In Michigan, 82 percent favor deer hunting (only 14 percent actually hunt deer). Antihunting does appear to have an urban flavor;

only 47 percent of the residents of Detroit support deer hunting. In Wisconsin 76 percent of 16- and 17-year-old approve of legal hunting, and 89 percent think it should remain a legal activity.

The International Association of Fish and Wildlife Agencies (IAFWA) recently conducted a study on general public perceptions on fish and wildlife, hunting and fishing. They found that nonhunters do not know who manages wildlife, but they do want wildlife managed. Also, nonhunters want more done for wildlife, but do not want to pay more to do it.

That's interesting since right now they pay almost nothing to manage wildlife. That study also showed that the two major hunting concerns that nonhunters have were that it be done safely, and that the animals taken should be used. Since hunting is extremely safe compared to other outdoor recreational activities, and since almost all game meat is utilized, the general public is not being betrayed. (Note, nonhunters did not rail on the ethics or morality of hunters or hunting, as we so often hear from the animal activists side. The general public apparently does not feel as strongly about those issues as animal activists.)

Studies published in 1996 by Montana Fish, Wildlife and Parks and the Missouri Department of Conservation show support for hunting. Ninety-six percent of Montanans believe they should have the right to hunt. Other beliefs were: 72 percent felt hunting reduced crop damage, 76 percent were opposed to hunting in state parks, and 59 percent believed that trapping was an important cultural tradition (40 percent thought it was cruel but 44 percent thought it wasn't).

Eighty-eight percent of Missourians approved of hunting for food, 59 percent approved of hunting to be with friends and family, and 59 percent approved of hunting to experience Missouri traditions.

Here is a very interesting statistic about trophy hunting. We've heard how most citizens oppose trophy hunting, yet, in Missouri, 44 percent approved of hunting for "an exceptional animal, like an older deer with big antlers."

Could a change in our use of the term "trophy" to "exceptional animals" help the public? Maybe so. And here is another interesting statistic from Missouri: 68 percent felt that trapping was acceptable as long as it was regulated.

Peoples Attitudes About Hunting And Antihunting

This study did show a need for more public education becauae a relatively high 23 percent believed that Missouri's wetlands "should be drained for better uses." Whoa.

One other conclusion of the IAFWA study was that people think wildlife conservation is important, but in the total picture, for most people, wildlife is not a significant issue. In fact, they find golf, gardening, and recycling more interesting than wildlife. This shows the need for a strong conservation education approach in the public schools.

Nonhunter Concerns About Hunting.—-In the 1980's the National Shooting Sports Foundation (NSSF) conducted interviews to determine what concerned nonhunters about hunting. They found *nonhunters have concerns that are antihunter and concerns that are antihunting.* Here is a list of those concerns.

Concerns Of Nonhunters About Hunting
1. Hunters kill other hunters accidently
2. *Wounded* animals die a slow death
3. *Wounded* animals die a painful death
4. Hunters don't have to know anything to buy a rifle
5. Leaving a *wounded* animal to die is sadistic
6. *Wounded* animals die a horrible death
7. Hunters *cripple* animals that are wounded but don't track them down
8. Hunters hunt in areas that are off limits
9. People get hurt while hunting
10. Hunters shoot animals they're not allowed to hunt

The major antihunting concern was *wounding*. It was mentioned in five of the top 10 concerns about hunting. The other five reasons were antihunter related. For example, there was concern about the safety of hunting and the fact that hunters are killed while hunting.

As a recreational activity, hunting is one of the safest of all sports. However, you never hear of a call to abolish those activities that are much less safe like football, skiing, boating, etc. More people die playing tennis and golf than by hunting.

How do nonhunters gain a perception about hunters? Here is a quote from the International Association of Fish and Wildlife Agencies: "If participants knew a good hunter, they had a good impression of hunters. If they knew a poor hunter, they had a poor impression of hunters."

That should tell you how important hunter behavior is today. Another 1995 nation-wide study confirmed how important hunter behavior is by showing that 62 percent of Americans believe that "a lot" of hunters violated laws or were unsafe hunters.

This study may be a reflection of just how far removed nonhunters are from what really happens in the woods, because 50 percent believe that hunters drink alcohol while in the field. While a few hunters may drink in the field, the vast majority do not. In my forty-plus years of hunting, I have never seen a hunter drinking in the field.

These two studies show that there is a great deal of misconception about hunting among nonhunters. They believe hunting is unsafe (when it is very safe compared to most outdoor recreation activities), that hunters are not educated about hunting and the ethics of hunting (when they do have to take a hunter education course before they can hunt; but perhaps more extensive training is required), and that wounding is a major problem (studies show that biologically wounding is not a factor, and hunter education programs focus on reducing wounding).

If hunting is to be accepted by the general public, then hunters must continue to improve their safety record, reduce wounding, and behave in an ethical manner at all times. The general public approves of hunting as a wildlife management tool.

Thus, for hunting to survive, hunters must show continued improvement in all areas, to be accepted by their nonhunting neighbors.

Conclusion On Attitudes About Hunting.—-The most extensive recent study on how 2,085 Americans view hunting was conducted in 1995 by the Responsive Management company in Harrisonburg, Virginia. They found that 73 percent of Americans approve of hunting while 22 percent disapprove. Eighty-one percent believe hunting should remain legal while 16 percent thought it should be illegal.

Eighty-five percent of adult Americans felt that people should have the freedom to choose to hunt if they wish while 14 percent disagreed. Clearly the majority of Americans still support the right to hunt.

"I was always adamantly opposed to hunting...Then, at the age of twenty-two, I went to live for a year with Inupiaq Eskimos on Alaska's Arctic coast, where I studied how they subsist and survive—and they taught me about their hunters' way."

Richard Nelson

Chapter 8

The Antihunting Movement*

Who are antihunters and why do they oppose hunting? Those are the questions that we will address in this chapter. We'll find that some folks are antihunting while others are antihunter. In other words, some oppose hunting, while others get upset about what hunters do.

We'll also discuss the major antihunting groups and note their role in this phenomenon known as the antihunting movement.

The Movement.—-The antihunting movement is growing, has a lot of money, and it has some appeal to a large segment of society. There are hundreds of local, state, national and international-level animal rights organizations and they get plenty of publicity from the press. Often celebrities are involved, greatly enhancing press appeal.

I first hunted in 1953. At that time literally no one questioned hunting. Even into the 60's and early 70's, there were few questions raised about recreational hunting. But during this time the animal activist movement was growing. This movement received a big boost from the publication of a book entitled *"Animal Liberation"* by Peter Singer in 1976. While criticizing the methods used to raise domestic livestock and poultry for meat consumption, Dr. Singer made the argument that animals deserve *equal consideration,* but not equal rights. His book led him into prominence as the philosopher whose writings and beliefs were a strong basis for the humanistic and animal welfare concerns for animals.

Dr. Singer does not feel that animals have legal and moral rights equal to humans, however, the movement that Dr. Singer stimulated has evolved to the place today where leaders of a couple of major groups believe animals have rights equal to humans.

*portions adapted (with permission) from "Know Hunting" columns, Bowhunter Magazine, February 1994 and December 1994.

Chapter 8

An important term in the evolution of antihunting is the word "*sentient*". Sentient beings are living animals that feel pain, and many animal rights believers feel this is where they will "draw the line." Animals that feel pain should be given equal consideration to humans. Those that don't feel pain, should not.

Hidden beneath this for some individuals is the feeling that the closer the animal is to humans in evolutionary terms, the more consideration they should be given. In other words, for some animal activists, primates should receive total consideration because they are more similar to humans than other animals, but fish get less consideration. For others, there is no such gradation. All sentient beings deserve equal consideration.

Tom Regan, Professor of Philosophy at North Carolina State University, has stepped to the lead as the spokesman encouraging a philosophy that all lives are equal. All life has "inherent" value.

This "equal consideration" philosophy creates real-world problems for wildlife managers because it means that domestic animals and wild animals are given the same consideration, and native and exotic animals must be treated the same. Even more weird, under this value system, we cannot accord greater importance to rare or endangered species than we can to common and abundant species.

When arbitrary lines (a moral obligation line) are drawn, problems arise because most state wildlife agencies have a shortage of funds. Because there are insufficient funds, that agency must set priorities on management projects. When priorities are set, then almost certainly some species will be favored over others. The animal rights philosophy strongly disapproves.

Who Are Antihunters?—-Rebecca Richards and Richard Krannich are sociologists at California State University and Utah State University, respectively. In 1990 they surveyed 1,020 subscribers to The Animals' Agenda magazine.

The results of that study (1991; "*The Ideology of the Animal Rights Movement and Activists Attitudes Toward Wildlife*", Trans. 56th North AmericanWildlilfe and Natural Resources Conference, pages 363-371) were as follows: 78 percent were women, both the east and west coasts were over-represented, ages 30-49 were over-represented (made up 57 percent of the sample, but are only 24 percent of our population according to the 1980 census), they were well educated, and had a high income.

Seven of 10 had no children, and two of the 10 that did had no children living at home. They were no more urban than the general population. Five of 10 are opposed to pro-life and pro-school prayer movements. As already mentioned, 90 percent owned an average of 4.7 pets. They were likely to be sympathetic toward liberal social movements.

A 1990 survey of folks who participated in a Washington, DC animal rights march showed that marchers were younger (average age was 30), highly educated (66 percent had a college education), but were underemployed. Most marchers (68 percent) were women, and 88 percent had been raised in urban environments.

They were critical of use of animals in agriculture and science. They belonged to the following organizations; People For the Ethical Treatment of Animals (62 percent), Humane Society of the United States (45 percent), American Society For The Prevention of Cruelty To Animals (35 percent), Friends of Animals (23 percent), Greenpeace (14 percent), and the Sierra Club (14 percent).

Their Likes and Dislikes.—-Subscribers to The Animals' Agenda magazine were asked to rank a series of animal uses from 1 = extremely wrong, to 7 = not at all wrong. Using leg-hold traps (1.06); using animals for cosmetic research (1.13); killing an animal for a fur coat (1.17); and hunting (1.49) were all viewed as very wrong.

Eating meat (2.74) and keeping animals in zoos (3.02) were in the medium wrong range. Near the bottom of the list was keeping a dog or cat as a pet (6.49) and neutering a pet (6.62).

When asked what they depended on for sources of information, the answers were as follows: Newspapers (27 percent), television (22 percent), magazines (19 percent), direct mail (16 percent) and radio (10 percent). Thus, the power of the press in this issue is a major one.

One last item, and it is a bit scary. More than half (52 percent) believe that "science does more harm than good". In Chapter 5 we discussed the science of wildlife management and how wildlife biologists were trained in universities. Wildlife research or management will not be readily accepted by those who believe that "science does more harm than good." Of course the medical sciences, agricultural sciences, and others will also be discounted. A strong bias that rules out input from science makes dialogue very difficult.

Many animal activists practice their beliefs by not wearing fur or leather products, not eating meat, opposing the use of animals for medical research, not owning pets (though one study mentioned above showed that 90 percent of animal activists owned pets and the mean number of pets owned was 4.7). But not wearing leather or eating meat does not mean that animal activists are not responsible for the death of animals.

For example, vegetarians *are responsible for the death of animals as all citizens are.* vegetables are raised on large agri-business farms where cultivated land was carved from wildlife habitat. In addition, herbicides are sprayed on such vegetables, also leading to the deaths of wild animals.

Then there are the costs of being a vegetarian. Ted Kerasote's Random House book titled *"Bloodties"* is worth reading. He makes many fine points in this excellent book, and one is on the costs of being a vegetarian.

Kerasote noted that *150 pounds of elk meat costs the planet 79,000 kilocalories of fossil fuel energy* while an equivalent caloric value in the form of Idaho potatoes costs 151,000 kilocalories of fossil fuel energy. He took into account the fuel costs of driving his car, and manufacturing the automobile, guns and ammo used to hunt.

He also included the costs in electricity to store the meat. For the vegetarian, he included the costs needed to run the farm machinery to harvest the potatoes and the costs to transport them from farm to market. Now get this, when he did the same figuring for *150 pounds of rice or beans*, grown in California, *the cost was 477,000 kilocalories of fossil fuel energy.*

Include the abuses of fertilizers and irrigation that takes water from streams and rivers that are over taxed, and you get a real feel for the problem. Kerasote concluded that growing his own beans and taking an elk during hunting season, close to home, was one small way he could help the environment. Interesting thoughts, because such inconsistencies in the vegetarian philosophy are rarely mentioned in animal activists literature.

Other Studies.——A 1977 study of members of the Fund For Animals (FFA) (an antihunting organization) who live in Michigan, showed an almost identical profile to those listed above. Respondents were predominantly female, urban, and well educated (W. W. Shaw, "*A Survey of Hunting Opponents,*" Wildlife Society Bulletin 5:19-24). Sixty-eight percent would support legislation making all hunting illegal and 72 percent have always felt that way.

For years, many believed that it was the antihunting organizations that created antihunting attitudes. Not so. In fact Shaw's study showed that 72 percent have always felt that way about antihunting legislation. Thus, as Shaw pointed out, such organizations don't create antihunting attitudes, they probably *organize* them with similar attitudes and *reinforce* their beliefs.

In this study Dr. Shaw asked respondents to rate the following reasons why wildlife is important. Interestingly, antihunters and hunters both picked the same first three reasons. However, the members of the Fund For Animals ranked "the importance for hunting recreation" as last, while hunters ranked it as fourth.

Members of the FFA also ranked the reasons of importance of the threats to wildlife populations. They selected loss of habitat, illegal hunting, and pollution as the top three reasons. Note that legal hunting ranked seventh out of eight possibilities.

It would appear that although FFA members are antihunting, they understand that legal hunting is not a threat to wildlife populations. (Note, that might be true for this group of antihunters, but there is no doubt that in certain situations some groups of antihunters would probably rate legal hunting as a threat to wildlife populations.) There is also no doubt some antihunting groups feel hunting bears over bait is a threat to the bear, even though data does not support that concern.

Members of The Fund For Animal Members From Michigan:

Felt that wildlife was important because
    1. Wildlife is a part of the ecological balance
    2. People enjoy viewing wildlife
    3. People enjoy knowing wildlife exists
    4. Wildlife is important to our culture
    5. Animals have souls like humans
    6. Animals are of scientific value
    7. Animals help the economy via tourism
    8. Animal are a food and fur source
    9. Animals provide hunting recreation

Felt the following were important threats to wildlife populations

1. Loss of habitat (human development)
2. Illegal hunting
3. Pollution
4. Commercial trapping
5. Unsound wildlife management practices
6. All-terrain vehicles
7. Legal sport hunting
8. Predation by other animals

Listed the following reasons for opposing hunting

1. I dislike the idea of killing for pleasure
2. I dislike the idea of taking the freedom of a wild and free animal
3. It is cruel and inhumane to the animals
4. Animals don't have a chance
5. It encourages an undesirable attitude of dominance over nature
6. It disrupts nature's balance
7. It destroys what is left of wildlife populations
8. It makes people insensitive to suffering
9. I don't like human behavior that involves violence
10. It encourages people to want guns
11. I don't like the type of people who hunt

Adapted from "*A Survey of Hunting Opponents*" William Shaw, 1977 Wildlife Society Bulletin 5(1), pages 19-24. Copyrighted with permission of The Wildlife Society.

The list of reasons FFA members selected and ranked for opposing hunting are interesting. Numbers 1, 4, 5, 8, and 11 center on the behavioral aspects of hunting. Numbers 2 and 3 focus on a perceived impact hunting has on the animal. And reasons 6 and 7 focus on impacts on the ecosystem.

This group of antihunters obviously feels that hunting is killing, and discounts the other components of the hunt. The moralistic attitude comes through as they feel that hunting is cruel.

Since they have no experience with hunting, antihunters do not realize that most animals escape during the hunt. Philosopher and nonhunter Ortega y Gassett (In his classic book, "*Meditations On Hunting*") thoroughly and beautifully discussed the fact that prey must always have the advantage over the predator (hunters). Escape must always be possible for a hunt to be ethical.

There is a paradox relative to technological advancements in hunting equipment. More advanced equipment usually means a more humane quick kill, but if there is too much equipment advancement then the chance for escape of the prey is reduced.*

Obviously, since most big game hunters are not successful then animals do have a chance, but also obvious is the fact that antihunters surveyed do not feel this to be true.

Based on reason number 7, antihunters feel that most wildlife populations have been destroyed by hunting. This is totally contradictory to the truth. Today we have more wildlife than ever before.

Is the antihunting bias so strong that facts and figures, and abundant wildlife populations go unnoticed? Or are wildlife agencies just not getting the message out to nonhunters? It's hard to tell.

Antihunting Groups.—-The top three antihunting groups in the country are the People for the Ethical Treatment of Animals (PETA), the Humane Society of the United States (HSUS), and the Fund For Animals (FFA). PETA was based in Washington, D.C., but in 1996 moved to Norfolk, Virginia. They have about 500,000 members and an annual budget of about $10 million a year. This is the fastest growing animal rights group in the world and they utilize celebrities and publicity stunts to keep a high profile.

The August 11, 1994 issue of the Philadelphia Inquirer, in a story on one of PETA's leaders, noted the following stars as PETA supporters; Paul McCartney, Kim Basinger, Alec Baldwin, Chrissie Hynde of the Pretenders, Bea Arthur of The Golden Girls, "Elvira" Peterson, Sara Gilbert of Roseanne's, models Naomi Campbell, Tyra Banks and Christy Turlington, and Kate Pierson of the B-52's.

PETA is especially active in anti meat and anti fur activities, and

---

*There is a thin line here that hunters must monitor. With modern technology hunting equipment could be developed that would increase the effectiveness and the kill during a hunt. But this would also shift the scale more heavily in favor of the predator over the prey. There is also the question of quick kills. One could develop grenade-like broadheads that would instantly kill an animal, but bowhunters would not want to use such devices because it would then be killing and not hunting. Drawing the line on equipment is more complicated than meets the eye.

at least one of their spokespersons has questioned keeping pet animals. According to the Washington Legal Foundation, the FBI has linked some of the employees of PETA with the terrorist group, the Animal Liberation Front (see *"America's new extremists: What you need to know about the animal rights movement"*, David T. Hardy, 1990, Washington Legal Foundation). In 1993 PETA budgeted $1 million for various educational activities aimed at public school teachers. According to *Animal People* magazine, their total 1997 budget was reportedly $10,681,269. Obviously the animal rights movement is big business.

The Humane Society of the United States (HSUS) is the largest animal rights group in the world with over 2 million members and an annual budget of around $35 million (published in Spokesman-Review newspaper, Spokane, Washington, 2/20/97). Many people mistakenly link HSUS with local animal shelters. HSUS has no formal relationship with dog pounds or animal shelters.

They are heavily involved with antihunting protests on National Wildlife Refuges, dog and bait bear hunting all over the west, but they also attack fur and eating meat. They have major programs aimed at public school teachers and students, and a separate organization that provides educational materials for public schools.

Over the past few years they have put millions into the antihunting referendums on various state ballots (see chapters 10 and 11). In recent years the salaries of their higher administration employees have come under scrutiny by other animal rights organizations.

The January 1996 issue of U. S. News & World Report wrote about this high salary issue (*"Charity begins at home?"*). Apparently one employee has filed a counter suit against HSUS, claiming that Paul G. Irwin, President of HSUS, received a salary of over $200,000 in 1994. The December 1996 issue of Animal People reported that at least 13 HSUS executives received more than $70,000 per year in 1994; and the CEO reportedly received $226,704.

According to the National Shooting Sports Foundation the "Humane Society of the United States is strongly opposed to the hunting of any living creature for fun, trophy, or sport because of the trauma, suffering and death to the animal which result." According to *Animal People* magazine HSUS's total 1997 budget was reportedly $39,492,711.

The Fund For Animals (FFA) is based in New York and was run by the late Cleveland Amory. They have approximately 250,000 members and an annual budget of around $4 million. This high profile organization utilizes movie stars to assist with various antihunting activities.

Of special note are legal cases; hunt disruptions including the protest of the buffalo hunt in Montana near Yellowstone National Park, trying to stop black bear hunting in California, and various attacks on the U. S. Fish and Wildlife Service and the U. S. Forest Service on bear baiting and bear hunting issues.

A friend wrote to the FFA for information on hunt disruptions. They provided tips that included: dress warm, arrive one-half hour before dawn, designate one person to deal with the media, do not allow yourself to be alone, wait in cars for the hunters to arrive, and stay with the hunter throughout his/her attempt to hunt. Keep noise down so that you do not drive deer to other hunters. No verbal abuse or physical contact. Stick to the issue of cruelty. Remain calm. Avoid breaking the law.

According to the National Shooting Sports Foundation "The Fund For Animals is unalterably opposed to the recreational killing of wildlife. Besides being a piteously unfair and cruel slaughter of innocent animals, sport hunting is also ecologically destructive. Despite claims to the contrary, hunters take a heavy toll on endangered and threatened animals." FFA's 1997 budget was reportedly $4,330,084.

The Friends of Animals is another long-existing animal rights group. They have been involved with a number of activities that are against hunting, and to my knowledge they conducted one of the few projects ever done by an antihunting group that actually benefited wildlife.

They provided funds via a partnership with the Senegal National Park in West Africa and the U. S. Fish and Wildlife Service to provide antipoaching support to protect an elephant population. The Friends provided $100,000, the USFWS $46,000 in 1993 and $39,000 in 1995. Apparently the desert population of elephants is showing the first increase in the past 10 years.

According to the National Shooting Sports Foundation, the Friends of Animals, Inc. states that "Hunting is cruel. It is socially unjustifiable. It is ecologically disruptive. Friends of Animals opposes hunting in all its forms." Their total 1997 budget was reportedly $5,082,387.

There is one other group that most citizens hear about in the news. The Animal Liberation Front is an underground organization that uses vandalism and violence to further the animal rights cause. They formed as a spin-off from the Band of Mercy, a 19th century antivivisection group from England. They have claimed responsibility for various terrorist acts including arson, break-ins, vandalizing fur stores, farms, slaughter houses, and medical research facilities.

Animal Rights Operations.—The American Professional Pet Distributors, Inc. (APPDI) noted that IRS figures show very high salaries for some of the animal rights leaders (note that APPDI would have a bias against animal rights organizations for obvious reasons). Animal rightists have attacked "puppy mills" which are farms where large numbers of dogs are raised to sell in pet stores.

Some puppy mills have gained national attention because of the lack of humane care of the animals. The Executive Director of APPDI, noted that overhead for some animal rights groups is high, with fewer dollars actually going to animal welfare activities. These figures highlight the self-serving hypocrisy of the animal rights movement.

The Director of APPDI stated, "Animal rights groups raise money by suggesting donor contributions will be used directly in efforts to help animals. However, the truth is that, increasingly, funds are being used instead to subsidize the huge salaries of animal rights executives."

I'll add that this is not true of all animal rights executives and their groups, but it is apparently true for some. And at least relative to high salaries, it appears to be true for the HSUS.

Here is another example of such expenditures by an animal rights group. The July 1992 issue of The Animals' Agenda magazine reported that the Doris Day Animal League spent 98 percent its 1990 budget on fund raising, public education related to fund raising, salaries and overhead. Does that mean that only 2 percent might have been used to stop things that are judged to be inhumane treatment of animals?

If true, do you believe the people who contributed to this

organization would be upset if they knew how their monies were spent?

Terrorism Activities.——The animal rights movement is a revolution, and terrorism is a big part of a revolution. What follows are accounts of the types of terrorism that are occur in the United States. Most do not focus on the antihunting movement, but they have been carried out by individuals and organizations that have antihunting philosophies, and are presented as examples of on-going activities.

Most were taken from newsletters of organizations or from newspaper accounts of the activity. In some cases arrests have been made and the cases have been legally concluded. For most however, no arrests have ever been made.

I first learned about animal rights terrorism when I read the December 15, 1987 issue of the Washington Post. It discussed a November 27th attack on five stores along Wisconsin Avenue in downtown Washington. It was "Fur-Free Friday," and someone with a pellet rifle shot holes through windows at five fur stores. Shots were also fired at a fur vault in Bethesda during business hours.

Red paint was splashed at the fur vault and at one other store. Apparently paint splashing of fur stores is common in other cities, but this was the first shooting that I could find written up anywhere. In the January 19, 1988 issue of the New York Times, there was a story indicating that Federal authorities were investigating several arson cases at research labs and meat companies.

The story noted that the FBI was looking into a $3.5 million fire that destroyed a veterinary lab at the University of California at Davis. Another story written by Marianne Yen appeared March 11, 1989 in the Washington Post, and it discussed harassment of fur wearers. In this article, a spokesman for the Fur Retailers Information Council reported that 350 acts of vandalism occurred to fur stores in 1988. Some activitists tactics are relatively harmless, although annoying, such as Krazy Glue on metal door locks to fur stores. Others involve destroying furs.

On August 13, 1991 a Department of Agriculture animal research facility on the campus of Washington State University was ransacked. According to newspaper accounts, the Animal Liberation Front contacted the Associated Press in Spokane, claiming responsible. They indicated that the reason this building was targeted was because

Washington State University participated "in research that benefited sheep ranching on American wilderness and fur farming of native wildlife."

A National Association For Biomedical Research Update indicated that the ALF claimed responsibility for a June 1991 fire at the Northwest Farm Food Cooperative in Washington and a break-in and fire at Oregon State University. Damage in the latter two incidents was estimated at $500,000.

The Animal Liberation Front has also claimed responsibility for torching a predator research lab of the U. S. Department of Agriculture in Millville, Utah. They broke into the office of Professor Fred Knowlton (who ran the research lab) at Utah State University and attempted to torch it. Fortunately they were not successful. Had they been, the entire Wildlife and Fisheries Department, as well as Forestry and Range Management, and their associated library, would have gone up in smoke. Even so, the damage was in the $250,000 range.

The Security Advisor reported that there were 610 worldwide animal rights incidents in 1993. Most (125) were directed against hunting, followed by 103 against health and beauty product testing, 89 against the meat industry, 81 against furs, 69 against zoos, and 68 against biomedical research facilities.

In March 1993, John Lilburn was found guilty of hunter harassment for stopping a hunter from shooting a buffalo in Montana. The Bozeman newspaper reported that 11 "animal rightists," some members of the Fund For Animals and Earth First, tried to keep hunters from shooting buffalo in March of 1990.

Lilburn was charged under a state law where it is a crime to disturb a hunter with intent to dissuade him or her from lawfully killing an animal. Lilburn appealed to the Supreme Court, but they refused to hear his case. He was sentenced to 30 days, but the sentence was suspended.

The September 1993 Safari Times reported that animal rights activist Rodney Coronado was indicted by a Michigan grand jury on five counts stemming from an alleged firebombing of an animal research lab at Michigan State University on February 28, 1992. They reported Coronado went into hiding but was apprehanded. He faces a fine of $1,250,000 and 50 years in jail.

We've all seen terrorism relative to emotional, revolutionary issues such as abortion. Understand though that relative to hunting and other uses of animals, we are dealing with a revolution. One part of revolutions is illegal activities, including terrorism.

Most citizens, regardless of their feelings about hunting, are opposed to violence. But such activities will always be a part of human society.

"I learned very early that you have to decide at the outset whether you are trying to make money or make sense—I feel they are mutually exclusive."

Buckminster Fuller

Chapter 9

Antihunting Is Not Environmentalism*

Environmentalists....people concerned about the environment. The environmental philosophy has evolved through the years, and it will continue to evolve. At the turn of the century hunters were environmentalists, and they still are today. They cared about the wildlife, and that lead to concern for wildlife habitat including wetlands and water.

Nonhunters care about the environment, today more than ever. Loving Mother Earth is a way of life for millions of environmentalists. Along with that goes another change. Today we find ourselves three or four generations off the farm. We have become so removed from reality that those opposed to the killing of animals are forcing wildlife agencies to do things that are not good for wildlife, and not good for habitat that is being degraded.

In situations where wildlife populations have exceeded their carrying capacity, our solutions make little sense. We want to feed all the surplus, or adopt them, or trap and move them.

In reality, in some of the overpopulated wildlife situations, we should be killing animals, and fast. But we don't. We're starting to become "preservationists" (do not touch anything), instead of conservationists (manage the resource).

Today, with the help of the press, there is another definition of environmentalism being used. The press often quotes antihunters as being environmentalists. This myth just doesn't hold up...antihunting is not environmentalism. And that is the subject of this chapter.

Changing Society.—-As a kid, I spent many hours on the farm. Our

*Portions adapted (with permission) from "On Your Side" columns in May, December 1989, December 1992 issues of Bowhunting News; "Know Hunting" columns in December 1991, February 1993 in Bowhunter Magazine.

Chapter 9

family lived in a rural area, surrounded by farms. No pavement, no neon signs, no taxi cabs, no interstate highways. Just kids on bikes, beagle dogs and ponies, dusty roads, cows, country churches, and green grass.

Every Sunday, right after church, we had a family dinner. Either mom prepared the food, or we went down the road to grandma's house. Often mom would prepare chicken. On Saturday afternoon, she'd give me a quarter, and I'd ride my bike about a mile down the road to farmer Blough's place. He'd go into the chicken coop, and catch two chickens by hand.

Right beside the chicken pen there was a chopping block with a sharp hatchet sticking in it. Mr. Blough would quickly remove the head of the first chicken. While it flopped on the ground he would do the second bird. After a minute or so, they would calm down and I'd place them in my bike basket and go home.

Mom had a bucket of scalding water, and I'd then remove all the feathers and clean the bird. The next day, we'd eat those birds. I never gave the killing of those birds for food any thought. Most of our neighbors got chickens in that manner.

Today, we still eat chickens. In fact we kill and consume millions of birds each year. But few children understand that these birds die so that citizens can eat fried chicken.

Society is changing and more and more people just do not relate to the death of animals. Why? And from this idealogy has evolved, perhaps generated by the press, a "new" environmentalist. The printed and spoken word has started to equate environmentalism with antihunting. This is a myth. Being an antihunter does not necessarily mean one is an environmentalist.

One reason is that most of us now live many generations removed from living off the land. Most of our parents did not live on a farm, but many of our grandparents did. How about our children or our grandchildren? They will be three or four generations removed from life on the land and all that goes with it, including hunting.

One major life lesson that one gets from living off the land is an understanding of the life and death cycles of animals, and how we humans use animals. Unless urbanites get to the country they have no way to relate to that, nor do they understand it.

Farmers have always understood that death is a part of life. They are utilitarians, using the land to produce the plants and animals needed to sustain human life. Farmers care about animals, they feed them, see that they stay healthy. But in the end, some of those animals and plants die, so that we might live. That is the perception, the reality, of living in the country.

Today most of us relate to wild animals through our knowledge of pets. When you relate through your pet, you tend to worry about individual animals instead of herds or flocks.

A society that does not understand or relate to the life and death cycles of animals often promotes unrealistic solutions to wildlife problem. That society wants to save all individual animals from the harshness of nature. I think that is why some animal activists want to; (1) keep all animals warm in winter, (2) keep all wildlife safe at all times, (3) keep all wild animals from starving in the winter by feeding individuals. (Read this in Hardin, *"Cultural Carrying Capacity: A Biologists Approach To Human Problems,"* AIBS Magazine, October, 1986). Nature just does not work that way.

Don't misunderstand. I am not opposed to feeding wildlife. I keep a bird feeder going in the winter in my back yard as do millions of other Americans. But my motive is not to save individual birds. I run a bird feeder because I like to see winter birds.

I do it for me, and really not for the birds, though I'm glad they benefit from the feed. Of course, winter feeders attract predators, and that is bad for the birds.

There are now some reports that winter feeders can contribute to the spread of diseases for some bird species. So, we take precautions, but we still feed birds.

Watching birds is fun and interesting, especially on cold winter days when we are trapped inside. However, if we took the millions of dollars and manpower hours spent feeding birds and redirected that into wildlife programs or saving habitat programs, would bird life benefit more in the end?

Good question, and it is one that won't be answered because humans (including me) like to feed winter birds and watch them at our feeders.

In our changing society we want to save and protect each

individual animal, even when it isn't possible or realistic. Every spring wildlife biologists get calls from people who find baby nestling birds like robins, flopping around on the ground. They want to know how to save them..or how to save baby rabbits, squirrels, or deer.

When I get such calls, I explain that it is difficult to save baby birds or mammals. It would require round-the-clock supervision, feeding every hour or two for at least two weeks. I also explain the sad news that when you are done, and place the survivor in the wild, they will probably die or be killed in a very short time.

Most people just do not want to hear that...even though it is true. How much further along would wildlife management be if that same person devoted the same number of hours spent trying to save a baby robin to an effort to save a local wetland that was being threatened by development?

Take all the local citizens in your town who try to save a baby songbird this year and multiply those hours, and convert that into time spent to save one 25-acre wetland. One could make a good case that the overall benefits of that wetland over the next 50 years would far surpass the ecological benefits of trying to save baby robins.

This does not mean that people should not attempt to save orphaned wildlife in their back yards. However, know that such rescue attempts are usually fruitless and many saved animals will die when released back into the wild.

In reality, with more energy and more volunteerism, we could have more bird feeders, more efforts to save individual songbirds, and more focus on local environmental issues and the ever-increasing loss of wildlife habitat. In that manner a changing society becomes a benefit to wildlife.

Loving Animals vs. Animal Lovers.—-Our system of wildlife management evolved for years under a hunting paradigm. Today we are asked to look at other approaches and some that animal activists want the public to pursue may cause more pain and suffering for the animals. In some cases, biological facts do not support the approaches taken by antihunting organizations. My guess is that some animal activists do not know the painful consequences nor the biological facts relative to their actions.

Dr. Garrett Hardin is one of the 20th century's top ecologists. His article (cited in the previous section) stated that the animal rights movement often forces state and federal agencies responsible for managing wildlife to do things that are not good for wildlife and are not good wildlife management practices. He made the point that when animal populations grow beyond what the habitat can support, the "environment is rapidly degraded."

In other words, there are consequences when we get too many animals. Dr. Hardin asked "what should concerned human beings do" when this situation (i.e., too many wild animals in an area) occurs?

His answer was simple, and one that most wildlife biologists strongly endorse. The answer was "get rid of the excess FAST." Though most people agree with his answer, animal lovers do not.

It is the "get rid of" portion that creates a problem for animal activists. Consider the following. Winter supplemental feeding is a remedy that is only rarely considered by wildlife managers as something beneficial to deer and other larger mammals.

Yet animal activists, well meaning though they might be, will take a situation where there are too many animals to make it through a normal winter and attempt to drum up public support for a winter feeding program. It is a common scenario relative to whitetail deer.

In reality, feeding deer in winter usually will only compound the problem, leading to further damage to the habitat. Several years ago in a New Jersey National Wildlife Refuge, there were too many deer for the habitat. A hunt was proposed, but antihunters suggested that the solution was for people to donate their Christmas trees after the holiday, haul them into the country for the deer to eat.

Not only is such a diet very unpalatable for deer, even if they did eat pine trees and survive, what would be done the following year after more fawns are born and the herd is even larger? More Christmas trees would not be the answer.

Dr. Hardin pointed out that the only real way to get rid of animals fast was to *shoot the excess*. He stated that if a person is truly interested in the welfare of the animal, this is what must be done. If we had too many deer 40 years ago, wildlife agencies would expand the hunting limits and we would remove excess animals quickly, in suburbs, in farm country, wherever they occurred. There would have been few complaints from citizens. That's not so today.

Chapter 9

Here is another example of where getting rid of the excess fast is sometimes made impossible by the animal activists, and then wildlife suffers. Populations of wild horses increase rather substantially every year. However, as Dr. Hardin pointed out, "the rate of increase of grazing lands (for those horses, and for wildlife) is a negative number."

In other words, horse numbers go up, amount of grazing lands goes down, and the horses as well as other native wildlife suffers. The Bureau of Land Management (BLM) has been given the job (by a law passed by animal activists) of running an adoption program for the public.

Wild horses and burros are rounded up, held in captivity, and put up for adoption, for a fee. Roundup is done by a helicopter, with the animals placed in holding pens. One can imagine that such a roundup is psychologically traumatizing to the wild horses.

Over the years this program has had its problems (though in recent years the program has been doing rather well). BLM does the best it can on a limited budget, but finances have not always been there. Holding unwanted animals for a long time has also been a problem, and finding enough homes for all the wild horses has been tough at times.

The holding and feeding costs alone run above $10-15 million a year. A sane solution would be for the BLM to survey the horse population every two years, and shoot the excess. It would be less traumatic for the horse *population* (obviously not for the individual horses that are killed), infinitely less expensive for tax payers, better for the habitat and wildlife population swould be better off.

Another example where habitat and wildlife suffer because of antihunter's solutions is trapping and transplanting excess deer from areas of high population. Most antihunters now understand that this option is not good even though it might sound like a humane solution.

The problem with trapping and transplanting is that studies show the animals die at a high rate once placed in a new environment, and it is an expensive venture as well. Worst of all, it does not solve the problem, for very soon, the numbers will increase and trap and transplanting would be needed again.

Because deer die with this approach, some states have chosen to disallow it as a solution to a high deer density problem. So what sounds like a humane solution is really an inhumane approach to the problem.

Recent research on transplanted moose was published by Robert Aho and John Hendrickson of the Michigan Department of Natural Resources. Radio collars were placed on 25 bulls and 36 cows moved from Ontario to Michigan. Animals were moved in January and February in 1985 and 1987, and no hunting was allowed.

By September 1989, eighteen (50 percent) of the cows were dead and eight (32 percent) of the bulls had died. Brainworm seemed to be the main culprit, killing 38 percent. Other causes of death were: hepatitis, liver flukes, drowning, gored foreleg, mired in mud, and falling from cliffs. One yearling was poached.

Let me make two statements on this work. First, my hat is off to the Michigan Department for bringing moose to Michigan. Although some moose died, the transplant appears to be a success. Second, even when there is no hunting, nature and man will kill some animals.

The May 1992 issue of the Safari Times reported that 16 of 27 blacktail deer that were transplanted from an urban park near Alameda, California to a wilderness area were eaten by mountain lions in less than two months. The deer had become a problem and residents requested the Game Department's help. The cost to move the deer was over $100,000. Shooting those deer would have been a better solution.

Bowhunts in such situations may have solved the problem and saved money to boot. One thing is certain; when you catch and move deer into new environments, studies show that most will die quickly. Not a humane alternative.

Dr. Hardin summed up the over-population problem in his article by stating that "the prime commandment (for humans) must be — Thou shalt not transgress the carrying capacity." Quality of life for animals decreases as population numbers increase. Fiddling with basic ecological principles (i.e., adopting wild horses, winter feeding of deer, trapping and transplanting when there are too many deer in an area) is not humane; it is not good wildlife management, and it is not what we should be doing for the benefit of wildlife *populations*.

Using Common Sense.—-In 1992 I had the opportunity to listen to a talk given by Robert Bidinotto, senior writer for Reader's Digest at the Northeast Association of Fish and Wildlife Agencies in Norfolk, Virginia. Mr. Bidinotto is not only an excellent writer, but a brilliant speaker.

He also has an excellent feel for the antihunting movement; he understands history, what antihunting and animal rights is all about, the dominant position of man on this planet, and he says it in a way that few have ever done before.

Yes, I am a real fan of Robert Bidinotto. Here is some of his common sense philosophy on the negative impacts of antihunting.

Bidinotto believes that radical environmentalists (animal rightists) morally reject the idea that we can manage wildlife by human intervention. It's the old "let nature take care of her own" philosophy that most wildlife biologists and Bidinotto reject.

An article in the September 1991 issue of The Animals' Agenda Magazine typifies this mentality. It stated that "left to their own devices, deer, like any other mammal, are regulated by natural factors, such as disease, extreme weather, predation, and the availability of food. If one factor (like predators) does not exert a significant impact in a particular region, the other factors assume greater importance."

It is true that if you stop hunting, something else will kill deer. If diseases don't, then extreme weather will. But the expense and damage to the habitat is huge, and the expense to the deer in terms of painful death and suffering will be tremendous. Apparently winter starvation is a terrible, painful death for deer.

Bidinotto points out that the public gets mixed messages. Biologists tell the public that scientific management is good and necessary. Moralist "environmentalists" via urban writers and television personalities portray such human intervention as bad and unnecessary. How does the public know who or what to believe?

In Bidinotto's words: "the scientific facts are frequently buried beneath mounds of pompous moralizing and pseudo-scientific claptrap." He believes these moralists are winning simply because "most people are far more comfortable with appeals to their values and emotions than with abstract scientific arguments."

However, Bidinotto believes that biologists and wildlife managers can appeal to people's common sense. He feels wildlife biologists should get out of the defensive mode and take the offense. Speak the language that people understand, clarify the public debate, and uphold the moral rightness of human intervention in nature.

To do this Bidinotto said biologists first must recognize that many leaders of the animal rightists are radical and uncompromising.

Bidinotto explained the history of this hands-off nature philosophy to his audience in Norfolk, and pointed out that "if these people get their way, all of you in fish and wildlife management will join the unemployment lines but you won't be alone there for there will also be no testing of medicines or surgical techniques; no hunting, circuses or rodeos; no bird cages or dog pens; no leather; no meat, milk or eggs; no use of animals, period."

At last a writer for a major publication who understands where all this animal rights philosophy is headed because this philosophy places animals ahead of man. Humans can die but animals must not. In Bidinotto's words: "beaver may change the flow of streams but Man must not. Locusts may denude hundreds of miles of plant life but Man must not. Cougars may eat sheep and chickens but Man must not."

Bidinotto's argument is that nature is our environment — the environment of Man. Deer may live there, but they do not make moral decisions, only Man does. He also believes that such animals do not have rights. If they did then Man really does not have rights.

Think about it. It is true.

If animals have rights, legal and moral rights equal to Man, then Man has no rights in nature. Man cannot be a wildlife manager. Man cannot do anything to the environment.

Bidinotto's examples are then true; beaver can build dams, but Man cannot. A philosophy that, if adopted in its totality, when pursued to its final destination, states that humans and animals are equal, makes little sense.

Do not misconstrue this philosophy. It is not saying that animal cruelty is good. It is not saying that Man should not continue to strive for more humane treatment of animals. It is not saying that hunters should stop striving to reduce all wounding. What it says is that Man is the pre-eminent being on this planet.

How do wildlife biologists get the message to the public that human management is good for wildlife? Bidinotto says we should show the public how brutal nature really is, and how animals suffer in nature. Use videos or films that show the brutal existence animals face in nature. Use photos to show how animals suffer if Man does not manage them.

I recently had the chance to watch the animals fighting video that has been extensively advertised on the TNT channel. It is bloody, brutal, vicious, and real. It shows death in nature, without the presence of Man. There is no doubt that nature can be cruel.

We're All Environmentalists?—-In the late 1800's and early 1900's man had a utilitarian approach to our resources. Animals were to be hunted, trees cut, grass was to be grazed. We used things, and we often abused them too.

This led to groups of people opposed to such activities. These new environmentalists had a different perspective on how we treat animals, trees, and grass.

They came from the cities, had little relationship as to how we used the land, but they wanted to escape to nature. Of course, their incursions into the woods also were destructive in some ways, but they didn't see it that way.

However, environmentalism grew, and it now is a philosophy, an ethic that is deep-seated and in direct conflict to those who want to cut trees, hunt animals and graze cows on public land. Loving Mother Earth became more than just a bumper sticker. It has become a way of life for millions of environmentalists.*

But hunters also evolved from the early 1900's as environmentalists. Their perspective was not one of total preservation, but rather one of using the commodities in our natural world, but doing so in an ethical, ecological manner. And so we had two different groups of folks who called themselves environmentalists.

Today there is a third group entering the scene. The media has taken to using the term environmentalist when speaking about animal rightists. I don't believe this is happening by accident. Animal rightists know their philosophy is not widely embraced by society, so they have become expert at integrating their agenda with that of other groups. So much so that most of the American public would probably

For a review of this topic, read Richard Knight's 1996 article ("Aldo Leopold, The Land Ethic, and Ecosystem Management"*) in the Journal of Wildlife Mgt. 60(3):471-474.

be surprised to learn that not all environmentalists are opposed to hunting.

Regardless of how it is painted in the press, *antihunting and environmentalism are not the same thing*. This is a myth. Let's consider this for a moment by examining an article from an environmental magazine. This article definitely gives one the impression that environmentalism equals antihunting, when in fact, the roots of environmentalism grew from hunting. The article was in the May/June 1990 issue of Environmental Magazine and titled "*Our Incredible War On Wildlife*" by Jude Reitman.

It began with a fair comparison of statements about hunting from those who favor it with statements from those opposed. However the article quickly moved to antihunting propaganda quoting liberally from the Humane Society of The United States. One quote questioned whether we should hunt animals to prevent starvation.

The author then skimmed the surface of a very complex topic, a discussion of how hunted deer populations leads to higher populations and higher numbers than non-hunted populations. It is an argument made time and time again by antihunting groups — that hunting causes more deer.

Simplifying the dynamics of deer reproduction to this logic is total foolishness. While it is true that when herds are undernourished due to lack of proper food from high animal densities, reproduction is depressed. And when you hunt these deer, lower the population, the weight of females will increase, their health improves, and their reproductive rates increase.

But to take this situation and stretch it to mean that the reason we have more deer today is because we hunt them is ludicrous. If we were to stop hunting deer, populations would shoot up for awhile, then growth would slow. The deer population would age as reproduction drops to near zero. Food availability would drop, and the first hard winter would lead to massive die-offs, starvation, and disease.

The article then goes on to state that wildlife agencies do the bidding of hunters because hunter license monies bring in $380 million a year (it's really $450 million) for wildlife management, and hunting equipment excise taxes bring in $110 million (it is really $155 million).

Mr. Reitman stated that since hunters control the purse strings, wildlife agencies manipulate the herds and habitats, and wipe out non-game species in the process. In general he intimated that all this is done at the expense of wildlife which is an over generalization at best.

He suggested that wildlife agencies burn habitat to the detriment of wildlife (when in fact controlled burning is a super management tool that benefits habitat and many non-game species as well), that they bulldoze and crush animals (I have no idea where he got this information, or how he can construe what wildlife agencies do for habitat management into crushing animals), that wildlife management policies are killing the farmer, and of course, there is the obligatory discussion of killing predators by the Animal Damage Control people.

After reading the article in Environmental Magazine it now appears that the term environmentalist refers to those who are saving the environment by opposing the killing of animals.

In the September 1990 issue of Audubon magazine, there was an article on page 16 titled *"Fakers' Legacy"*. It quoted a book (*"The Nature Fakers"*) by Ralph Lutts (Fulcrum Publishing, Golden, Colorado), and noted that the environmental movement in the late 1960's and early 1970's was filled with sentimentalism, romanticism, emotional attachment, rather than scientific understanding.

If true, then it is a real change for environmentalists. Our first conservationists understood science but it appears that this is changing.

Outdoor Life, in an article about the antihunting movement in their October 1990 issue, listed several environmental groups as fence straddlers on their stance on hunting. It said that the National Wildlife Federation, the National Audubon Society, World Wildlife Fund, The Nature Conservancy, and the Wilderness Society are fence straddlers and that others, such as the Sierra Club lean toward the antihunters. Then they note other environmental groups as totally antihunting (Earth First, Defenders of Wildlife, and others). It appears that environmental groups that were once prohunting are changing.

A survey done by Utah State University is cited in the March 1991 issue of The Animals' Agenda magazine published by the Animal Rights Network, Inc. This survey of subscribers to the Animals' Agenda magazine showed that 98.4 percent identified with the environmental movement.*

The group in Minnesota which attempted to stop all bowhunting

*Animal rightists work hard to encourage the confusion between their philosophy and that of environmentalism. The two moyements are completely incompatible.

in that state evidently thinks it is environmental, and are called Friends of Animals and Their Environment (FATE). Apparently these people truly believe they are environmentalists because they are against hunting.

Does this mean that all environmental groups are antihunting? Not at all. Several years ago there was a small controversy over membership beliefs in the National Wildlife Federation. Apparently there was a discussion at an annual meeting that left some people feeling that the NWF may have anti leanings.

My experience with this very powerful pro wildlife management lobby group is just the opposite. The NWF has always been a strong supporter of wildlife management and hunting as a tool for the same. But the separation of antihunting from environmentalism is getting to be a thin line in many organizations, and it is getting harder to walk that line.

Robert Redford has been a spokesman for the NWF, and he was active in getting Proposition 117 passed in California banning mountain lion hunting and limiting lion management. However, the NWF is nevertheless a strong advocate of hunting.

In a February 1991 editorial, Jay Hair, then director of the NWF, discussed the attacks of antihunters, and noted that "such controversies detract from the environmental issues we face." Dr. Hair pointed out the main problem with the antihunting movement (and I might add, with antihunters who call themselves environmentalists), is that a growing number of Americans "are losing their connections with the land and the wild resources that we outdoor people enjoy so much."

This may well be the crux of the problem. Hunters are out there and understand how great nature is, and they understand how nature works. I think a fair number of antihunters, and most nonhunters, would be more tolerant of hunting if they spent time in the woods and studied nature.

Hike through deer yards in the dead of winter and view what nature is really like. Watch the predator-prey cycles in action. Some antihunters who call themselves environmentalists probably do not understand the difference between the words "conservation" and "preservation."

They think these two buzzwords mean the same thing. They

believe that preservation is the way to go; that it helps the habitat and wildlife. That's not always so.

That concept is not in our wildlife textbooks. Antihunters that believe that we write wildlife management textbooks to justify our hunting, are not only wrong in their philosophy, but they also discount many thousands of highly trained professional wildlife biologists.

In the September 1990 issue of The Leader, a newsletter of the National Wildlife Federation, George Hulsey discussed being in an environmental work session with a woman who leaned toward being an antihunter. Apparently she listened to the environmental discussions and then indicated that "you people (hunters) are hard to hate."

She found that the hunters in the meeting felt just as strongly about the environment as she did. They always have. Hulsey suggested that all hunters should become leaders in the environmental movement. By doing so hunters will be showing others that they are good people. But then, relative to environmentalism, they always have been.

Watching certain television talk shows might give the feeling that hunters are bad people, and terrible citizens who do awful things to animals and their environment. Reading the article in Environmental Magazine gives the impression that wildlife agencies are bad people who do terrible damage to animals and their environment.

That is not so. Wildlife agencies make mistakes, but their reason for being is to be the steward of wildlife, a job they have done well for many years. I'm sure that some antihunters are good environmentalists who understand environmental problems and work hard to protect the environment. I also understand that some hunters and antihunters know little about the environment, and could care less about helping to save Mother Earth.

My major concern as a hunter, an ethical sportsman who not only cares about animals, but also cares about our environment, is that the press and others are jumping on board a bandwagon that equates antihunting with being an environmentalist or a conservationist. The truth is that for years, hunters as a group, have been strong conservationists and environmentalists, and that tradition continues today.

"The deer hunter habitually watches the next bend; the duck hunter watches the skyline; the bird hunter watches the dog; the nonhunter does not watch."

Aldo Leopold

SECTION IV

THE APPROACH TO ANTIHUNTING

Chapter 10. Antihunting Strategies*

In 1990 the first state ballot referendum was passed that affected how we manage wildlife. Up to 1998, this antihunting strategy was used successfully on quite a few occasions. However, at that time the Ballot Issues Coalition was formed and their strategies to offset this antihunting activity have been very successful.

Even so, state ballot referendums have been the most successful antihunting strategy. Often in such referendum votes, citizens make decisions on issues that they know little about. Even so, the votes take place and usually the wildlife resource is the loser.

There have been several myths perpetuated that concern bowhunting. One myth is that bows do not kill, and that many animals are wounded, then go off to die a painful death. And that is another myth...that broadheads are painful. Bows are now used more than ever to curb deer numbers in suburban situations.

However, when such proposals are made, antihunters rush to another myth in an effort to stop the bowhunt. That myth is the one that implies that bowhunting is not safe. Not only is bowhunting very safe, all hunting is safe. In this chapter we'll discover that hunting is safer than golf!

What follows is a close look at the state ballot issues and the other antihunting strategies that have been used.

Voter Referendum.—-Antihunters have used many different strategies to stop hunting. Some have worked better than others, and thus have been adopted over and over again. By far the best strategy with the most success is a voter referendum.

*Portions adapted (with permission) from "On Your Side" column, Bowhunting News, May 1991. "Know Hunting" column, Bowhunter Magazine, October 1994.

The process is relatively simple, but it requires work. Citizens can get issues on the state voting ballots by securing a specified number of signatures on a petition before a predetermined deadline. Once the legal signatures are obtained, the legislature in some states then has a chance to act on the issue. If state politicians do not vote in legislation, then the issue goes to the state's voters.

In other states, the referendums do not go first to the legislature, but are voted on directly in a state-wide ballot during election periods.

Many citizens question allowing the public to make decisions on issues for which they have no training and little knowledge or understanding. Indeed, few of us would think about advising firemen or police or emergency squad workers how to best do their job by changing laws via a referendum. Yet citizens are presently making major decisions that greatly restrict how to best manage wildlife species.

Wildlife biologist Ron Regan of Vermont has suggested that "constituent groups (citizens) can and do make bad biological or ecological choices and requests." While that is probably true, our democratic form of government depends on the option of allowing citizens to make such decisions but the results are a mixed bag.

Several such referendums have passed in western states in recent years (see Chapter 11 for black bear and mountain lion examples). Those have worked so well that antihunting forces are presently attempting many more.

In 1990, proposition 117 stopped mountain lion hunting in California. The battle was a bitter one, but in the end, the vote brought an end to lion hunting. Then in 1995 the legislature passed a bill to put this issue up for a revote. The California Senate passed the bill by a 26-8 vote. The House passed it 44-30.

The reason for a reconsideration of lion hunting was the death of two women by cougars in 1994. Proposition 197, which would have rescinded Proposition 117, then went up for state vote on March 26, 1996. Though prohunters spent millions to get 117 rescinded, antihunters again prevailed by defeating Proposition 197 by a whopping 58 to 42 percent.

In 1994 another major referendum issue was passed in Arizona. Proposition 200 stopped trapping on all public lands in Arizona.

During the period before the November election both sides battled back and forth on this issue. The fight was emotional and expensive, but in the end the antihunters won by a large majority — 58 to 42 percent.

The passage of Propositions 117 in California and 200 in Arizona stimulated many more referendum voter issues, and will lead to many more in the future. This is the best and most successful antihunting strategy used today.

The Humane Society of the United States published a paper on their strategy in winning Proposition 197 in March 1996. They convinced the public that this was about trophy hunting lions rather than about managing a troublesome mountain lion population. They also focused the majority of their media blitz in large metropolitan areas like Sacramento and San Francisco.

A controversial and emotional video was run at no cost by many television stations. Apparently similar tapes of lions falling from trees were shown in Massachusetts and Idaho, where voter referendums on bear hunting occurred in November, 1996.

As an example of how effective this strategy has been, consider the following antihunting-related ballot issues voted on in November 1996.

A. Alaska. Ballot measure No. 3. Groups that led the signature gathering (22,074) were the   Defenders of Wildlife and the Alaska Wildlife Alliance. This initiative passed and thus it is now illegal to hunt wolves on the same day you fly. The motive of this measure was to stop the wildlife management agency from shooting wolves as a form of predator control on the same day they fly.

Most biologists with the Alaska Department of Fish and Game feel that this will impair their ability to manage wolves and to bring back herds of caribou and moose to localized areas where they have been depleted. Antihunters feel that the recovery of caribou and moose is just to benefit recreation hunters, and suggest that it is the hunters who have caused the loss of moose and caribou.

In truth, the loss of caribou and moose in localized areas is caused by many factors, not the least of which are native subsistence hunters who have grown in numbers in recent years, and are putting heavy pressure on big game animals. At the same time, wolf protection has led to unprecedented high numbers of these predators.

These factors, and others, have led to this problem. Aerial shooting is a practical and economically feasible solution. It apparently won't happen any longer.

B. California. An initiative was up for vote that would have reinstated mountain lion hunting and repeal the 1990 ban. It failed by a large majority (42 percent voted in favor of it).

C. Colorado. This referendum needed 54,000 signatures to get on the ballot, but 120,000 were secured. Led by the People Allied With Wildlife, this referendum, voted on in November, 1996, stopped all trapping in Colorado. Interestingly the Colorado Wildlife Commission started the ball rolling in the fall of 1995. They shortened the recreational trapping season and reduced the number of species that could be trapped from 16 to eight. They established a season for coyotes, rather than allowing them to be hunted all year round. Though it is probably true that the steps taken by the Commission made sense, some feel that the decision of the Commission was an effort to compromise the situation. This capitulation strategy did not work in Colorado.

D. Idaho. Proposition No. 2 was defeated in November, 1996. It would have banned bear hunting between March 1 and September 1, hound hunting for bears and bait hunting for bears. The initiative was led by the Idaho Coalition United for Bear (CUB). They needed 41,250 signatures and submitted 43,000 to get this on the ballot. This effort to ban bear hunting in Idaho was defeated when 61 percent of the state's voters voted against it.

E. Massachusetts. This initiative was called the Massachusetts Wildlife Protection Act, and it bans all forms of trapping, and the use of dogs to hunt bears and bobcats. Antihunters gathered 64,928 signatures in 1995, and the issue went to the state legislature where it was rejected (i.e., not enacted into law). An additional 10,821 signatures were needed to get this on the November, 1996 election ballot.

That was accomplished, and the citizens then voted in favor of the referendum to ban trapping and the use of dogs to hunt bears and bobcats. In addition, this referendum also eliminated the requirement that five of the seven members on the wildlife commission hold a hunting or fishing license and eliminated the requirement that they must have held a hunting or fishing license for the previous five years. This will help to insure that nonhunters serve on the board. The group leading this initiative was Protect Pets and Wildlife (ProPaws), and the referendum passed by a wide margin (64 percent in favor).

F. Michigan. Proposal D was a referendum that would have banned the use of dogs and bait for bear hunting and would have stopped bear hunting from March 1 to August 31.The petition needed 247,000 signatures by July 5, 1996, and over 341,000 were gathered. This initiative was led by the Citizens United For Bears (CUB).

However, to counter to this antihunting initiative, on July 5th the Michigan Legislature passed Public Act 377 that allowed the citizens to vote on another referendum (Proposal G) in November, 1996. This referendum amended the Natural Resources and Environmental Protection Act that grants the Department of Natural Resources the exclusive authority to regulate the taking of game in Michigan.

Thus, if passed, it would have left all decisions on conservation of Michigan's wildlife up to the Natural Resources Commission. This Commission would decide if it is good wildlife management to stop fall bear hunting plus bait and dog hunting. The November vote showed a huge support for Michigan bear hunting.

Proposal D was defeated (70 percent against) and Proposal G passed with 74 percent in favor. The Michigan DNR still has the exclusive authority to regulate the taking of game, and it is still legal to bear hunt in that state.

G. Oregon. Measure No. 34. This referendum would repeal the 1994 referendum that stopped bear/cougar hunting with dogs and over bait. The prohunting group that led this fight was named "Don't Let The Wackos Get Away With Their Lies This Time" (I am not making this up).

When bear hunting with dogs and over bait was stopped in 1994, it led to a drop in the 1995 harvest of 764 bears, 53 percent less than the 1994 harvest. This was no surprise; it was just as biologists had predicted. The result of this decreased harvest was that bear nuisance complaints rose 39 percent and 205 problem bears had to be killed.

This referendum would have put the power of wildlife management back into the hands of the Oregon Fish and Wildlife Commission, and would have given them exclusive authority over hunting regulations. Hunters needed 73,261 signatures and they gathered 90,000. To no avail. because the referendum failed with 59 percent voting against it in November, 1996.

H. Washington. Referendum 655 stopped the taking of bear, bobcats and mountain lions with dogs, and the hunting of bear with bait. The Washington Wildlife Alliance needed 181,667 verified signatures to bring this to a state vote and got 225,500. In November, 1996 this referendum passed by a wide margin (64 percent approved). You now cannot hunt bears over bait nor can you hunt bears or mountain lions with dogs in the state of Washington.

J. West Virginia. Constitutional Amendment No. 1 protects the West Virginia Department of Natural Resources from funding raids on hunting license monies by any special interest. In the past various groups (not antihunting) have attempted, via politicians unfamiliar with federal laws, to take hunting and fishing license monies and use them for state activities other than fish and wildlife management.

Federal excise tax monies are given to all states on a 3:1 basis as long as all state license funds are used for fish and wildlife management. Thus, any such raiding of hunting license monies leads to a loss of millions of dollars in any one state. States do not want to lose that 3:1 match, so raids such as this never happen, but this constitutional amendment will guarantee it won't happen in West Virginia. In November, 1996 it passed by a wide margin.

Because of what happened at the ballot box in 1996 (the loss of hunting and the way to manage some species of wildlife in six of the nine ballot initiatives), some prowildlife groups joined forces and formed the Ballot Issues Coalition (BIC).

Groups that joined BIC included some of the major prohunting organizations (Safari Club International, National Rifle Association, Archery Manufacturers and Merchants Organization, Foundation for North American Wild Sheep, the National Shooting Sports Foundation, the Pope and Young Club, and others). They orchestrated the 1998 campaigns in states where antihunting ballot initiatives were on the ballot, and the results were considerably different than in 1996.

Of five initiatives that would have negatively impacted hunting and trapping, four were voted down. Here is the summary of the votes for the ballot referendums in November, 1998.

A. Alaska. Ballot Measure No. 9 would have banned the use of snares to manage wolves. The vote was 36 percent in favor and 64 percent against.

B. California. Proposition 4 would ban the use of animal traps and poisons. Hunters and trappers lost this battle by 57 to 43 percent.

C. Minnesota. Here a constitutional amendment was made (Amendment 2) that established hunting and fishing as a "valued part of our heritage that shall be forever preserved for the people and shall be managed by law and regulation for the public good." This was not a ballot initiative as Minnesota does not have such a process. Rather this was a measure sent to the voters by the legislature. It worked the same as a ballot referendum, and it passed by a wide margin, of 77 percent for and 23 percent against.

D. Ohio. Issue 1 would ban dove hunting in Ohio. Doves are delineated as song birds in some states and game birds in others. But the battle was fought and decided on the issue of whether the state wildlife agency should maintain control over management of wildlife. The public voted against the ban on dove hunting by a 60 to 40 percent majority. The Wildlife Legislative Fund of America helped fight this initiative.

E. Utah. Proposition 5 centered on the referendum process by requiring that a two-thirds majority must be met to pass any initiatives in Utah. That passed by 57 to 43 percent.

How did the Ballot Issues Coalition turn the tide on the referendum voting? They used the same strategies that have been so successful for antihunting organizations. They hired big time firms to help them develop polished television propaganda. They spent their money wisely and got material in front of the public in a timely fashion. And they appealed to the emotions of voters on these ballot issues.

Attack Bowhunting.—-This strategy has been used since the early 1970's, but it has only recently become a major problem. There are several issues in attacking bowhunting. The most heavily utilized issue is to focus on wounding.

The argument made by antihunters is simple and straight forward; the bow is a primitive hunting implement, so it must not kill very efficiently. A second argument is that the broadheads used cause pain and suffering as the animal dies a lingering death. Though neither argument was substantiated, they were given credence by the publication of a book, *"The Bowhunting Alternative"*, that was published in 1989. This book discussed a Texas Parks and Wildlife unpublished report that quoted high wounding rates.

The major thrust of the book was that bow wounding losses were very high, and that bowhunters could not shoot accurately. Though the lack of science in this book has been questioned, it received great notoriety from the antibowhunting forces.

The Fund For Animals (FFA), and other antihunting groups reinforced the materials in the book, disregarding subsequent published data and summaries of bow wounding data. They decided that 80 percent of all deer shot with arrows were not found by the hunter and later died from their wounds.

Thus, if this were factual, for every 100 deer shot with bows, another 80 deer are left in the woods. To carry the extrapolation further, in a state like Michigan where the 1991 bow kill was around 100,000 deer, then another 80,000 deer would be left in the woods following the bow season. It is worth noting that immediately after the Michigan bow season approximately one million gun hunters take to the woods for the firearm deer season. One would assume that they would find thousands of dead deer left by bowhunters. Conservation officers contend that few such dead animals are found.

There have been two major studies done where ground searches were made following bowhunts. One was a masters' thesis done by M. L. Lohfeld at Rutgers University in 1979. He found the unrecovered wounding loss was 11 percent following a controlled hunt in a New Jersey state park. (Unrecovered losses include animals killed but not found by bowhunters, and also deer killed but illegally abandoned by violators).

The second study was another masters' thesis done by J. S. C. Herron at the University of Wisconsin-Madison in 1984, and he found that bow wounding losses were nine percent. Even though these two studies were available, the perception of high losses was still perpetuated by the press and antihunting leaders. As an example here is a quote from the October 20th, 1991 issue of the Houston Chronicle by Dana Forbes, director of Fund For Animals. She described hunting "with the bow and arrow as a cruel way to hunt deer because the animals usually don't die immediately."

Such newspaper quotes were very common, especially from 1990-1995. During that time frame, newspapers all over the country carried letters to the editor written by antihunters that were filled with quotes citing the paltry Texas wound data.

Thus, there was a need for some good scientific data on bow wounding losses. So, Jay McAninch, biologist with the Minnesota Department of Natural Resources, and I, put together a massive and expensive study at Camp Ripley, Minnesota. The study utilized university graduate students, sophisticated hunter interviews, and remote sensing to determine wounding rates and wounding losses.

After four years of study, the conclusions were that a maximum of 13 percent of all bow-wounded deer had the potential to go off and die later. At Camp Ripley, for every 100 deer shot, a minimum of 87 were recovered by the hunter. A maximum of 13 percent were wounded and not found by the hunter. These are listed as "unaccounted" for. If all unaccounted for wounded deer died, the loss would be 13 percent. If some of those deer lived, as they most certainly would, then the wounding loss would be less than 13 percent.

Though attacked by some antihunting groups, this study has been accepted by the professional wildlife community as a good estimate of what the maximum, potential bow wounding loss is for deer. It is not 80 percent; at the most it is 13 percent. Biologically, the difference is huge.

In recent years there have been two other major bow wounding studies published. In 1995 the Washington Department of Fish and Wildlife released a new study on elk mortality*. The study focused on poaching but also listed bow wounding losses.

Previous studies suggested relatively high elk bow wounding losses, but sample sizes were very small. In this study 335 adult elk were radio-collared and 165 died over a four-year period. Legal hunting accounted for 59 percent of all mortality; poaching 15 percent. Cougar predation and winter kill was 15 percent, and all other losses, including gun and bow wounding, totaled 11 percent of all mortality.

Archery hunters took eight of 26 radio-collared cows that were harvested, and only one of 70 marked bulls. Nine marked animals

*"An Analysis of Elk Poaching Losses, And Other Mortality Sources in Washington Using Biotelemetry." Smith et al. 1995, Washington Department of Fish and Wildlife, Olympia, Washington.

were shot with rifles and lost, only one was shot with a muzzleloader and lost, and *only one was shot with a bow and lost.* This is a most interesting study. It clearly showed that as with deer, most elk shot with arrows either die quickly and are found by the hunter or recover from their wounds.

Finally, a 1995 study in South Carolina followed the hunting success of experienced bowhunters who shot deer from tree stands.* Sixty of 61 deer shot were recovered by the bowhunters, yielding an extremely small wounding loss.

Since bows shoot over very short ranges, they are often proposed as a method in urban deer-problem areas where guns cannot obviously be used. When such proposals are made, antihunters often suggest that bowhunting is not a safe form of hunting.

In fact, few sports are as safe as bowhunting. There is an average of one mortality per year in bowhunting. The Hunter Education Association noted that 1989 showed an all-time high for bowhunting accidents. There were 21 reported accidents resulting in three fatalities.

If we consider that each year there are around 100 deaths due to lightning strikes, 40 deaths due to bee stings, 20 deaths due to dog attacks, 16 deaths in football, and three deaths due to black widow spider bites, bowhunting is safe. And, nonhunters are never involved in bowhunting accidents.

There is a large misconception that all forms of hunting are dangerous. In fact, recent data from the National Safety Council shows that hunting is very safe. Football showed 3,313 injuries per 100,000 participants; volleyball had 622; golf had 185; fishing had 173 (mostly from drowning); ping pong had 15; and hunting had seven.

Yes, it is true. Far more people per 100,000 participants get hurt playing golf, fishing, or ping pong, than by hunting. When looking at accidental death rates, hunting is higher than some sports, but still below fires, poisoning, suffocating, football, golf, fishing, skiing, etc.

Hunter Harassment.——From 1988-1994 hunter harassment was a popular antihunting activity. Harassment usually took place at a National Wildlife Refuge or State Park. The antihunting strategy was

*"*Efficiency of Archery Hunting For White-tailed Deer on Medway Plantation.*" Morton *et al.* Proceedings, 49th Southeast Fish and Wildlife Conf., 1995.

two-fold; to get publicity, and to test state hunter harassment laws.

Harassers would follow hunters through the woods, sometimes taunting, sometimes quiet. Since the hunt was legal, such harassment soon led to legal battles and state laws enacted to protect hunter rights.

The situation at McKee Beshers Wildlife Management Area in Montgomery County, Maryland was typical. This state area was opened to bowhunting to help reduce environmental damage caused by an overpopulation of deer.

Antihunters conducted harassment of bowhunters and got some publicity. They returned the next year to continue their harassment. However, this time they were greeted by a Protect Whats Right booth set up by the Maryland Bowhunters Society.

On September 14, 1991, the opening day of the Maryland bow season, the Maryland Bowhunters Society held a Celebration of Conservation Success day at the wildlife management area. Over 250 sportsman attended, many attired in coats and ties. They set up the Protect Whats Right booth, presented scientific information on wildlife to the press, and took the play away from the 35 animal rightists who attended. This prowildlife management event was so successful that the Maryland Bowhunters made it an annual event.

With the passage of the new "Crime Bill," hunter harassment is now illegal in all states. In addition, hunters have begun using the approach implemented by the Maryland Bowhunters Society, and this has greatly reduced publicity, and thus, greatly reduced the use of this strategy.

Local Ordinances.—-Introducing or enforcing local ordinances is often used, especially in suburban situations where growing deer herds cause many problems. There have been several strategies used.

One attempt is to stop hunting locally. Here the antihunters protest the bowhunt or gun hunt (though gun hunts are rare in suburban situations) to the County or Township, and public hearings are held.

The next step is to introduce local ordinances to stop bowhunting. Another strategy is to pass a local ordinance against shooting a bow. Obviously, if you can't shoot a bow you can't bowhunt. In Montgomery County, Maryland, this strategy was used, based in part upon safety of the bow.

As Americans continue to build homes in rural areas, encroaching on deer habitat, the need for bowhunting will continue. Princeton Township in New Jersey is a typical example. Hunting was stopped in the early 1970's, deer herds ballooned, gardens and shrubs got hammered, auto-deer collisions increased many times, and citizens complained. Bowhunting was successfully used and antihunters got very upset.

Another strategy was used in 1992 on Prudence Island, Rhode Island where 150-180 deer were harvested each year. Portsmouth is the government seat of this small island, and they have a city ordinance that states if 20 percent of the registered voters sign a petition, a special ballot must be held.

Antihunters initiated a petition to stop hunting on the island. They got the required number of signatures needed to force a vote, but they didn't succeed in stopping hunting. The ballot vote was won by prohunting forces in the Town of Portsmouth by a wide margin (75 to 25 percent). Apparently deer damage impacted lots of people, and they did not want to lose control of the only viable method left for herd control.

In most states the Department of Natural Resources has the statutory authority to manage wildlife. When any local government bans bowhunting then the state game agency must challenge them so that management regulations do not become fragmented.

The Threat of Negative Public Opinion.—-In the fall of 1991 the small town of Vonore, Tennessee decided to allow bowhunting to eliminate a major deer problem. Auto/deer accidents were high, but when the mayor announced the bowhunt, the Fund For Animals threatened to bring in protestors.

The mayor canceled the bowhunt because he had only three policemen, and felt the protestors might get hurt by local hunters. This strategy has not worked in many instances, and thus it is not used very often.

"Whenever we deny our instincts, we create problems for ourselves, those around us, and the world."

James Swan

Chapter 11

Mountain Lions and Black Bears; To Hunt or Not to Hunt*

Mountain lions and black bears have been a major focus for antihunting organizations. Myths and misinformation abounds. Even though state wildlife agencies have good population data showing that both species are extremely abundant throughout their range, many citizens believe these animals are endangered.

Another myth is that once hunting seasons are canceled, no lions or bears die. Truth is that in states where hunting seasons have been canceled, increasingly large numbers of problem bears and lions have to be killed each year. Sometimes the numbers of problem animals killed approaches the once-legal hunting harvest. Also when hunting seasons are canceled, the state losses the license monies and excise taxes it once used for managing these two species.

One might then think that citizens would want management to take precedent over preservation. But that is not the case. This whole affair is quite complex and differs from state to state. What follows is a bit of history and the present-day situation relative to the ongoing saga of mountain lion and black bear management, or lack thereof.

Mountain Lions.—-Thirty years ago I saw my first mountain lion in the wild. I was bowhunting for mule deer in the Colorado mountains near Douglas Pass. The really big bucks were feeding in aspen meadows at night, and then moving to bedding sites in the rim rocks at the top of the mountain during the day.

As I moved along a cliff in the rim rocks my path was blocked by a fallen spruce tree across the steep trail. There was only one way

*adapted with permission from "On Your Side" column, Eastern Bowhunting, Jan. 1991; "Know Hunting" columns, Bowhunter magazine, Feb. 1992, Jun, Oct. 1994, Jun., Oct., Dec. 1995, Feb, Apr 1996.

through, and as I climbed over the tree, a lion ran from a small cave right below me. It ran up the trail, stopped to look, and then disappeared. That memory will be etched in my mind forever.

Most people never see a mountain lion in the wild. Yet this species engenders a great deal of emotion and concern for many people. In the antihunting arena, mountain lions have been a primary focus.

In June 1990, California residents voted on a state referendum, Proposition 117, banning all mountain lion hunting. The referendum passed by a margin of approximately 200,000 votes. To the naive, the proposition sounded quite good. It was called "The Wildlife Protection Act," and the name does have a ring to it. But the overall affect on humans and mountain lions has yet to be determined. Preliminary indications are that both have suffered, and the state wildlife management agency has also suffered as this Act was the first major step in redirecting wildlife management dollars in California.

When the Act passed, mountain lions were doing very well in California. Some speculated that there were more lions in California at that time than in any state in the country (officials showed more than 5,100 cats). They were far from endangered, as many people were led to believe.

The history of California mountain lion management showed they were a bountied predator from 1907-1963, and over 12,000 lions were killed during that period (an average of 219/year). Populations increased over those years, from 1963-1968 they were a managed nongame species; under that status they were not protected.

To protect cougars they were listed as a game species from 1969 to 1972. (You can set long or short seasons on game species, or totally close a season. Thus, making an animal a game species is one way to protect them.)

There was a lion season in 1971 and a short portion of 1972 before a moratorium on recreational hunting was imposed in February, 1972. In 1973, 21 problem lions were killed. Lions were again classified as game animals in 1986, and the California Department of Fish and Game recognized the need to manage lions and unsuccessfully attempted to open lion hunting in 1987 and 1988. Over the ensuing years many problem cats had to be killed.

Mountain Lions and Black Bears; To Hunt Or Not To Hunt

In 1990, because of the concern that lions would be hunted, antihunting organizations led an effort to get signatures on a petition that put a referendum on the voting ballot. These groups included the Fund For Animals, the Mountain Lion Foundation (with board members Doris Day, Rue McLanahan, Robert Redford, Mrs. Jimmie Stewart, and others), Defenders of Wildlife, Sierra Club, Environmental Defense Fund, plus many television and movie stars. The referendum was Proposition 117, and it passed in 1990.

Proposition 117 banned lion hunting but it also stated that $30 million per year for the next 30 years (a total of $900 million) was to be placed into an account to be used to purchase mountain lion habitat. Remember, mountain lions were doing very well in California; habitat was not a problem.

Note too that at that time the financial situation of California was a bit on the downside, to say the least. This $30 million expenditure per year was not realistic, nor needed. And this $30 million was not to be new monies; instead it had to come from the existing budget of the fish and game agency, thus causing a negative impact on active wildlife management programs.

In essence, this new law, if fully enforced, would have compelled the state wildlife agency to spend $30 million a year to buy habitat for mountain lions, when in fact, lions were at or near an all time high in population numbers. Removing that $30 million from ongoing successful wildlife programs would have been a disaster for the state.

Fortunately, that hasn't happened because this portion of the Wildlife Protection Act has not been enforced. One last thing. Proposition 117 also stated that the $30 million could not be used for population surveys to estimate numbers of mountain lions. Go figure.

Cougar habits (see next paragraph) make it difficult to get a good handle on their numbers, and it is costly. Without new funds, the state game agency has found it hard to estimate lion numbers, but they have done as good a job as is possible given limited resources and the species involved.

There are several reasons that mountain lions are so vulnerable to antihunting activities. First, they are extremely difficult to count. Cat biologists say that all members of the cat family, including mountain lions, are very difficult to census. Any animal that travels alone, has a home range of over 50 square miles, is predominantly active at night, and is extremely wary, is difficult to census. Without accurate data, it is easy for critics to claim that lions are endangered.

Second, because of antihunter propaganda and for other unexplained reasons, the general public believes that mountain lions are endangered. In truth, we find that in almost all regions of the United States where good populations exist, lion numbers are rising.

The number of California mountain lions is growing every year. In 1988, Dr. Bart O'Gara, noted mountain lion biologist from Montana, stated that the mountain lion was declared a game animal in Montana in 1971 and every year thereafter, his track counts of lions have showed an increase indicating that hunters can have permit hunting and still have an increase in numbers if that is the public wish.

Although hard to prove, it is common sense that more and more people hiking, biking and jogging in what was formerly uninhabited (by humans) lion country, can create a lion-man problem. This is compounded by not having any hunting which will lead to lions being less wary of humans. This obviously can create a major problem. Human-lion conflicts exist throughout the west, and they create the potential for human deaths, even in states where hunting is legal.

Consider the suburban areas around Boulder, Colorado, along the eastern front of the Rocky Mountains, where deer hunting has been curtailed or stopped (due, in part, to public opinion and because the area is suburban and gun hunting might be dangerous). With burgeoning deer populations, and a sprawling suburban human population, a growing and less wary lion population has moved into town to feast on the deer.

In addition, some domestic dogs have been killed and eaten by mountain lions around Boulder. With more and more people hiking and living in what is lion habitat, human-lion interactions have increased.

It is in these suburban situations, as well as in parks where lion hunting is not allowed and human use is high, that problems can occur. There have been five mountain lion attacks in Colorado between 1991 and 1998. Two of the attacks were fatal, and four of the five involved small people, running, and alone. Here is a summary of all five attacks in Colorado:

Mountain Lions and Black Bears; To Hunt Or Not To Hunt

1. Idaho Springs, January, 1991. Eighteen year old jogger was killed by a 110 lb. lion. It's been postulated that he may have been bent over tying his tennis shoes when attacked. This position might have given an unwary mountain lion the impression that he was an animal...prey species. The lion was later killed at the scene, returning to feed on the victim.

2. Rocky Mountain National Park, July 1997. A 10-year-old boy was killed by an 88 lb. female lion. The boy was running ahead of his parents on a trail. The lion was later killed.

3. Cortez, non-fatal attack on a woman. She was taking samples from a stream and fought off the lion by stabbing it in the eye with forceps. The lion only weighed 60 lbs., was apparently very old with worn teeth, and was not in good condition. It was killed by the state.

4. Mesa Verde, 1997. A four-year-old boy was running ahead of his parents. A 75 lb. lion in good condition attacked the boy, but his family fought it off. This same cat had approached others in that area two days before. It was later killed.

5. Roxborough State Park, 1998. A 24-year-old man, small in stature, fought off a lion with a pocket knife. The lion was small and never killed.

These incidents are not unique to California or Colorado. A four year-old boy was attacked and killed in his Montana back yard in 1989. There were 123 incidents between humans and lions in Montana between 1989 and 1995. The state responded by increasing the lion hunting quota, and lion incidents were reduced in 1995 to half that of former years.

The 1989 issue of the Wildlife Society Bulletin (a scientific journal) has a most interesting article summarizing all cougar attacks in the United States. Dr. Paul Beier from the University of California, documented 10 deaths and 48 nonfatal injuries by mountain lions in the United States from 1890 to 1990.

There were nine fatal attacks during that period. Five of the nine fatal attacks (one attack had two deaths) occurred since 1970 (note this is up through 1989 and there have been other deaths since). As a sign of this increasing problem, the author noted that *there were more fatal attacks during the past 20 years than during the previous 80 years.*

Most attacks occur in the summer, perhaps reflecting increased human activity in wildlands in those months. Dr. Beier noted that cougar populations have increased markedly in recent years in British Columbia, California, Colorado, Nevada, Texas, and Wyoming. Other states probably show similar increases, but data has not been collected. There have been five lion-caused human fatalities in California since 1909 (up through 1989).

In recent years, lion attacks in California have increased. There were five nonfatal attacks of California citizens from 1992 to 1995. In September, 1993 a state park was closed because of a mountain lion scare. The lion that caused that stir was a problem animal, and officials attempted to kill the cat.

Antihunters protested and this, in part, led to the reopening of the park to hikers. Within a few days a 10-year-old girl and her dog were attacked. She survived but the cat had to be killed.

Because mountain lion populations are on the rise, the California wildlife agency has been issuing many more permits to kill problem lions. From 1990 to 1994 over 408 problem cats were killed in California under special depredation permits. Ten cats were killed in 1994 after they threatened or attacked humans.

Two women were killed by lions in California in 1994. In April in El Dorado County a 40-year-old woman was killed. In December, in San Diego County a 56-year-old woman was killed.

As further indication that mountain lion populations are healthy and growing, consider the article in the Sept. 3 1997 issue of the New York Times. They reported that from 1984-1993 lions killed 60 sheep a year in Colorado. Since 1994 that figure has jumped to 1,200, with 1996 damages totaling $500,000. At the same time the numbers of lions legally killed by hunters in Colorado has increased five times to 391.

The article suggests one reason is that "these hunters (lions) may be losing an ancestral wariness of humans." Colorado Biologist Tom Beck notes that "we recognize the woods are not risk free. But if you have a large predator showing highly unusual behavior and losing its normal wariness around people, that animal is a risk to human safety and likely needs to be destroyed."

There are problems elsewhere and the consequences are serious and sad. Cindy Parolin, 36, was killed by a mountain lion in August, 1996, in British Columbia. She was riding horseback with her three children near Princeton, 120 miles east of Vancouver. A 59-pound lion (which is a small lion) spooked a horse and then attacked the six-year-old child when he fell.

Cindy beat the cougar with a stick while her other youngsters carried the injured child to safety. The lion killed Cindy, and was later shot as it stood over her body. This fatality occurred in a province where there is mountain lion hunting.

As more citizens in states vote yes on referendums to stop lion hunting, and as people become more active in what was once lion habitat, we can expect to see cougar attacks increase. What once was uncommon under a wildlife management scheme is now becoming all-to-common with less management.

Is it too logical to consider more hunting of mountain lions to reduce people/lion conflicts, especially when lion populations are on the increase? Maybe so. There is no question from a biological management standpoint that the species can sustain a recreational hunting season without a negative impact on numbers.

Hunting can possibly reduce numbers in certain localities, make cats more wary of humans, and thus reduce human/lion interactions. Though this approach seems rational, the truth is that society is changing and urban values differ a great deal from the rural values we all once held.

A recent public survey in Wyoming showed that only 25 percent agreed that hunting mountain lions with dogs should continue. Interestingly, over 75 percent favored the right of a rancher to kill a problem lion and 84 percent favored removal of individual lions when there was a depredation problem.

A more recent (1996) Colorado study of citizens living along the eastern foothills (Colorado Springs, Denver, Boulder) is also enlightening. Around 80 percent hold positive attitudes about mountain lions. Ten percent want to have lions killed that are seen in residential areas. Less than 20 percent want lions killed that have killed a pet. Between 50 and 60 percent want lions killed if they have injured a person.

This is a major value change in modern society. Thirty years ago, if a lion attacked and injured a human, it would be hunted down and killed. No questions asked, and no one would have been upset, not even those who live in large cities. Today, in large cities in eastern Colorado, almost half of the population says such lions should not be harmed.

Finally, only 67-78 percent want lions killed that have attacked and killed a person. Thus 22-33 percent do not want to exterminate lions that have come into a residential area and killed a human. Interesting, and the message to wildlife managers from those 22-33 percent is quite clear. Leave things alone; do not kill problem lions.

When Proposition 117 was passed in California to stop mountain lion hunting, the belief among antihunters, and those that followed them and voted for the proposition, was that its passage would end all mountain lion killings in California. One got the impression from Hollywood types that these lions would now live in total peace and harmony with the world.

The truth is that real nature in California just doesn't read the script. Since Proposition 117 went into effect, mountain lion encounters with people have increased dramatically.

Now here is the paradox. In 1971, when the last hunting season was held for cats in California, around 100 lions were killed during the hunting season. One animal was killed by special depredation permit. Without legal recreational hunting, under special permits, the state is killing more lions each year than when there was legal recreational hunting. Antihunters led the fight to save them from hunters, and the result is that more lions have to be shot because of problem interactions with humans each year than in the 1970's. We are killing just as many lions in California each year on average now then when there was recreational hunting.

Obviously there are just too many cougars in parts of California. As further indication of this, the December 1994 National Geographic noted eight of 32 radio-collared lions were hit by cars in southern California. Torres *et al.* (1996; *"Mountain Lion And Human Activity In California: Testing Speculations"*, Wildlife Society Bulletin 24, pages 451-460) noted that increasing domestic sheep depredation was probably related to an increasing lion population.

Pet predation is on the rise where new housing developments are being built in lion habitat. When pets are killed by lions, then humans are living too close. Even so, the majority of California citizens do not want lions hunted. In March, 1996 they voted on Proposition 197, which would have overturned Proposition 117 and allowed lion hunting. It was defeated by a wide margin.

Problems are not just limited to California. On election day in November 1994 Oregon voters passed Amendment 18 making it illegal to use bait and dogs to hunt bear and mountain lion. Final tally was around 52 percent for Amendment 18 and 48 percent opposed.

Let's consider the total Oregon hunting harvest and the mountain lions killed as a result of damage complaints for the past five years. In 1992, 187 cats were harvested, and 22 killed after complaints. In 1993 160 animals were harvested, and 31 more after complaints. In 1994, 144 were harvested, 35 after complaints.

After bait and dog hunting were stopped let's see what happened. In 1995, 31 cats were harvested, and 67 from damage complaints. In 1996, 47 lions harvested and 94 more after complaints. In 1997, 61 were harvested, and 98 after complaints. The trend is fairly clear. While the estimated Oregon lion population went from 200 to 2500 in the past 30 years, once dog and bait hunting were stopped, the total mountain lion hunter harvest dropped dramatically, while the damage complaint kills soared.

From 1992 to 1994, the total cat mortality in Oregon was 209, 191, and 179 respectively. After the ban, from 1995-1997, the total cat mortality was 98, 141, and 159 respectively. Note that in 1997, the total mortality was higher than the hunter harvest in 1994, and that was before the ban.

Obviously, a ban on bait and dog hunting has not dropped the total mountain lion mortality; it just has decreased revenues to manage cats, and created safety problems for cats and people. Although Oregon has not had a human death nor many attacks from lions, it will happen.

As in California, in November 1996 a referendum was introduced in Oregon to overturn Amendment 18 and allow lions to be hunted. Again, as in California, this referendum was defeated by a wide margin.

California and Oregon are not alone in this issue. Washington also has a lion problem. With the passage of Initiative 655, the normal 45-day hound hunting lion season was eliminated in Washington in 1996.

Until then the cougar harvest from all forms of hunting was 230 per year.

In 1995, Washington had to kill six problem lions and handle around 380 complaints. In 1996 when hunting was stopped in the middle of the year (reducing the season to eight days) the state had to kill 43 problem lions and handle 495 complaints. The kill in 1996 (178), though considerably below average, was not as low as expected, and this was attributed to the fact that cougar hunters realized this was there last chance to use hounds to hunt lion, so they hunted all eight days.

In 1997, there was no hound hunting and the total cougar kill dropped to 132. I don't have the harvest figures for 1998, but the game agency there lowered the lion tags from $24 to $5 to encourage more hunters to hunt lions (even though doing so without dogs is rather iffy). Meanwhile, the cougar populations is estimated between 2,400 and 3,200, and problem animals are on the increase and 1998 complaints are at an all-time high.

Many trained lion biologists are working for state wildlife agencies. Hopefully voters in western states will chose to let these biologists properly manage the lions. Mountain lions are great animals. They do need the protection that game species get, but they also need the management that wildlife agencies and hunting provides.

But do not expect common sense to prevail. It is likely that more and more western states will vote to terminate management of lions by stopping hunting.

Black Bears.—-Colorado citizens voted 70 to 30 percent in 1992 to stop spring bear hunting and all bait and dog hunting for bears. In 1994, Oregon voters also banned bait and dog hunting for bears. With these two victories, antihunting groups at the national level recognized an opportunity to put a large chink in the hunter's armor. With 340,000 bears nationwide and hunting legal in 27 states, any ground swell of support to stop bear hunting would have major impacts on a state's ability to manage bruins. That fear is now a reality.

The Colorado vote was preceded by much discussion and debate.

Mountain Lions and Black Bears; To Hunt Or Not To Hunt

In 1991, the Colorado Division of Wildlife and the Wildlife Commission modified bear hunting. They lengthened the spring season by two weeks, but reduced the licenses available for spring bear hunting. They also increased the number of bear permits for the fall season.

Citizens were not happy with this compromise and succeeded in getting Amendment 10 on the ballot for 1992, leading to the vote mentioned above. Hunters and farmers were concerned that the loss of bear hunting was a first step to restrict or eliminate other hunting and trapping in Colorado.

In-state supporters of the elimination of bear hunting said that would not happen; they only wanted to stop bait and dog bear hunting. Out-of-state antihunting groups, on the other hand, indicated that this was just the first step in stopping all hunting and trapping in Colorado.

Regardless of whether one feels the referendum is the way to manage black bears or not, it is state referendums that control the future of bear management. To understand the future, let's consider the past.

What is it about the black bear that has made this species the target of antihunters? There are several possible factors. One recent scientific report indicated that many people view the bear as intelligent, appealing and similar to people. Such an image would obviously alter any management practice that involved killing bears.

Many citizens also believe that bears are human-like, cuddly, warm, soft, a friend of man, comical, a teddy bear, etc. Again, this is not an image that leads to an acceptance of hunting bears as a management tool.

Beyond speculation, studies show that *many urban citizens believe that black bears are an endangered species.* When folks in Colorado were asked why they opposed a spring black bear hunting season, 30 percent did so because they felt black bears were endangered. Studies show that 20 percent of Michigan citizens also think black bears are endangered. With over 11,000 black bears in Colorado, and populations growing, it is obvious that this species is not endangered, but many people remain unconvinced.

One might assume that this lack of knowledge stems from so many Coloradans living in an urban environment. However, that apparently is not the case. The Colorado Division of Wildlife Report No. 15 published in 1990 showed a tremendous increase in urbanization in Colorado.

In 1950, 60 percent of the population lived in urban areas. By 1980 it was up to 80 percent. This separation from real nature might explain the lack of knowledge people have about bears.

However, another journal article (*"Colorado Black Bear Hunting Referendum: What Was Behind The Vote,?"* by Cynthia Loker and Daniel Decker, Wildlife Society Bulletin 23:370-376, 1995) showed that this urban issue was not as important as believed.

Fifty-four percent of those living in medium to large cities supported Amendment 10, while 51 percent were opposed. The fact that just a little over half of urban citizens voted to stop bear hunting is not a strong argument that being urban is the reason for the vote.

In fact, many rural Colorado citizens opposed bait and dog hunting for bears. Thirty-one percent of those living in rural areas or on farms or ranches were in favor of Amendment 10 while only 28 % opposed it. Chances are that the 30 % who felt that black bears were endangered came from both urban and rural areas of the state. Regardless, this point indicates why many people voted to stop bear hunting; they thought bears were endangered.

Not only was the Colorado vote not related to urban life, it also was not related to a knowledge of the issue. Both hunters and nonhunters were very willing to vote to stop certain forms of bear hunting even though they knew little about the issue. A 1991 study (*"Study of Colorado Registered Voters and Black Bear Hunters: Attitudes About Hunting Black Bears in Colorado,"* Colorado Division of Wildlife, 1991) showed that just prior to the vote to stop black bear hunting, 48 percent of all registered voters had heard nothing at all about spring black bear hunting issues.

Even more interesting, 34 percent of those that had heard nothing held a hunting license, and seven percent indicated they were black bear hunters. Another 42 percent of the public indicated they had heard very little about the issue, and 45 percent of those were hunters, and 28 percent were bear hunters.

Thus, 90 percent of the voters who put an end to bear hunting in Colorado had heard little about the issues and some were bear hunters.

Mountain Lions and Black Bears; To Hunt Or Not To Hunt

All of these studies have led some to believe that most supporters of Amendment 10 in Colorado were not antihunting; they just were opposed to bear hunting over bait and with dogs.

Another major factor in the Colorado black bear vote was that antihunters and a small percent of hunters became bedfellows in this issue. Fourteen percent of the supporters of Amendment 10 in Colorado were active hunters and another 12 percent had previously hunted. Strange bedfellows indeed.

The same trend held for Michigan when the bear hunting debate got hot and heavy. A 1994 survey conducted by Dr. Ben Peyton of Michigan State University showed that 42 percent of active Michigan hunters who responded to a questionnaire were opposed to bear hunting with dogs and 29 percent were against bait hunting. Even more interesting was a 1992 Michigan survey of bear hunters. It showed that almost 33 percent of bait hunters opposed dog hunting and 33 percent of bear dog hunters opposed bait hunting.*

Competition between hunter types makes it convenient and effective to pit them against one another. Antihunting groups have seized the fact that some hunters feel that bait and dog hunting are unethical, and are using this as part of their campaign in what might be a stepping stone to stop all hunting. The strategy is simple. Use the appealing issues of dog and bait hunting for bears that has attracted some hunter support as a strategy to convince the nonhunting public that there are problems. Convey to the public that the problem with hunting is using bait and dogs to bear hunt...nothing more.

Also let the public know that some hunters oppose some forms of hunting. Using this approach, bait and dog hunting have caught the attention of not only strong animal activists, but borderline antihunters, and some hunters as well.

A consideration of bear hunting data from Michigan shows how a strategy of pitting one form of hunter against another will work. Sixty-two percent of Michigan's bear hunters *only* use bait while six percent *only* use dogs. Another eight percent use dogs but may start the chase at bait. Another 18 percent use more than one method.

---

*The bear ballot initiative in Michigan was largely organized and supported by an irate landowner (and a hunter) tired of bear dog hunters trespassing on his property. Language to prohibit the use of bait was added to the ballot iniative later to gain support of a broader group of animal activists.

In fact, only six percent hunt *without* dogs or bait. Thus, when you have a situation where dog hunters feel that bait hunting is unethical or vice versa, and a high percentage of the bear hunters utilize such hunting methods, hunting will lose in the end. Antihunters know this and they will encourage such a strategy.

Bear biologist Tom Beck rightfully lays some of the blame for the antibear hunting phenomenon on wildlife professionals (see Beck, T. 1998; *"Citizen Ballot Initiatives: A Failure of the Wildlife Management Profession"*, Human Dimensions in Wildlife 3(2); pages 21- 28). He noted that we have permitted hunting methods for bears that are prohibited for most species (baiting, dogs, spring seasons), and suggested that this approach would logically lead to problems.

What is the issue for the pressure to eliminate dogs and bait hunting for bears? If it is a concern for the physical and mental health of a bear then the issue is one of animal welfare. If there is a belief that the bear has a right not to be hunted, then this is an animal rights issue (see Peyton, R. B. 1998. *"Defining Management Issues: Dogs, Hunting and Society"*, presented at 53rd North American Wildlife and Natural Resource Conference, March 20-24, Orlando, Florida).

Dr. Peyton pointed out that "animal rightists play an important role in dog-hunting issues because they often initiate challenges to hunting methods." He then went on to note that "the factor which sways the voting public will most likely be animal welfare and not animal rights concerns."

For example, in Colorado, the voters were concerned about the welfare of cubs during spring bait hunts, and that is an animal welfare issue. An interesting survey was done in Michigan, and it showed another animal welfare issue, the concern for the dogs used in bear hunting. Twenty percent of respondents who were opposed to bear dog hunting stated concern for the dogs as a reason primarily while only 11 percent of that group mentioned concern for the bear (see Peyton, R. B. and L. D. Grise. 1995. *"A 1994 Survey of Michigan Public Attitudes Regarding Bear Management Issues."* A report to the Wildlife Division, Michigan Department of Natural Resources, Lansing, Michigan 84 pp). The use of dogs seems to be a major influence in voter attitudes.

Most of my childhood friends owned beagles. I did too. Hunting rabbits with beagles was as common as the Internet. It was not viewed as bad, unethical, and in fact, beagles were fairly benign. No one gave them a second thought; in rural areas the beagle was a normal part of the landscape.

Apparently nonhunters today have a different perspective. Peyton and Grise questioned nonhunters (excluding antihunters) in Michigan about rabbit dog hunting while they were questioning them about using dogs to hunt bears. They found that 66 percent of Michigan nonhunters opposed bear hunting with dogs, but a seemingly and surprisingly high 48 percent opposed rabbit hunting with dogs.

If hunters don't understand that society is changing, this statistic should give them a strong signal. But, to me, there is sadness here, because the loss of support for beagle hunting means a loss of what rural families have done for many years. Beagle hunting was a family affair and it seems more obvious every day that society today needs more family activities.

Dr. Ben Peyton has broken down the response to public challenges on dog and bait hunting to two approaches. He calls one a "capitulation" approach where the public draws a line on what is an acceptable form of hunting and what is not. (See Peyton, R. B. 1995. *"Their Own Worst Enemy."* Michigan Out-of-Doors 49(12): 30+.).

The argument is that by capitulating to the antihunters and eliminating unacceptable forms of hunting, the nonhunting public will then support other forms of hunting (i.e., hunters and/or wildlife agencies that manage game animals will capitulate to nonhunters in deciding what is an acceptable hunting method).

The second strategy is the "hard line" approach. This approach is based on the premise that you do not yield on one form of hunting because that is the first step to a loss of other forms of hunting.

Right now, it appears the "capitulation" approach is being more frequently practiced among wildlife agencies. When you consider the citizen view on using dogs to hunt rabbits, it lends credence to the idea that capitulation can be a problem for an escalation of antihunting issues. But the welfare issues cannot be ignored.

Even some wildlife professionals (includes biologists, managers, professors, etc. but all had degrees and jobs in wildlife and/or fisheries) who support hunting have publicly come out against bait and dog hunting for bears. In fact, a recent survey showed that 57 percent of biologists felt that the use of dogs to hunt black bears should be abolished. Only 27 percent felt it should continue.

I believe that capitulation is a mistake that will lead to a loss of other forms of hunting. Even though antihunting leaders say that bait and dog hunting for bears is the problem, once bait and dog hunting is stopped, animal rights activitivists will attack other forms of hunting — forms that are supported by most hunters and wildlife biologists...forms that are more ethically acceptable to the public at large.

While I support the democratic nature of our government that allows it to happen, I believe that hunters and biologists who line up with antihunters on this bait and dog hunting issue are making a serious mistake. Ron Regan (a wildlife biologist from Vermont) agrees.

In the Summer 1996 Newsletter of the Northeast Section of The Wildlife Society Regan acknowledged that state biologists are public servants, but such biologists should not capitulate to an irresponsible, though often well-intended, course of action, at least until social or political pressures become unbearable.

He further suggested that we (state biologists) should be willing to exert ecologically-responsible leadership in the midst of adversity.

I agree. My suggestion to those who feel a form of hunting is unethical, don't do it. But by making your feelings known publicly, and helping pass antihunting referendums, you are helping antihunters gain more support for the defeat of other forms of hunting and wildlife management.

Capitulation will work with citizens who truly do not like one form of hunting, but approve of others. Capitulation will not work at the state level simply because antihunting leaders and the press will educate the general public on their perception of reality. The hunters perception will not be portrayed, and more referendums will pass.

Of course some will say that in our free America, everyone should be able to express their opinions on a subject. I agree with that as well. There are no simple answers here.

The capitulation approach predictably leads to an attack on other forms of hunting. The question is, what will hunters give up next? Other forms of dog hunting like using dogs to hunt rabbits? How about using decoys for duck hunting? What about hunting deer near apple trees because that is a form of bait hunting? How about hunting geese because people feel it is unethical to shoot an animal that mates for life?

Antihunting leaders will lead the news media on such forays just as they have done on the bear bait and dog issue. The October 1996 issue of Time magazine wrote a negative story about the bear bait and dog issue *("Hunting's Bad Sports")*. They quoted Lynn Fritchman, a hunter and the leader of the antibear hunting issue in Idaho. "If we all want to be hunting in 40 years we'd better do away with practices that are now viewed as repugnant."

Likewise in the High Country News, October 1996, wildlife biologist Tom Beck from Colorado stated that "we must change or we will cease to exist."

These suggestions have two presuppositions. One, that citizens drive such issues and dictate policy rather than antihunting groups and their subsequent publicity releases. Two, for the leaders of antihunting groups, the issue is bait and dog hunting. If these suppositions are true, then elimination of bait and dog hunting as a compromise will mean that there will be no further, immediate attacks on bear hunting...or other forms of hunting.

That is one view. Another might be that in supporting these antihunting issues one is step-by-step leading nonhunters down a path where much of our wildlife management programs will be lost because of a calculated, planned loss of one form of hunting after another.

Can that happen? Maybe. Consider what happened in Colorado.

When the Fund For Animals helped organize and support the passage of Amendment 10 in Colorado, they apparently gave some antihunters (and hunters too) the impression that the issue was only bait and dog hunting for bears. However, two months after the vote to stop bait and dog hunting for bears, the Fund returned to Colorado in an attempt to stop mountain lion hunting with dogs, all bow hunting for bears, and to get all hunting scents and lures classified as bait so that they could also be banned.

This was not well received by some animal rights and hunting groups in Colorado. The December 23rd, 1992 issue of the Rocky Mountain News headlined that "Opponents of spring bear hunt say Fund For Animals lied about goals."

Sherri Tippie, founder of Wildlife 2000 (a Colorado group that wanted bait and dog hunting for bears stopped, and supported Amendment 10) apparently felt that the original goal of the Fund was only to stop bait and dog bear hunting. When the Fund For Animals returned, many Colorado animal activists realized that the Fund wanted to stop all forms of hunting.

Tippie was quoted as stating that "hunting groups aren't going to trust any of us again."

What we have here are Colorado citizens who are not totally antihunting, but they did not like bait and dog hunting for bears. In this situation the antihunters did not respond to national leaders in the animal rights movement when they called to abolish other forms of hunting beyond bait and dog hunting for bears and lions. In fact the folks in Colorado felt betrayed by the Fund For Animals attacks on hunting, and did not want to be a part of that.

Thus, my fears that the attacks on bait and dog hunting are a ploy and that other attacks will follow have not become reality to date in Colorado. Only time will tell whether further attacks will come, and whether a capitulation approach will lead to further management problems. In the meantime, hunters need to understand that all people who vote against certain hunting activities are not necessarily against all hunting.

Having said this, if you are going to draw a hard line and not capitulate, where do you draw that line? In chapter 6 we noted that there are five components of hunting. These are: Skill development, scouting, shooting, recovering the animal, and preparing the meat. Are there forms of hunting that do not have all these components? Yes there are and hunters need to acknowledge that fact. Although such shooting (it's not hunting) is rare and few participate, these things do occur.

Almost no hunters would support letting an animal loose in a small pen and shooting it. OR releasing penned mallards to fly over duck blinds on their way to the marsh. OR hunting a wild boar in a forty-acre pen. OR shooting an elk in a five hundred acre enclosure. These are not hunting activities, they are shooting activities.

What should the hunting community not defend because the activity doesn't qualify as hunting? Where does one draw a line in the sand? Dr. Peyton feels that hunters should separate hunting from all other nonhunting activities and then take a hard line.

And where the line is drawn is part of this issue. The placement of that line will vary from one person to another. My choice is to draw the line where almost all hunters do.....a line that allows bait and hound hunting for bears because those have all the components of hunting. Shooting animals in small enclosures or animals released from pens does not. I agree with Dr. Peyton and feel that such activities should be stopped. I don't call that capitulation, I call it common sense. Also important is the fact that such activities do not fit the definition of hunting.

Now let's consider what has happened in Colorado since bear hunting was reduced. In 1993, I predicted (Bowhunting News, Feb 1993) that this move would lead to many more negative encounters with bears including some where humans would be seriously hurt. Sad to say, my predictions were correct. The September 2nd, 1993 issue of The New York Times contained an interesting story by Alston Chase (*"Too Many Bears"*). It seems that Colorado black bears are doing aggressive things and the article said: black bears are normally shy and these events are virtually unprecedented.

What events? In July a black bear consumed the body of an apparent suicide victim in Colorado. In August a black bear broke into a trailer and killed and ate a man. Biologist Kathi Green noted that the Colorado Division of Wildlife does not normally get calls on bear problems until late July, but they received their first call that year in April, and later received 25 per day. The article noted that there was plenty of food for bears, and intimated that the problem might be the canceled spring bear season.

"It is too soon to say that discontinuing the hunt is the cause of the misbehavior, Green said. But bear population explosions and the resulting behavioral changes fit an emerging pattern."

Just when mountain lion hunting was stopped in California, the canceling of spring bear hunting in Colorado did not lead to the end of the killing of bears. The February 1994 issue of the Rocky Mountain News indicated that 71 problem bears were killed in 1993 while there were only five problem bears killed in 1984.

Nationwide we find that for several reasons, bear attacks are up. From 1972 to 1982, there were two human fatalities and 22 injuries. From 1983 to 1987, there were four human deaths and 26 injuries.

And from 1988 to 1994 there were three deaths and 23 injuries. The cause for such activity is probably the same two reasons that mountain lion encounters with humans have increased. One, people are more and more active (hiking, living, etc.) in bear country. Two, without hunting, bears become less shy around people and this leads to negative interactions.

It appears that when hunting is decreased, negative bear encounters with humans increases. Since the stoppage of hunting has such important ramifications for humans, let's consider the latest in antibear hunting activity for states and provinces.

British Columbia.—-Apparently politicians have been making decisions on bear management that have reduced harvest by limiting the number of bear hunters. On June 14, 1996 a black bear stalked, attacked, and killed a 53-year-old rancher named Sevend Satre in central British Columbia near Tatlayoko Lake.

Mitch Kendall, Wildlife Conservation officer in that area noted in an article appearing in the Williams Lake Tribune that "bear complaints in this area of British Columbia have gone up by 300 percent in the last three years, and the reason is obvious." (referring to the reduction in bear hunters).

Antibear hunting groups are also active. The Western Canada Wilderness Committee wants to end all trophy and recreational hunting for bears in British Columbia. They are actively attempting to get a voter referendum on the ballot to end bear hunting. In mid-August 1996, in remote Liard River Hot Springs Provincial Park, British Columbia, 37 year old Patti McConnell was attacked and killed by a black bear. Raymond Kitchen of Fort Nelson, B. C. was also killed when he tried to save Mrs. McConnell. Her son and another man were mauled, but not killed. A tourist escaped, got a gun and killed the bear.

Other such attacks have occurred in B. C. in recent years. In 1995 bears injured six and killed one human and in 1996 they injured 11 and killed two.

California.—-In 1990 California antihunters used an interesting approach to stop the black bear bow hunting season. They sued, invoking a state environmental law that required an environmental impact statement to be written before any hunting season could be held.

Mountain Lions and Black Bears; To Hunt Or Not To Hunt

Writing such documents is time-consuming and costly, especially since they had to be written for each species hunted in California. The antihunters won the law suit.

The same type of suit occurred in 1991 with the same results. But in 1992, the wildlife and fish agency in California took to the courts, and went through the pain-staking process of adhering to demands of antihunters. As a result, there were no negative comments filed by antihunting groups against the environmental impact report on the black bear bow season in California.

Bowhunting was then reinstated. Even though antihunters predicted that a resumption of hunting would lead to the demise of the black bear, bear numbers have been increasing. The California Department of Fish and Game reports that they have between 17,000 and 24,000 black bears, the highest estimate in 10 years.

In 1995, 12,169 hunters took 1,484 bears. (State hunting regulations require Fish and Game to shut down the season once the yearly kill reaches 1,500). The dedicated California biologists deserve much credit for their hard work in preserving the major source of revenue that is used to manage bears hunting.

Florida.—-The situation in Florida is a little confusing to most people. Habitat is limited, and where there is good habitat, there are good numbers of bears and hunting is allowed. Where there is not habitat, there are few or no bears. The bear was listed as a threatened species, but that has been recently removed. About 50 bears are taken each year, and habitat loss is a major problem. Bear numbers are relatively low, but stopping the hunting won't help the bears due to lack of habitat.

It is handy and even politically correct (for some) for antihunters to blame hunting for the lower numbers of black bears, but that apparently is not the case. In fact, bear numbers are rising and state estimates now approach 3,000.

Idaho.—-A referendum was on the ballot to stop bear hunting with the vote in November, 1996. It failed to pass. For details, see chapter 10.

Louisiana.—-Bear hunting is being stopped, but not because of antihunters. The subspecies of black bear here has not been legally hunted since 1986, and in 1992 it was placed on the federal list of threatened species. Loss of habitat apparently is a major problem.

Michigan.—-A recent study (*"A 1994 Survey of Michigan Public Attitudes Regarding Bear Management Issues"*, A report to the Wildlife Division, Michigan DNR, May 1995) showed that almost half of the citizens know little or nothing about the activities of the wildlife agency.

Seventy-eight percent knew that black bears live in Michigan but most did not know whether there were too many or too few animals. And 20 percent of those who knew bears lived in the state thought that they were an endangered species.

Worse, that same group felt that legal hunting, habitat loss and poaching led to the endangered status. However, this survey showed that the public supported hunting in principle. A referendum was on the ballot to stop bear hunting with the vote in November 1996. It failed to pass. For details, see chapter 10.

New Mexico.—-Their spring bear season was curtailed in 1993, but apparently this was in response to a drop in black bear numbers. Antihunters stated that hunting caused the decline. but there is great debate as to how much hunting had to do with the decrease. If New Mexico gets good rains you can expect bear numbers to increase. In the meantime, bears are estimated to be 5,000 and the annual harvest around 370.

New York.—-Governor Cuomo vetoed a bill that would have continued the use of dogs and bait to bear hunt. He was quoted by an animals rights magazine article as saying "the notion of authorizing this advantage to bear hunters seems inconsistent with the sense of sport? Isn't human superior intelligence and use of weapons advantage enough?"

Ontario.—-As of 1996, black bear hunting was facing a threat. This impacts many Americans since some 70 percent of all Ontario bear hunters are Americans. Bears bring $40 million into the economy each spring. However, this is being threatened by a coalition called Animal Alliance that wants to end all bear hunting in Canada, and they have started their attack in Ontario.

Apparently the Federation of Ontario Naturalists (FON) and the World Wildlife Fund (WWF) conducted a survey, and stated that "a majority of Ontarians want hunting of black bear in spring either stopped or reduced."

In fact, they reported that supposedly 49 percent of the public wants bear hunting banned. Apparently Animal Alliance will attempt to use the same strategy antihunters used in Colorado; get bear hunters who oppose bait hunting to join their cause, develop a major media campaign, use any legal issues, and use the illegal international traffic in bear parts to add fuel to the fire. And, as in Colorado, they will claim that too many females are being killed and putting the population of 100,000 bears in jeopardy.*

Oregon.—-After dog and bait hunting were made illegal the 1995 bear harvest dropped by 764 bears, 53 percent fewer than the 1994 harvest. No surprise, it was just as biologists predicted.

What is the result of this decreased harvest? Bear nuisance complaints rose 39 percent, and 205 bears had to be killed. A referendum was on the ballot to reinstate bear hunting after it was curtailed in 1995. The vote took place in November, 1996. It failed to pass. For details, see chapter 10.

Utah.—-From what I can learn, in 1992, antihunters threatened to put a referendum on the ballot to stop bear hunting if the Wildlife Board (the equivalent of Game Commissions in other states) did not curtail spring bait hunting. So, in August of 1992, the board terminated spring hunting starting in 1993. Watch for a referendum on the ballot to eliminate bear hunting in Utah in the near future.

Washington.—-A referendum to stop bait and dog bear hunting passed in November 1996. For details, see chapter 10. The consequences of this closure are just now becoming apparent. There are between 12,000-15,000 bear hunters in Washington, and they can harvest one bear per year.

Approximately 10 percent of these hunters are successful. Initiative 655 eliminated hunting by 1,000-1,300 hound hunters and 1,700-3,500 bait hunters. This initiative reduced bear harvest in Washington about 50 percent.

---

*As this book goes to press, the Ontario government has announced that the 1999 spring bear season has been canceled. The decision appears to be a political one, and it also appears to be permanent. The government promised to help all the guides and lodges to recoup their losses, but at press time has only offered them $250 per hunter for the 1999 spring hunt. The guides will lose $10-12 million, and will receive compensation totaling around $2 million.

Chapter 11

The present bear population is 25,000, but population density varies within the state. In areas of high bear density, stopping of bait and dog hunting will cause a growth of up to six percent per year. This means that such areas will suffer higher bear damage complaints. In areas of low bear density, the growth may only be one to three percent, and bear complaints will not be high.

Hound hunters killed an average of 267 bears per year from 1992-1995. Bait hunters killed an average of 529 bears each year. (But since the bait kill was only 322 in 1994 and 353 in 1995, the average measured over four years may not represent what will happen when bait hunting was stopped in 1996. The reduction in the kill from the loss of bait hunting will probably be in the 350 range each year).

Hunters who stalk-hunt bears have taken an average of 427 bruins a year. Thus, the average annual harvest from 1992 to 1995 was 1,223. In 1995, when bait and dog hunting were legal, there were approximately 360 bear complaints and eight problem bears were killed from March-December (no data kept prior to March, 1995). In 1996 there were 556 bear complaints and 20 problem bears were killed. There were 70 bears trapped and relocated, and bears killed 60 livestock animals. When bait and hound hunting for bears is lost, expect increased problems and livestock losses.

The Department of Fish and Wildlife recently projected the economic losses from no bear bait or dog hunting. The annual revenue from the sale of resident and nonresident licenses, transport tags, and hound permits is $560,000. Local economies gain an additional $1.15 million each year from bear hunting. From the total of $1.7 million, an estimated $511,400 will be lost.

Of special importance is the portion lost from license and tag sales that formerly went to the Department of Fish and Wildlife. I estimate that about one-half of the $560,000 income from licenses and tag sales will be lost.

Thus, the Department will have to solve the increased bear complaint problem, trap and relocate bears, and shoot problem animals, with half the monies they formerly had for all of bear management. In essence, what we have here is a situation where the game agency has a more difficult job to do and much less money to do it with.

The obvious solution would be for the citizens to reinstate bear hunting with dogs and over bait. That probably won't happen, at least not in the near future. Thus, the Department of Fish and Wildlife has their hands tied. They must be creative and attempt to manage high bear densities with the hunters they now have which are stalking hunters on foot.

Where there are high bear numbers and complaints, watch for the state to allow hunters two bears a year in an effort to curb density. Where public safety is a concern, again we might see bear bag limits increased. The most efficient methods of harvesting bears, especially in local situations where bear densities are high, are by hounds and over bait. Can't do that now.

Thus, the game agency will need extra funds (from the legislature) to hire wildlife officers to help with bear problems, especially near urban areas where public safety is of major concerned. Either that, or they will have to hire hounds men to help the agency control the bears. Both options will cost money— an estimated $500,000 a year for each—and what a shame. Why? Because the problems were relatively small when bait and dog hunting were legal.

Conclusions.—-States that have good data on their bear populations will be in better shape to defend hunting seasons and bear management. Consider Wayne Pacelle's (Humane Society of the United States, but worked for the Fund For Animals when these comments were made) statements in the September 1992 issue of Animals' Agenda Magazine: "In some states, the bears, already outgunned, are also outnumbered by the hunters. Pennsylvania, for instance, with 96,000 licensed bear hunters has only 7,500 bears."

Does that give the reader the impression that the reason there are no more bears in Pennsylvania is because of bear hunting? Sure, but that is not the true situation. Bear habitat in Pennsylvania would support 20,000 bears, and the Game Commission has scientific data to back that up.

Bear damage complaints have led the Commission to hold the bear numbers at 7,500 so how do they manage their bears to benefit all citizens? By hunting.

Consider this quote from the same magazine article: "Fortunately, most bear hunters come home empty-handed; otherwise, the population would be quickly extirpated."

Such statements are obviously given to create the impression that legal hunting will wipe out bears. This is not so, and wildlife agencies deserve better than this kind of logic from leaders of the antibear hunting factions.

Wildlife agencies work hard to manage bears and other species. They would never allow hunters to extirpate bears.

Pennsylvania has superior data on black bears, better than any other state. Virginia is getting good data right now as is Arkansas, Louisiana, and many others. They will need it to defend their management.

Bear biologist Gary Alt, of the Pennsylvania Game Commission, summed up his frustration with antihunting groups attempting to stop hunting there when he said: "we see them (antihunters) one day a year during bear season and the other 364 days they're not concerned about bears. I wish they would put their efforts into something constructive."

Though hound and bait hunting has come under fire, a recent New Hampshire black bear study published in the winter 1994 issue of the Wildlife Society Bulletin showed that male bears were considerably more likely to be harvested than females during bait and hound hunting. Males made up 73 percent of the bait harvest, 71 percent of the hound harvest and 52 percent of the stalk harvest.

Since harvesting male bears has little overall impacts on total bear numbers, it appears that hound and bait hunting would be better for overall bear numbers than other forms of bear hunting. Yet, the antihunters have led the stoppage of these two forms of hunting, while stalk hunting still goes on. The reason, stalk hunting is viewed as being more ethical, even though this form of hunting kills a much higher percentage of females compared to the other methods.

Another result of the study was that hound hunters were more selective and passed up more shots (53 percent of the time) than other hunters. Bait hunters also passed up shots (25 percent of the time). Stalk hunters only passed up shots 17 percent of the time.

Still hunting (i.e., stalking), which is the only legal way to harvest bears in Oregon, Washington, and Colorado, leads to a higher percentage of females in the harvest. In addition, hunters are less selective, and may take more females and younger bears. Simply stating that hound hunting and bait hunting are unethical is an oversimplification of the situation.

Oversimplification or not, the public makes the final decisions. A recent survey of Wyoming residents showed that 65 percent opposed baiting and only 33 percent favored spring bear hunting. So even though stopping bear hunting leads to growing bear-human encounters, and some are fatal, we'll probably see it stopped in more states.

One argument against hunting black bears is that numbers are declining due to poaching for gall bladders, and as trophies for hunters. However, data shows just the opposite. Black bears are thriving and growing in numbers in most states. Of course this growth occurs while legal hunting continues. Thus there are more bears for *all* citizens to see, and hunters are creating the funds used for this recovery. They pay for the research via license fees and hunting equipment taxes.

Consider West Virginia. There the black bear is at an all time high with a tremendous range expansion occurring throughout the state. Black bears are now found in many counties where they were formerly extirpated, and a trap and transfer program (paid for almost entirely by hunters) is the major reason for this growth.

Tennessee, North Carolina, and Arkansas black bears are also showing dramatic increases in recent years. The black bear is a prime example of a species that has been maintained because of the interest of hunters, yet it has captured the imagination and interest of nonhunters because they are exciting to see in the wild.

Christopher Carter of the Oregon Department of Fish and Wildlife recently took a look at the fiscal effects of the cougar hunting ban (1998; *"Fiscal Effects of Voter Initiatives to Ban Certain Methods of Bear and Cougar Hunting: Oregon's Experience,"* Human Dimensions of Wildlife 3(2), pages 29-41). They found that bear tag sales dropped by 20 percent the year after the ban (1995) and cougar tag sales dropped by 35 percent.

This led to revenue losses of $88,000 in 1995. Harvest success rates tumbled for both species in 1995. In 1996, the game agency extended the deadline for buying a bear tag from August 31st to September 30th, and this led to a complete recovery in bear tag sales.

Carter suggested this increase was caused by deer and elk hunters buying more tags hoping for an incidental harvest of a bear while hunting other species. Cougar tags were changed from controlled hunt tags to general season tags, and this led to a recovery of sales in tags for that species too.

Although the harvest of both species did not return to pre-initiative levels (in fact it was considerably lower), the changes made by the game agency helped sell more tags and thus fiscal losses (at least the direct losses from license sales) did not occur.

It has been difficult to explain bait and dog hunting to nonhunters and even to other hunters who have never experienced that activity. It will be just as difficult to explain the values of harvesting rabbits with beagles, male elk during the rut when they are less wary, a deer near a cornfield where it feeds, a deer under an oak tree where it eats acorns, a deer that was called to the hunter by the hunter, a goose shot over a field of decoys, a bighorn sheep that was bedded down, etc. to those who have never been in the woods.

Unless the voting public has sufficient information on the above types of hunting, or has actually participated in such activities, their perception of fairness may be a bit skewed. Their ideas of what actually occurs may not be a true perspective of reality. I am not saying that it is wrong for someone to oppose bait or dog hunting for bears.

I am saying that bait and/or dog hunting is not what many nonhunters think it is, relative to fairness of the hunt. And I am saying that bait and dog hunting is not the real issue for some involved in setting policy on this issue.

Their real issue is far more involved and far more threatening to a very successful system of wildlife management. The hunter needs to maintain the moral high ground by using peer pressure to eliminate all illegal behavior by hunters. They also must expose nonhunting neighbors to the values of hunting, to the benefits of hunting that have existed for one million years.

When referendums appear on the state voting ballot that are not good for wildlife, even though supported by well-intentioned but uninformed citizens, hunters should be prepared to spend the money and time needed to defeat such initiatives.

Mountain Lions and Black Bears; To Hunt Or Not To Hunt

Uninformed citizens by voting on referendums to stop hunting are making management decisions that severely impair the state biologists from management of bears and mountain lions. States must provide timely information to their citizens before antihunting activists take charge of a potentially volatile and emotional situation.

As citizens spend more time in bear and mountain lion country, and build housing developments within or near bear and lion habitat, keeping these species somewhat wary of man will become essential for human safety. With that behavior will come continued negative encounters.

In July 1996, there were three black bear maulings within a month. An eight-year old Girl Scout was swiped in the face while sleeping on a camping trip in Arizona. Later that week on the same mountain, a bear mauled a 16-year old counselor in her tent at a 4-H campsite. The bear was killed and the girl underwent 12 hours of major skin graft surgery.

Finally, a boy camping in the Angeles National Forest in California was mauled, and the bear was later killed. I know it is an oversimplification to say that hunting would solve such problems, for it won't, but it is true that as bear and lion hunting decreases, such attacks will increase.

Todd Malmsbury, spokesman for the Colorado Division of Wildlife, noted that more and more animals are exposed to humans in Colorado. According to an Associated Press news release he stated: "I'm not arguing in favor of hunting them (referring to lions), but when they were hunted regularly, they had a good reason to fear us. Now they don't."

Am I missing something here? We should be arguing in favor of hunting. Colorado has about 3,000 lions, over 11,000 black bears and huge numbers of coyotes, yet hunting and trapping of these species, even though it was formerly done under restrictions that allowed sustainable harvest, is restricted more and more.

True, bear and lion are still harvested in Colorado, but the Division of Wildlife is under increasing pressure to curtail the amount of hunting and trapping.

In 1998, the Montana Department of Fish, Wildlife and Parks and the U. S. Forest Service announced an end to a ban on hunting mountain lions in the federal Rattlesnake Recreation Area near Missoula. The reason? Too many human/lion encounters, including attacks.

They attempted to have a hunt four years earlier, but public outcry prevented it from happening. Only three or four subadults or females will be harvested with only bows and handguns used for safety reasons.

Elsewhere, animal attacks on humans will continue to rise in the west and there is not a simple solution. Almost assuredly the movement of people into lion and bear habitat is a major part of this problem, but there can be little doubt that legal, ethical, recreational hunting, done under the principles of sustained harvest, could reduce this problem.

It has worked for years, but now some members of society are forcing us to turn away from it.

Mountain Lions and Black Bears; To Hunt Or Not To Hunt

"...the main reason bear hunting has become the Achilles' heel of so many state wildlife agencies is that they have never understood how human societies perceive bears."

Tom Beck

SECTION V

WHAT EVERYONE SHOULD KNOW

Chapter 12. Factors That Affect Attitudes*

Why The Public Thinks Wildlife is Accessible.—I recently attended a social dinner, and during the evening began chatting with someone about various environmental matters. Eventually the discussion turned to hunting, and in particular, my bowhunts for the past year. I mentioned a Saskatchewan bear hunt, and my friend's date immediately became interested. She said: "I assume you didn't bait hunt for bears, because that is so unfair and unethical."

Believing this was not the place to debate the subject, I tried to skirt the issue. But she continued her questioning so I mentioned that indeed I did bait hunt, and the bears did fairly well. I didn't see a bear during my week-long hunt.

Her look of disbelief was immediate and incredulous. She had never hunted, but from television and the media, there was no question that she believed hunting bears over bait was a sure thing and the bears had no chance.

Black bears just stumbled around bait sites, and any dolt could shoot one at any time of the day. Actually, her belief is fairly typical because many people have the impression that hunters can go to a bait site any time and see a black bear. It's not so.

In 1990 the National Audubon magazine carried a very interesting essay by Peter Steinhart. Steinhart's essays are always outstanding, but this one, *"Electronic Intimacies,"* was especially good. In it he talked about watching animals on television. In fact, it centered on how close we can get to animals via television.

Fifteen years ago, if you saw a leopard kill an impala on television,

*portions adapted (with permission) from Feb. and July 1991 "On Your Side" columns in Bowhunting News.

that was an eye grabber. You were glued to the tube. Can you imagine what it would be like to personally see a leopard streak across the dusty plains and nail an impala with a death grip to the neck?

Well, the next best thing is watching it on television. Today, such television shows are relatively commonplace. Flick on your local public television station or cable's Discovery Channel, and you see predators taking prey over and over, again. Lynx take snowshoe hares, great horned owls take hares, tigers take sambar deer, lions take zebras, and snakes eat mice. It is as common as Marty Stauffer's grizzly bears eating Alaskan salmon. We've seen it over and over again and as Steinhart points out, *we believe it is accessible,* and easy.

Steinhart noted something else very interesting — *television wildlife shows take the waiting out of watching,* and he is right. Hunters don't need to wait hour after hour in their tree stand to see a deer, just turn on the boob tube and you can see a hunting show where the animal always comes by within five minutes.

Steinhart says that television makes wild animals seem as if they are readily accessible. Right again.

Animals in the wild must behave just as they do on a 30-minute television show. If it is a show on elk, then just turn on the TV and there you go: bugling elk, cows giving birth to calves, wolves killing calves; it's all there, the whole bit, and all in a 30-minute program.

How easy can that be? Elk must be running around everywhere. Elk hunting must be so easy that it isn't fair to the animal. Yes, to the uninitiated, one could easily get such an impression from watching television.

People flip on the PBS channel, the Discovery Channel, a National Geographic Special, an Audubon special, a Marty Stauffer production, and they see wildlife. Yes, this is the same wildlife and nature that hunters see from his/her treestand, but an entire life of hunting is sandwiched into a 30-minute or one-hour program.

It discounts the many hours a hunter spends in the woods when they see no deer because who would want to watch that? I understand why hunters enjoy those hours in the stand, even when they aren't seeing deer, but would television viewers understand?

When I hunt, I might hear a turkey gobble as I settle in for a morning hunt. Then a pileated woodpecker chattels off down the valley, and later that morning I get a glimpse of that rare woodpecker as he zips overhead in their wavering flight. A cardinal calls from my tree, and a squirrel scampers past sometime during the morning.

I glimpsed a deer walking along a field edge just as daylight filtered through the trees, and it was a great morning hunt. I didn't even draw my bow. I didn't see a red-tailed hawk hammer a chipmunk, or a red fox grab a ruffed grouse. I didn't see a peregrine falcon chase a mourning dove, and I missed that bobcat capturing an early morning rabbit for his first meal of the week.

Television viewers saw all of that and more. And they didn't have to sit very long, nor must they move from their living room comfort to do it.

If wildlife is so accessible, so easy to see, then I should be able to go to my local state or national park, and watch the same things seen on television. Right? I believe, as does Steinhart, that many people actually think free roaming wildlife is as accessible as it is on their television. I believe such wildlife television programs are part of the reason some citizens are opposed to hunting.

As with my friend's date, many people believe that animals are very accessible, and thus hunters have an unfair advantage. If people actually believe that deer walk by every minute, since they do so on television, then is it a surprise they think that hunting is too easy, and unfair to the animal?

It's no wonder some people are disappointed when they go to a national park for a vacation. They expect to see wildlife around every bend in the road, in every field, and grazing everywhere. Steinhart, in another Audubon magazine essay entitled *"Dreaming Elands"* pointed out that animals are a big part of mans thoughts. Even our terminology is tied to animals.

As he noted, the stock market is "bullish" or "bearish," you get "mad as a hornet," and people are "sly as a fox." From early times people developed fables about animals and believed them.

One researcher has shown that almost half of the American public actually believes that an ostrich buries its head in the sand when faced with danger. Now think about that one for a moment. A predator runs after an ostrich, and it sticks its head in the sand? What a dumb evolutionary strategy that would be. First ostrich to use it would die.

Chapter 12

So would the second and the third, but such beliefs are passed down from fables to cartoons, and from television to the human mind.

Childrens books, television, and parents perpetuate media myths. Don't "Teddy Bears" behave like real bears? Aren't wolves bad? Don't they eat small children? Don't wild animals, when they are not shot by a bad hunter, get old, walk through a green grassy meadow to a small hill overlooking a pristine blue river, curl up in the sun, and go to sleep (die)?

If you answered "yes" to any of these questions, then you've been watching too much television. Nature just doesn't work that way.

Many authors point out that man needs wild animals. I agree there is that need, but there is also a need to fully understand how nature works. For example, would it be a surprise to learn that most wild animals do not die of old age?

Instead, they get eaten by a predator, get run over by trucks, are poisoned by chemicals, kill each other, and some die from being shot by hunters. These same authors point out that one major way to get people to understand nature is to get them out of the cities. Only then can we educate them about the life and death struggles that occur in the woods. That is one of the beautiful things about hunting. Hunters are out there, and we see wild nature every time we go hunting. Hunters see death as a part of wild nature when they go hunting, and they actually participate in the life death struggles.

Wild nature is not wrapped in cellophane and labeled. It is not captured on film and readily accessible on television. Sitting in a tree stand lets us understand what real nature really is. People can experience it. No, one doesn't have to be hunting to experience nature but they need to be out there. And you need to be out there either alone, or in a very quiet setting, to see things occurring as they really do. Nothing is artificially added; no sweet music in the background. no cutting or splicing. Just real nature.

Most folks don't do these things very often. (Bird watchers are the exception. They are out there watching nature during all seasons of the year). Other than bird watchers, duck blinds are empty except during hunting season. What a waste of a good blind.

If we abolish deer hunting in an eastern state like Rhode Island,

Wisconsin, New Jersey, or Pennsylvania, will those who led to the demise of deer management by eliminating deer hunting really understand much about the suffering that such an act would cause? Probably not.

If deer hunting is stopped in your state, when the next severe winter moves through, who will be out there trying to save the deer? Will those who voted "no" be there? Will they contribute the millions of dollars to manage wildlife? Will they take to the fields to help save the animals?

My guess is that many won't even know winter deer are in trouble. Many hunters will be out there though, because they participate in the realities of nature every day. They understand that wildlife is not accessible, that it is precarious, and that nature is cruel and unrelenting.

Antikill Is An Easy Message To Sell.——Killing animals can be easily made to sound so simple and so bad. The message to sell is simple: "If you want to save animals, stop hunting because that is how animals get killed."

Now doesn't that sounds rational? Those hunters must be killing every moving animal; it is a wonder there are any living animals left at all. For many citizens today, that sounds like something that makes sense.

No matter that all the monies raised through sportsmen's excise taxes and licenses have brought most wildlife species to all-time high levels. Ask hunters what species have recovered from population lows over the past 50-60 years and you will get answers like the wild turkey, whitetail deer, antelope, black bear, and elk, but those are game species. OK, then let's try river otters, ospreys, or peregrine falcons. Hunter dollars are used to manage non-hunted species.

Many hunters know this, but some nonhunters do not. The November 1990 issue of Audubon magazine contains a most interesting article (*"Fuzzy-Wuzzy Thinking About Animal Rights"*) by Richard Conniff. He discusses the point that the antitrappers have an easy message to sell (just as the antihunters do). "You want to save the animals? Stop wearing fur." Sounds great, except as Conniff points out, "most of us never wore fur in the first place."

Maybe the message is too easy because the media, especially the talk show people, are really picking up on discussing and challenging hunting. Moderators of such shows have little understanding about the brutality and complexities of nature, and they do not understand the economic incentive for wildlife management. Who are the people who can get prohunting media attention? Movie stars of course, but also musicians, athletes, politicians, etc. Do any of these fellows hunt? You bet. How about bowhunting? You bet.

Entertainers and sports stars like Don Johnson, Ted Nugent, Wade Boggs, Jack Nicklaus, Travis Fryman, Bo Jackson, Walter Peyton, Aaron Tippen, John Anderson and many more.

Good, then hunters can get these guys on television and they can help the cause. It isn't quite that simple.

Some will not go public with strong statements that are prohunting because it would hurt their advertising ratings. Some may just not feel comfortable being the spokesman for hunting rights. Some may lay back on most issues, just to protect their own privacy. I wouldn't quarrel with any of those reasons, even though I wish some of the stars that hunt would help more than they do.

The hunters cause is a good cause. Prowildlife management, proenvironment, proconservation, but I wish we had more people like Bo Jackson and Ted Nugent who have impact with nonhunters and speak out on the values of hunting. Goodness knows, there are plenty of such people adding emotions to the antihunting cause.

We need to reach nonhunters with educational statements about hunting and its role in conservation. Nonhunters need to know that much of the non-game research that goes on in their state is paid for by hunting dollars. Can that be done on television talk shows? Maybe, but probably not very easily.

It's fairly boring to talk about hunting and its role in conservation. Talk shows often thrive on controversy. They want people to get excited and have heated exchanges because it apparently sells. Would a discussion of the economic incentive for wildlife management do much on such a show?

I'm afraid not.

One can easily defend hunting from a biological basis, but when you get to the moral issues, of whether it is right or wrong, then some people agree it is right while others think it is wrong. A television debate on hunting does little to help.

In fact, I think it probably hurts hunting. And the talk shows don't really want anyone who will bore the audience with biology. Biologists tell the antihunters, "trust us, we know what we're doing."

They will not trust us because they don't know enough about the resource. So do we beat them into submission with ball bats? We may have to approach things that way occasionally, but if we look at the big picture, we can't win with the ball-bat approach.

Celebrities might make inroads by supporting and pushing things that no one can oppose. Ted Nugent is a strong and outspoken spokesman against drugs, and that is a message that no one can oppose. When hunters do a talk show they need to sell hunting just as a flyfishermen sells fishing. They need to be Mister Nice Guy.

Remain quiet most of the time, but get your points across. Listen, smile, and let the audience understand the truth that most hunters are not bubbas or rednecks who only care about the kill.

I wish we could see former President Bush making strong statements about the economic benefits of hunting. I wish that we could see Jack Nicklaus make subtle, but important comments on television about how much he values bowhunting for deer every fall in Montana. Or that his hunts with his son are important times in his family life. That is what is needed.

"It is more difficult for the modern hunter to understand as much about the psychological issues of hunting because it has become an activity to be crowded into one's schedule, rather than being the core of one's life and identity. We have become more like the dog than its ancestor the wolf."

James Swan

Chapter 13

Urban Deer Problems and Solutions*

Thirty years ago one seldom heard urban citizens complain about deer damage. Today we find urban deer problems everywhere. It is a complex problem and the solutions are not simple. I wrote this chapter because there is so much misinformation given to the public about the urban deer problem.

The truth is that there are too many deer living close to people. Damage takes many forms including loss of human life. But there are several myths being promoted about the deer problem.

One common myth perpetuated by antihunters is that hunting causes deer numbers to increase. This is not an accurate picture of what happens, and I will discuss it in this chapter. Another myth is that if we stop hunting, the deer herd will be just fine if we "let nature take care of her own." As a wildlife biologist, this one really bothers me because when we implement this strategy, deer and deer habitat suffer. The truth is that such an alternative is extremely inhumane and come the first severe winter, starvation leads to huge deer die-offs, and a rather sad spectacle in the field.

Another myth is that contraception should be used to control deer instead of hunting. The truth is that the science for sterilizing deer, or using contraceptives, is not developed enough to do so in the field. In fact, on a large scale, it is very likely that such techniques will never be effective in the field.

Antihunters suggest that deer be trapped and moved from urban problem areas. Deer can be trapped and moved, but the truth is that

*portions adapted (with permission) from August 1993, October 1995, August 1996 "Know Hunting" columns, Bowhunter Magazine and from June, July 1993, March, April 1994 "On Your Side" columns, Bowhunting News and "*Deer On The Pill*" article in the December 1993 issue of the Pennsylvania Sportsman magazine.

almost all moved deer die in a very short period. Thus, such movement is inhumane. But there are ways to control deer numbers in urban situations and those will be discussed herein.

Hunting Creates Deer?—-Whitetail deer herds have exploded in recent years across most of their range. As deer numbers increase, state wildlife agencies scramble to harvest more deer. Added doe permits are given out; added seasons like muzzleloader hunting have been expanded to help control the herds.

In parts of some states there are not enough hunters to control the deer. Though bag limits are liberal, a deer hunter can only utilize so many deer and this further lowers the ability of hunters to control deer numbers.

Even though hunting is used as a management tool to *control* deer numbers, some antihunters and organizations suggest the reason for deer increases is *because* of hunting. Their theory is that hunting first causes deer herds to decrease. Then as more food becomes available to the remaining deer, they are healthier, have more twins and reproduction increases as does the population.

This description is an extreme oversimplification of the complexities of wild nature. Hunting deer is done to keep deer at levels that are acceptable for most members of society. Some citizens, like farmers, want fewer deer. Others, like hunters, want more deer. What wildlife agencies must do is juggle all interest groups and find a population level that not only is ecologically sound, but allows citizens to enjoy seeing deer if they so desire.

People have settled all lands that were once deer habitat, and in so doing, they have reduced or eliminated the natural predators of deer. Obviously you cannot bring natural predators like mountain lions or wolves into suburban areas (even though some animal rights activists have made such suggestions), and you cannot feed deer in such situations for very long.

Feed 10 this year and you'll have 30 to feed next year. Thus, hunters have replaced wolves, cougars, bears and coyotes as major deer predators.

What Happens With No Hunting.—-When deer numbers increase, they seriously affect the seedlings and ground plants that grow in an area. This can negatively impact nesting songbirds, mammals, amphibians and reptiles. If we stopped deer hunting (i.e., if we eliminated predation), deer herds would explode. Does would have fewer and fewer fawns (breeding activity would decrease, abortions would increase, fewer fawns would be born, and of those born, more would die than normal), and thus the deer herd would age.

Once the herd exceeded the carrying capacity, large numbers would die from starvation, diseases and parasites. Ground vegetation would be seriously overbrowsed, and lead to large decreases in plant diversity that might last for years.

Wild flowers would be lost. Tree seedlings would be eaten and the forests would change. Major hard winters would lead to massive deer suffering, starvation and die-offs.

But hunting does lower deer numbers, and this helps plant life to increase and improves the ecosystem as a whole. The increase in ground vegetation leads to healthier deer, and healthier deer do have higher fawn survival. But to suggest that hunting has led to the numbers of deer we have today is a shallow consideration of an extremely complex ecological situation.

In the situation just described, to not remove some deer would be inhumane. The old adage, "let nature take care of her own" might have once applied to the pristine world before man settled the land in large numbers, but it definitely doesn't apply today. The scales of nature have been reset by man.

The Urban Deer Problem.—-Deer herds have grown everywhere in recent years, including in urban areas. Hardly a day goes by when a local newspaper does not publish an article on excessive deer numbers in urban areas.

The February 12, 1991 issue of The Washington Post headline read: "Protected by hunting ban, herd overruns New Jersey Township." The March 5, 1991 issue of The Evening Sun (Baltimore) carried a headline article, "Deer threaten park's ecosystem." An April 1991 issue of the New York Times Magazine ran an extensive piece on "Deer on your doorstep" that received wide circulation and acclaim. The April 11, 1991 issue of the Chicago Tribune discussed deer problems in Elk Grove Village, Cook County Forest Preserve, North Shore, Lake County, and North Brook, all near Chicago. The Detroit News carried an article describing how "Prolific bambis become real pests."

Urban and suburban deer eat gardens and chew on valuable shrubs. They consume endangered plants in state parks.

Even worse, high numbers of deer threaten human lives. Most citizens become relatively tolerant of deer destruction to vegetation and gardens, but they get downright mad when humans become severely ill from Lyme Disease or are killed in auto/deer collisions. Consider Lymes Disease. There were 465 cases reported in Maryland in 1995 alone. Other states show similar high numbers of this serious and debilitating disease.

Auto/deer collisions are also on the rise. In the Detroit, Michigan area from 1980-1990, auto-deer accidents jumped 308 percent (777 accidents). Wayne County accidents jumped 302 percent with 193 accidents in 1990 alone, while Macomb County saw a 269 percent increase. The Detroit Free Press stated that "46,784 drivers (Michigan) struck deer in 1990, up 120 percent since 1981. Six people were killed and 1,857 were injured."

An article written by wildlife professors at Utah State University in the 1996 Wildlife Society Bulletin showed that for 1991 the conservative number of road-killed deer in the United States was at least 500,000. Several studies are cited on the costs of such collisions.

One Colorado study estimated costs at $500 per collision. A Michigan study showed losses at $1,600 per collision; New York $1,415; eastern Washington $760; Vermont $1,881; and Utah $635 for 1985 and $1,200 for 1992. If from all these studies we take an average of $1,500 lost for each deer hit (for 1998 values), and multiply that by the numbers of deer-car collisions each year (for 1991 there were 538,000 reported from only 31 states and only half of all such collisions are reported), the total yearly losses are a whopping $ 1 billion dollars (see Conover, J. R. *"Monetary And Intangible Valuation Of Deer In The United States,"* Wildlife Society Bulletin 25(2):298-305, 1997).

Whoa. There is also loss of human life and suffering caused by injuries. An estimated 120 people/year are killed in animal-car collisions nationwide, and there are thousands of people injured.

For example, from 1972-76, 17 people were killed and 3,289 injured in deer/car collisions in Michigan. In Vermont, 11 people died and 1,886 were injured in deer/car collisions from 1981-91. Top deer/car collision states from 1982-1991 were Wisconsin (76,626 in

1989), Michigan (44,374 in 1991), and Pennsylvania (43,002 in 1990).

Deer cause economic losses in other ways too. Agricultural crop damage is estimated to be $500 million a year, and timber losses approach $750 million a year (see Conover paper). No doubt about it, deer cause tremendous economic losses to citizens, and terrible human losses as well.

Why do we have so many deer living in our suburbs and towns? Part of the problem has been caused by increasing deer herds. Deer are very adaptable and have increased everywhere, including our suburbs and cities.

But a major factor has been we humans have moved into deer habitat. We build housing developments right in the middle of good deer habitat. We then stop gun hunting for safety reasons, and we plant gardens and shrubs which deer really like.

Since firearm hunting cannot be safely done near or in cities, citizens seek other solutions. Bowhunting has proven successful in thousands of such situations. Indeed, in New Jersey, where human populations average over 1,000 people per square mile, bowhunters commonly hunt in close proximity to thousands of private citizens.

Encounters and problems occur, but they are rare, and these bowhunters harvest deer. In 1992, the New Jersey bowhunters harvested more than 36 percent of all the deer taken in the state.

Bowhunting is a viable deer management tool in suburban environments, but anithunters are not happy with this alternative. They encourage the public to force wildlife agencies to trap and transplant animals — even though this alternative has been proven to be inhumane because it often leads to deer deaths shortly after they are moved. In fact, the knowledge that trapping and moving leads to death has become so well known that this alternative is rarely used any more.

Contraception; Probably Not The Solution.*—- There has been considerable publicity in recent years about using contraceptives to control deer numbers instead of hunting them. This alternative is often suggested by antihunters, and in so doing is made to seem that this is

* For a great review of the basics of immunocontraception and the inherent and unsolved problems therein, see Muller *et al.* ("*Theory And Practice Of Immunocontraception In Wild Animals.*" Wildlife Society Bulletin 25(2):504-514, 1997)

the answer to the urban deer problem.

Initially, the idea of contraception had some deer hunters concerned. They believed that when contraception was adopted as a management tool, recreational hunting would be lost.

"Sweat is pouring from their (hunters) foreheads," said Wayne Pacelle, then spokesman for the Fund For Animals (but now with the Humane Society of The United States). "A successful contraceptive program could eliminate the key justification for sport hunting - the need to control wildlife populations." (quote from a March 25, 1993 article in USA Today, *"Battling Animal Overpopulation-Deer Herds At Heart Of Park Conflict"*).

However, it now appears that contraception cannot work on large areas for many reasons because there is an ocean of problems between theory and reality. Even so, it is interesting that people believe we can easily contracept deer when it is very difficult to contracept humans.

Humans already know exactly how to control births via contraceptive techniques, yet population growth in most parts of the world continues at astronomical rates. We have the pill, the delivery system, the knowledge, and plenty of money, but we haven't solved the problem.

Humans cannot utilize contraception to control reproduction in all parts of the world, yet we are to believe that we can control an entire deer population via contraception. It's a real stretch, but before we rule out the possibility, let's study the situation and see where we are relative to deer birth control and the loss of hunting.

There are areas near and within urban environments where gun hunting cannot be safely used to control deer numbers. In such areas, biologists must consider methods for control that have not been used to any extent in the past.

Bowhunting often can be used in such situations, but there are a few places where even bows cannot be used to control deer numbers. Enter the world of animal contraception.

The Humane Society of The United States has supported deer birth control research and has lead urban people to believe contraception will solve their deer problems in the near future. Consider the statement of Marie Kochochis, a spokeswoman for the

Concerned Citizens For Fox Chapel (near Pittsburgh, Pennsylvania), where police sharp-shooters have been used to curb urban problems: "she would prefer a less violent means of culling the herd such as contraceptive darts, expected to be available soon."

Animal activists commonly give the perception that animal sterilization is a viable alternative to reduce deer herds, but this is not the case. Contraceptive darts will not be available for deer control any time soon.

Yet citizens are being led to believe that contraception will be available for deer control. Though it may be true that within 10 years contraception in one form or another may assist controlling deer in small, localized herds, their use in other situations may never occur. The reason is that there are lots of problems with attempting to sterilize deer.

Wildlife birth control can take several forms. One approach is to use antifertility drugs. In the early 1970's one researcher induced fetal loss in penned deer by administering diethylstilbestrol, a synthetic estrogen, into the doe. In order for such an approach to deer birth control to work in the wild, an effective system of oral delivery must be developed.

Deer must ingest the contraceptive material. Deer are grazers and browsers, eating vegetation, and that means that delivery by ingestion is almost impossible. Even if you could get them to eat the drugs, how would you control the dose?

However, other delivery systems have been tested for getting the contraceptives into deer. A dart-delivered "Bio-bullet" shows real promise, but multiple booster injections are still required, seriously limiting any use in the wild.*

Bio-bullets have been used to treat horses and deer in limited situations. But even if a delivery system can be designed, there are many unanswered questions and problems in using fertility agents. For example, how will such fertility chemicals affect non-target

---

*If you have to get multiple bullets into the same doe to guarantee infertility, how would you   identify that doe for the second shot, and how would you get close enough for shots? Even if you need only one bullet for infertility, getting enough bullets into enough does in the wild will be difficult, if not impossible. Maybe in very small, controlled areas, but not in the normal wooded habitat where whitetails are found.

species (i.e., things that eat deer)? Will these chemicals cause behavioral side effects? Can such chemicals be an environmental hazard in nature?

There are no answers to these important questions at this time.

A second form of birth control is getting much more attention by researchers. This approach is known as "immunocontraception" and heres how it is supposed to work. The idea is that a substance (a vaccine if you will) is injected into the female deer, and she builds up antibodies against this substance.

The process is similar to humans getting measles shots, or polio vaccines, or allergy shots when we were kids. Inject a vaccine (the antigen) into the body and the animals immune system will build up antibodies against that antigen. Then the next time the antigen comes into the body, the animal will fight it off and reject it.

That is an oversimplification, but the process is basically similar. Now what antigen is being given to female deer? The "antigen" that is getting the most press for deer contraception is PZP. There are a layer of proteins that surround the unfertilized egg in females, and these are known as "ZP" (zona pellucida) proteins.

ZP surrounds the doe's egg cell and it may reduce the ability of a sperm to penetrate and fertilize the egg. Over the past several years researchers have been injecting pig ZP proteins (hence the name "PZP") into female captive deer. The female deer builds up antibodies against these ZP proteins, and when sperm enters the deer, fertilization is blocked.

So far researchers have had to give deer several shots of PZP to render them infertile, and then only with penned animals. Since it would be virtually impossible to give wild does multiple shots via dart guns, researchers are now working on a one-shot system.

This research is now underway in several places in the eastern United States. But even if a one-shot system is developed, many biologists have concerns about the use of contraceptives in the wild. In May, 1993 a Subcommittee (on Contraception in Wildlife) of the International Association of Fish and Wildlife Agencies (this is a national group that represents every state game and fish agency) released a report on this topic.

That report raised many questions. For example, if there is

repeated immunization with ZP will it lead to permanent sterility in deer? We don't know. Since deer with ZP immunization cannot get pregnant, will this lead to repeated estrus cycles lasting for months? We don't know.

If we get long estrus periods will this lead to energy problems for does since they will be chased by bucks for months instead of days as now exists? Since this would take place in winter, will the added stress and loss of weight lead to mortality? Here we do have some answers. The April 1997 issue of the Journal of Wildlife Management has a most interesting article on a study of deer behavior after being given hormone shots to render does sterile (see McShea *et al. "The Effect Of Immunocontraception On The Behavior And Reproduction Of White-Tailed Deer,"* J. Wildl. Manage. 61(2): pages 560-569).

It answers some of these questions. Penned does given two shots (four weeks apart) of PZP produced no fawns the first year and only one of 10 produced fawns the second year. Seven of nine does given one-shot of a contraceptive (PZP) produced fawns. In most situations in the wild, giving does more than 1 shot of hormone would be impossible, thus, the fact that the 1-shot dose did not work means that at present deer contraception is not viable for herd control.

The study showed a more serious negative impact and begs the question of whether we should be "fooling with Mother Nature." When does were given PZP, they stayed in heat. In response, bucks extended their breeding season in this captive Virginia herd and mating behavior was observed in early March. The authors noted that "the changes in activity indicate that food-limited populations may become further stressed by the extended breeding season."

Other studies showed that a 10 percent reduction in deer body fat in the fall resulted in a 15 percent increase in winter mortality. Thus, since PZP causes extended breeding behavior into the dead of winter, if used in the wild there is a high probability that excessive body fat would be used, leading to higher mortality.

On the other side is a study done by McShea *et al. ("Behavioral and hormonal responses of white-tailed deer to immunocontraception with PZP."* Abstract, Contraception in Wildlife Management; Denver CO, 1993) that suggested that even though does continued cycling throughout the winter, dominant bucks reduced their reproductive behavior. If that is true, then the potential problem would not be as severe.

PZP has had some success and shows some potential for use in the wild. PZP has been tried on horses and successful applications of the vaccine required an initial treatment plus several inoculations over a short period of time, plus an annual booster. More recent efforts show some success at developing a single-dose vaccine, with costs at $25 per treatment. The wild ponies at Assateague Island, Virginia have been inoculated via darts from the ground. In that situation, a one-dose system is working.

In a 1992 paper in the Journal of Wildlife Management, John Turner and his colleagues reported that they developed a successful method to deliver the immunocontraceptive in captive, unrestrained deer using PZP antigen (see Turner, J. W. *et al. "Remotely Delivered Immunocontraception In Captive White-Tailed Deer,"* J. Wildl. Manage. 56: pages 154-157).

All of the seven does in captivity failed to produce fawns. All of this research shows that giving deer an inoculation of PZP, then giving them a second and third inoculation three and six weeks later, in captivity, stopped the production of fawns.

At Fire Island National Seashore in New York, two shots of PZP given in 1994 led to only 28 percent of does having fawns in 1995. Pretreatment fawning rate was 90 percent. Thus, there is potential for PZP to work in isolated, small, wild populations, but obviously we need more research to get a clearer picture of this aspect of immunocontraception.

Dr. Victor Nettles, a wildlife biologist and veterinarian with the Southeast Cooperative Wildlife Disease Study at the University of Georgia, also has real concerns. He questions: Will does that have very long estrus periods because of contraceptives be more subject to predation? If you give a pregnant animal a contraceptive product, will she abort? Could contraceptives cause young females to suffer body growth defects? Could PZP type contraceptives cause anaphylactic shock in vaccinated does that are then exposed to deer sperm?

This question is similar to the one doctors often ask before they give you a shot, are you allergic to any medicines? If you are, and you get the shot, you may go into anaphylactic shock.

If people react to some foreign "shots" in this manner, maybe deer will too. Though there are many other unanswered questions, there is one unresearched question that really scares many biologists. With PZP, and other antigen-type contraceptives, how well they work depends on the deer's immunological system.

Will deer with the best immune systems build up antibodies better than deer with poor immune systems? If they do it is possible that deer with the best immune systems will become sterile, and those with poor immune systems will become pregnant.

"So what?" you say. If the scenario I've just painted is real, then only the strongest deer *will not* get pregnant. The weakest deer *will* get pregnant. If we have to treat 80 percent of a deer herd to control deer numbers (as some models suggest), and only the weak get pregnant, there is a real potential for causing major impacts on wild deer herds. Could it be possible to shift the gene pool to favor those weak animals?

Fooling around with Mother Nature could lead to all kinds of problems if done on a wide scale in the wild. True, we don't know for sure whether this will happen, but my point is that we need more research, tons of it, before we begin to use fertility control in the wild.

Robert Deblinger, Assistant Director for Wildlife Research for the wildlife agency in Massachusetts believes that we might use wildlife birth control in limited areas where hunting is not safe. I agree.

"But the research would have to come a lot farther for us to know on what scale it could be applied," Deblinger noted. Even Phillip Robakiewicz, a biologist for the Massachusetts Audubon Society (who says he is a "proponent of animals rights") noted potential problems similar to some outlined by Nettles. Robakiewicz was concerned about putting hormones into deer that might be eaten by humans or other animals.

Researchers cite other potential problems in a paper in the 1992 issue of the Journal of Wildlife Management. They noted "significant tissue response" and swelling when PZP was injected. Previous researchers found abscesses in 12 percent of vaccinated horses. This same wildlife journal paper noted that the effects of PZP injections on fetuses was unknown nor whether the "PZP treatment effect in deer is reversible."

As with other studies, these researchers also noted that PZP-treated does continued to cycle after not becoming pregnant and suggested that this may "affect long-term patterns of behavior and social organization." They also noted the problem of injections in the field, getting access to the deer and how to tell treated does from untreated ones, so as not to reinject a sterile doe.

The paper also mentioned other studies "that show changes in ovarian morphology and function associated with immunocontraception that may lead to long-term, possibly irreversible, infertility."

Is permanent infertility what we want? Maybe yes, but probably no.

Cost is another factor for urban communities dealing with an overpopulated deer herd. New research shows that using deer contraceptives is not only very expensive, it is impractical. The study was done to determine the practicality of controlling deer in Minnetonka, Minnesota.

Assuming a one-shot contraception was used, and none have been developed yet, the cost to treat one doe was $533. To stop the growth of the herd, 75 percent of all yearling and adult females (a total of 183 deer) need to be treated. Realize that getting drugs into that high a percentage of all females would not be possible, but assuming you could, what would it cost? Try $97,539 for the first year alone. Obviously municipalities cannot afford this alternative.

The International Association of Fish and Wildlife Agencies report on contraceptives also raises unanswered questions about legal issues. Does the state have the legal authority to promulgate rules related to the chemical fertility control of deer?

New Jersey believes that their wildlife agency does have that power. New York also believes that it has the legal authority for their wildlife agency to control the use of fertility agents in the field. West Virginia passed a law in 1996 mandating that the wildlife agency will control any future use of contraceptives in the wild. Other states need to investigate their authority. States also need to develop "policy" on how, when, where, and if fertility control chemicals will be used. New York has written such a policy.

Other states are investigating or are in the process of writing such policy. The report also noted that no wildlife contraceptives have been registered with the federal government. Nor have any such contraceptives been approved.

So you see that immunocontraception and other forms of sterilization in deer are a long way from being used in the field. Will they ever replace hunters on a state-wide basis?

Even the researchers funded in part by the Humane Society of the United States feel that we are a long way from field use on a wide scale. Jay Kirkpatrick has been quoted as saying: "If you compared the current state of wildlife contraception to a weapons system, what we have here is a slightly pointed stone attached to a crooked stick. Right now, we're in the process of straightening out the stick."

He also stated in a USA Today article that "if somebody thinks a few guys with dart

guns are going to seriously affect hunting, they're smoking something really good."

I know that hunters are concerned that contraception will replace hunting. It now appears, and has even been acknowledged by a few leaders in the animal rights movement, that deer contraception cannot be used except in very, very small areas (100 acres or less). And there is still years of research remaining before contraception can be used for deer anywhere in the wild.

The report of the International Association of Fish and Wildlife Agencies concluded: "It currently appears that this technology may have application on some limited isolated or confined populations where hunting is not feasible. However, its eventual use on wild, free-ranging populations appears in question."

Some Bowhunting Case Studies.—-If contraception probably cannot work to control urban deer problems in most situations, what might work? One answer that is being used by more and more towns is bowhunting. Bowhunting has been used very successfully in many suburban and urban situations.

Consider just a few case studies of this use. In the 1993 journal, Bulletin of New Jersey Academy of Science, Dr. Len Wolgast and John Kuser published a paper entitled, *"Bowhunting Stabilizes A New Jersey White-tailed Deer Population."* Here is a summary of what has happened in Princeton Township, New Jersey relative to bowhunting as an effective control measure for deer.

In the 1970's the deer herd in Princeton Township grew at a rapid rate. As the herd grew, auto/deer collisions also grew. There were around 75 auto/deer collisions in 1974, 105 in 1980, 200 in 1986 and 172 in 1992. Why did the herd grow so rapidly?

First, in 1973 the Township passed a no-firearms-discharge, (hence no gun hunting) and during the next 14 years there was a 600 percent increase in deer-car collisions. The area also had excellent edge habitat for a growing deer herd. Plus, there was no gun hunting and this allowed the herd to grow from around 150-200 deer in 1971 to 1,000 in 1986.

Bowhunting was initiated in the township in 1972 but participation was low and no deer were harvested. By 1982 a limited number of bowhunters took 40 deer. In 1983 the mayor appointed a deer committee and after reviewing all the alternatives they opted to have a shotgun hunt.

Public sentiment was measured by an opinion survey, and they opposed the gun hunt. However, from 1984 to 1991, the public had to face higher incidences of deer related problems. Lyme disease was growing and auto collisions did too. In 1991 bowhunters took 245 deer, but a survey done in that year showed that township residents felt that the cultural carrying capacity was exceeded and they favored increased gun and bow hunting.

So, the township amended its no-discharge ordinance to allow shotgun hunting during the either-sex season. The present status is as follows. Bowhunting is taking around 150 deer each year. Bowhunting harvest has shown a steady increase since 1972. Deer populations have appeared to stabilize at around 800-1,000 deer. Auto-deer collisions have leveled off since 1984. The new added gun season appears to have helped stabilize the herd, but bowhunting definitely helped stabilize the deer herd before there was gun hunting.

The next two examples show that a combination of bowhunting and some other form of gun hunting can be used to control or stabilize deer herds. Rock Cut State Park is a 2,500-acre park near Rockford, Illinois. In 1987 the park had 73 deer per square mile and many associated problems.

An either-sex archery hunt was held in 1988 and 1989. This reduced the deer herd to 55 deer per square mile by 1990. The Department of Conservation again had a bowhunt in 1990, but followed it with sharpshooting by gunners. The 1990 program placed a heavy emphasis on bow harvesting does, and required them to kill two does before they could try for a buck.

This requirement was probably too stringent, but even so, 80 deer were taken. This was an increase of 60 percent over the harvests of 1988 and 1989. In 1991 the Department of Conservation lowered the doe quota to one before hunters could try for a buck. Again the bow kill was satisfactory.

But the costs are a key factor in this study. In 1990 it cost the state $233 for every deer killed by sharpshooters after the bow season. (This sharpshooting was done at night at bait stations by trained marksman. Baiting was done in ravines so that no safety problems occurred in the highly urbanized area). Phone costs, mailings, gas, etc. only cost the state $83 for each deer taken by bowhunters. Clearly the bowhunt was the most economical of the two alternatives.

In the greater Rochester, New York area, similar problems occurred due to high deer numbers. Deer-vehicle collisions and crop damage led to many citizen complaints. A Citizen Task Force obtained public input in an effort to balance the diversity of opinions on how to solve the problem. The Task Force had two goals: to determine an appropriate deer density for the area, and to determine a way to achieve this deer density.

Thirty-two percent (126,400 acres) of the area was classified as residential. Another 12 percent was industrial and business. Clearly this was a highly urbanized area. There were some scattered farms making up 30 percent of the area, and an additional 21 percent was classified as undeveloped or vacant. Five percent of the area was in suburban parks and one 965-acre park was the site for the heaviest debate on deer herd control (Durand Eastman Park within the Town of Irondequoit. Deer density in the park is over 87 deer per square mile).

Auto-deer collisions in this Rochester area were incredible. There were 260 carcasses removed from roads in 1980 and 650 in 1990. This represents only about 20 percent of the total car-killed deer. Thus, for this area, the estimate of vehicle damage was between $1.3

and $3.6 million a year.

Within the Rochester area, only bowhunting was allowed (the Task Force reached a consensus to allow bowhunting). Wildlife officials increased the bow doe permits in the area to allow further harvests.

However, within the Town of Irondequoit bow and gun discharge was prohibited by a local ordinance. So, the Task Force suggested culling deer by professional marksman within Durand Eastman Park.

Antihunting groups including the Humane Society of Rochester and Monroe County, the Fund For Animals, Animal Advocates of Upstate New York, and the Humane Society of the United States fought this. It went to the New York State Supreme Court and the deer removal was upheld.

Despite vocal opposition, 80 animals were culled from the park, but the full results of the impacts of bowhunting on the Rochester area deer herd remain unknown. It obviously is a complicated situation with many stakeholders hanging on to their turf and values.

Clearly, deer need to be removed and bowhunting is safe and economical. Yet, many citizens continue to fight.

Although the land owned by the Illinois Power Company is not urban, it does show how successful bowhunting can be to reduce deer numbers in a small area. An archery-only deer hunt was started there in 1991. Bowhunters could harvest as many does as they wanted, but they had to take a doe before trying for a buck. During two years 303 deer were taken from 1,000 acres of timber on the area. The deer herd was reduced on this area by 68 percent in two years using bowhunters alone

The suburban Chippewa Nature Center in Michigan had 35-40 deer per square kilometer and there were vegetation and deer-auto collision problems. After seven years of problems the center held a bowhunt in 1992. Fourteen bowhunters killed 49 deer (1/4 of the total deer herd in the center). All but one were does and fawns. Because of controlled publicity and good hunt preparation, public reaction was very favorable. Only quality bowhunters were selected.

Some of the most successful bowhunts in urban areas occur in Minnesota. In the Hennepin Parks area near Minneapolis, two bowhunts were held in 1992 in two suburban communities. One was in Kings Point where 50 hunters were selected in a random drawing. They had to hunt on 270 acres of woodlands and they had to do it in pairs. There was no shooting proficiency test, but only those hunters who demonstrated a positive and cooperative attitude relative to the hunt rules were selected.

Hunters had to take the Bowhunter Education Program and attend a pre-hunt orientation. Bowhunters killed 29 deer in seven weeks and had a success rate of 58 percent. The Eagle Lake area ran a similar hunt with similar rules. Here 25 hunters killed 15 deer in 130 acres in four weeks. In both cases the programs were deemed a success. This success has led to an expanded bowhunting program in over 25 suburban areas in Minnesota.

Here are some examples. The Dakota County Minnesota Park had almost 60 deer per square mile in 1994, while the desired ecological level was 15-25. Bowhunters hunted weekday mornings only, three days per week and removed 108 deer in three years, 93 of which were does. That exceeded the goal of removing 100 deer in three years. The Minneapolis water filtration plant had 31 deer on their grounds. A bowhunt was approved and in one day, 16 archers removed 22 deer with 26 shots.

More Case Studies Of Urban Deer Problems.—-There are hundreds of case studies where various control methods have been attempted. Part of the purpose in presenting the following material is to give readers information they might use in their neighborhood if an overabundant deer problem arises.

River Hills, Wisconsin—This Village is an eight-square-kilometer suburb near Milwaukee. In the mid-80's residents began complaining of vegetation damage and car-deer collisions. A citizens committee recommended sharpshooting with guns to remove deer, but government officials of the village decided to trap and transplant.

Between 1987 and 1991, 348 deer were translocated, but due to high mortality of these deer, the Wisconsin Department of Natural Resources discontinued authorizing such moves. Over 43 percent died within one year. The average time they survived once moved was 285 days. Of those moved, 94 were hit by cars, indicating a real problem with translocating deer in some areas. (Though not mentioned in this situation, moving diseases from one area to another is also a problem when trapping and translocating deer). And it costs money;

in this study, costs ranged between $273 and $400 per deer to trap (doesn't include transportation costs nor costs of trap construction).

In another example of the costs for moving deer, the May 1992 issue of the Safari Times reported that 16 of 27 blacktail deer that were transplanted from an urban park near Alameda, California to a wilderness area were eaten by mountain lions in less than two months. The deer had become a problem and residents requested the Wildlife Department to help. Cost to move the deer was over $100,000.

Another problem with translocating is a lack of suitable release sites (most areas have all the deer they can hold). Interestingly, in River Hills since 1991, the deer have been trapped alive and given to deer game farms where most are killed. I would think that this would bother citizens who were opposed to hunting the deer.

Suburban Areas Around Chicago—The problems caused by a high deer population in these suburbs are the same as reported in the other cases. However near Peoria there were also four deer-plane strikes at an airport. In one 5 1/2 square mile area there were 100 deer per square mile (whew!!! That is a very high density and would lead to serious problems for vegetation, wild flowers, tree regeneration, etc.).

The goal was to reduce deer numbers in this area to 15 deer per square mile using trained firearm sharpshooters. In the winters of 1985,' 86, '87 they shot 334 deer and a few were trapped and translocated. In 1987 near O'Hare Airport, 54 deer were shot by sharpshooters in one month. At the Lake City Forest Preserve antihunters tried to stop a sharpshooting program in 1988 and 89. However, the shooting went ahead and was judged to be humane. They also used a capture and kill approach, and citizens felt this was inhumane.

Angel Island, San Francisco—Columbian black-tailed deer on this small island were in terrible shape due to overpopulation. Obviously the habitat was suffering as well. A hunt was suggested but an anti group forced a trap and removal program. In 1981, 215 deer were trapped and removed at a cost of $100,000 to capture, relocate and follow-up monitoring of 15 radio-collared animals.

Only two of the 15 were alive after one year. Only an estimated 15 percent of the 215 released deer survived one year with many dying from car collisions and many were eaten by mountain lions.

By 1984 the island's deer population again increased so antihunters suggested chemosterilizing the deer. The Society For the Prevention of Cruelty to Animals treated 30 does but stopped because they just couldn't catch enough animals. Since then Park officials on the island shoot 20-30 deer per year with guns.

Ardenwood Regional Preserve Near Oakland, California—The town voted to remove all the deer from a fenced preserve. The Humane Society said they should sterilize the deer, but the state wildlife agency said "no" and trapped and removed them. They collared and released 27 deer. Only one was alive at the end of one year.

Six were eaten by lions, one by coyotes, one was hit by a train, one died in a fence, and one was hit by a car. The other deaths were from unknown causes. The message is clear. Trap and remove leads to death of the animals.

Ipswich, Massachusetts—Deer on a 1400-acre barrier beach island were in poor health and starving, and at the same time there was increased Lyme disease (by the mid-1980's 30 percent of local landowners tested positive for this disease), and there was severe over-browsing of vegetation. A hunt was proposed in 1983 but canceled due to anti activities.

It was later approved by local and state government authorities, and using selected firearm hunters the herd was reduced from 350 to 60 after four years of hunting. Hunters had to be local, have five years of experience, take a safety course, go to a pre-hunt orientation, and pass a gun shooting proficiency test. Public approval has grown as deer numbers have successfully been controlled by hunters. In 1990 the town gave approval for the gun hunt to continue for the next 10 years.

North Oaks, Minnesota—There are situations where hunting just is not possible. This community conducts a trap and shoot removal, plus some shooting. The trap and shoot approach is "far more feasible and acceptable than shooting." Two people run 25 baited clover traps in winter. Deer are shot in the traps with .22's. They have taken 250 deer from urban areas in one year, but deer keep moving in from outside.

Summary.—I once believed that involving antihunters in the decision-making processes of wildlife management would resolve the problem. I still want to do that; it does help in some situations and many animal activists can work within the system.

But for certain situations, in some urban areas, when the antihunters lose all of their legal options to stop a hunt and the decision is made to kill some deer, some very emotional people resort to threatening, intimidating and sometimes illegal activities.

In such situations, a handful of citizens can create problems for city political leaders, local wildlife biologists and others who support killing deer. When antihunters do nothing but resort to excessive and continual legal actions, the usual result is that during all the delays, deer numbers continue to rise, vegetation suffers, and so do the deer.

From the examples I've presented, it's easy to see that there are combinations of ways to solve an over-abundant deer problem. Contraception probably is not viable, nor is trapping and moving the deer.

Bowhunting works, and trapping and shooting will work. Costs must be considered, and be a part of any plan to reduce deer numbers.

"In elaborating what he came to call the "land ethic,"Leopold rejected the notion that humans can simply stand aside and leave nature to her own devices."

Jan Dizard

Chapter 14

A Different Perspective On Trophy Hunting*

Hunting has always given me a multitude of benefits. As Dr. Randall Eaton recently expressed... "I don't hunt to control game herds. Nor do I hunt to support wildlife conservation. If I did, I'd buy all the licenses, permits, tags, and stamps...and stay home and watch hunting videos. I hunt because I love to hunt." (In *"Tell It Like It Is,"* Bowman's Journal 1 (1), Autumn 1999). And the benefits are many (see chapters 3 and 4).

Dr. Donna Minnis noted that "describing hunting by labeling it as "sport hunting," "meat hunting," or "trophy hunting" depicts hunting as providing only one purpose" (e.g., for recreation, food, or trophy, respectively) (In *"Communicating A Pro-hunting Message: Pitfalls To Avoid,"* Proceedings Annual Conference of Southeastern Association of Fish and Wildlife Agencies, 1997). When we reduce hunting to just one dimension (e.g. "trophy hunting"), we do it a disservice.

Hunting for quality animals is a part of my bowhunts for deer. I'll take the first legal deer I can to make sure there will be meat in the freezer over the winter. Then I will become selective and attempt to harvest a larger deer. In so doing, I will pass up many shots, observe lots of deer behavior, and spend many hours in the woods.

This chapter discusses what trophy hunting is. I've written it because people have a mental image of what trophy hunting is, but it differs from my real-life experience hunting quality animals.

---

*Portions adapted (with permission) from August and September 1993 "On Your Side" columns in Bowhunting News and from the 4th edition record book of The Pope and Young Club. Dr. Randall Eaton has recently released two excellent videos and a book. "The Sacred Hunt" and "The Sacred Hunt II: The Rite of Passage" and "The Sacred Hunt; An Anthology" speak to the history and evolution of man as a hunting animal. Contact Dr. Eaton at PO Box 280, Enterprise, OR 97828.

Maybe they see an image of the rich, illegal hunter who wants to kill the biggest animal at all costs. Though that may be what trophy hunting is to a few, it is not what trophy hunting is to most and it never has been.

We Evolved As Trophy Hunters.—-Equating illegal activities to the legitimate trophy hunter is like equating drunk drivers to all motorists who drive cars in a legal and safe manner. The real trophy hunter is actually one of the most ethical of all hunters, and understands nature and the outdoors more than most. Here we will look at the many positive aspects of trophy hunting.

In 1978, Randall Eaton wrote a classic paper on *"The Evolution of Trophy Hunting"* in the very first issue of a journal called Carnivore. His hypothesis was that man evolved not only as a hunting animal, but also evolved as a trophy hunting animal. The argument is compelling, and may help explain why modern hunters are so prone to put animals on their wall, antlers on the garage, bear claws around their neck, mounted animals in their office, etc.

His argument is relatively simple. Eaton believed that the highest social status went to primitive hunters who were the most fit and who killed the most and biggest animals while citing much scientific, anthropological literature to support his theory. He showed that male hunters benefited when competing for females if they advertised their hunting prowess.

For example, male members of the King Bushman could only marry after they killed a large herbivore. Another study showed that a female Bushman female could not marry outside her culture, but cited one exception when a male who was not a Bushman was allowed to marry a Bushman because he was an exceptional hunter. In short, good hunters had an advantage when seeking a mate and perpetuating their race.

Most early primitive peoples advertised their hunting success by displaying trophies. Most primitive peoples still do today. Eaton noted that the Akoa pygmies wore elephant hair bracelets. Bushman cut strips of hair from antelope they killed and made bracelets for their wives. Others could tell the species of the animal taken by the color of the hair on the bracelets.

More difficult trophies were then recognized as being taken by Bushman who saw the bracelets on the wives. There are other examples of how primitive hunters gained status and wives via hunting and killing trophies.

Mbuti pygmies killed large antelopes and gave them to the parents of the bride-to-be before the parents allowed a marriage. Alaskan Eskimos had to kill a series of animals, culminating with the polar bear prior to a completion of the marriage eligibility. Eskimos killed grizzly bears even though they were not used for food. Trophy hunting? Probably.

Males became chiefs of the Sciriono peoples of the Amazon Basin based on their hunting abilities.

One could argue that chiefs and leaders of primitive peoples became such because their fathers were the leaders. In other words, they inherited their leadership. Eaton contented that good hunters became the leaders and chiefs.

One study showed that chiefs were selected by nonhereditary means in 13 of 18 hunting cultures but in nonhunting cultures, chiefs succeeded each other because they were sons of chiefs in 93 of 160 such cultures. The conclusion? Good hunters became chiefs. Thus, there was selective advantage to being a good hunter. Eaton cited many examples where this was true.

Among Tikerarmiut Eskimos the most prominent males were those who hunt whales. The Nootka, northwest coastal Indians, hunted whales "as a test of valor." Various Indian societies of South America show the same thing — male status depends on hunting success. The Kayapo of the Amazon Basin hunted jaguars as trophies to prove their bravery. The Waiwai of the Amazon achieve status by hunting. Many Plains Indians killed grizzlies as a symbol of power.

Pastoral societies that raise livestock also must kill predators to protect their cattle. The males of those peoples (the Zulu, Suk, Turkana, Marakweet) wear leopard skins to advertise their trophy hunting skills. Examples could go on and on, but the conclusions are rather obvious. Since the best hunters got the most and best women, and had the highest social status among the males, such hunters probably had an evolutionary selective advantage.

They would breed more, they (and their families) would eat more protein and hence survive better. In other words, the best hunters, and the hunters who killed the biggest animals (i.e., the trophy hunters), would survive and would evolve.

The best hunters displayed bravery by killing large predators. This gave them status, but it also reduced competition in their hunting areas for prey. By reducing competition for food, there is again a selective advantage to being a good hunter.

But Eaton pointed out that killing large trophy predators might also be ritualistic, "done in such a way as to give individuals the opportunity to demonstrate warrior skills." Eaton also pointed out that paintings and sculptings of Paleolithic hunters emphasized the head which suggests an emphasis on killing trophy animals.

Nootkan war chiefs used charred bone from wolves or mountain lions to paint their faces before raiding other Indians. Authors suggest that bone from these predators provided power. Even in war, the best hunters seemed to have the advantage.

Eaton also suggested that in some hunting cultures, art originated from hunting trophies. He also suggested that "picture writing could be traced directly to trophy art." His paper has an interesting discussion about the role of lion hunting in the evolution of the Pharaohs in Egypt and the importance of trophy hunting to the Greeks. Greek coins had hunting scenes on them.

He also noted that Plato advocated hunting as a part of the training of young men. Eaton even suggests that some dancing evolved from imitating "animals to enhance hunting success." He suggested that acting might have evolved from dance.

Eaton noted that "eight different monarchies of Europe are symbolized by the lion (as are seven in Asia by the tiger). He points out that we still utilize trophies as important symbols of society. Taverns known as the "Red Lion Inn," automobiles named after trophy animals like cougar, bobcat, mustang, and jaguar. We give "trophy cups" to people who win races, competitions, and Eaton suggested that this form of trophy may have originated in the late upper Paleolithic hunters of Europe, "who may have used trophy skulls as drinking cups."

Finally, Eaton pointed out that people today attack trophy hunting "as an expression of male ego" and he stated that this is biologically correct. "However, the moral judgment against trophyism is not necessarily valid," he said.

A Different Perspective On Trophy Hunting

It Is Ethical.—-Though humans probably evolved as trophy hunting animals, many in society today are opposed to trophy hunting. Even so, most hunters keep some form of trophies, whether it be antlers from last year's deer, or hides and furs from animals they have harvested. Some go one step further and make jewelry from their animals.

Some convert parts of the animals into art. Last year I had a western fringe leather coat made from six deer hides. And, yes, I have a "trophy room," my den, where some of my best animals are located. In fact, I do all my writing in my den. It is a rather private place, a bit separate from the main part of my home.

Why do I keep such trophies? Is it because I want to possess the beauty of the animal? Is it because I want to remember the hunt? Is it something more subtle whereby I subconsciously want to maintain my tie to my evolutionary past? Is it a way for me to let others know that I am a good hunter, a skilled hunter?

My guess is that keeping trophies is something that we do for all of these reasons. John Madson, in a paper given at the Montana Governor's Symposium on North America's Hunting Heritage stated: "Ten thousand years ago the hunter might have stood by a fire and recounted the great deed to his clan brothers, while the old men nodded their approval and stripling boys back in the shadows listened in wonder. It hasn't changed much. The trophy hunter, the ethical killer of the great stag, or bear or ram, still commands attention by the fire as he recites his deeds. His peers still salute him, the old men still nod and remember, and boys still dream of tomorrow's hunts."

The 4th edition of the Pope and Young record book has two very important chapters on trophy hunting. *"The Truth About Trophy Hunting"* by Bill Krenz, and *"The Value of Trophy Hunting"* by Jim Dougherty are must reading for all serious hunters. These chapters point out that trophy hunting is misunderstood, and as I noted earlier, it is misunderstood by not only nonhunters but by some hunters as well.

Antihunters and others suggest that trophy hunting kills off the best animals and thus damages the herd. John Madson points out that "neither the mathematics of genetics nor the observed facts of breeding within wildlife populations add support to that contention."

You will hear this argument from antihunters over and over in the future, but no scientific studies back up this claim. For the common species that we hunt there is no biological proof that shooting big animals affects the reproduction of the species in any way.

Jim Dougherty pointed out that trophy hunting is not the "fabricating (of) reputations" that a few hunters feel that they need to satisfy their ego. However, it is these guys that we read about; they give us all a bad name, they give trophy hunting a bad rap that it does not deserve.

Bill Krenz noted that trophy hunting is not a science but a philosophy. Trophy hunting has always been a philosophy. It was a philosophy for primitive peoples, and it still is today.

As Krenz pointed out, there is a big difference between a science and a philosophy. Anti trophy hunters think the science of killing is the same as the philosophy of trophy hunting. Not so.

Krenz noted that with science you have an "external reward" to prove your accomplishment. With a philosophy the reward is something internal, and it's hard to measure. The philosophy of trophy hunting doesn't involve ego as much as it involves honor, self respect, achieving something, and responding to challenge.

The key to trophy hunting is not the science, and it is not in killing trophies. It is the philosophy, the value to each trophy hunter, and the way it was done. The key to trophy hunting isn't the killing, it is the hunting, and the hunting is the philosophy.

It must be totally ethical, totally legal, and totally in keeping with good biology and good wildlife management. As Krenz and Dougherty point out, the most important aspect of trophy hunting is not the kill, but rather how we hunted.

I'm reminded of a story told to me by brothers Gene and Barry Wensel about a huge buck they had hunted for at least a year. While bowhunting, one of them came upon that buck in the river and ice on the shore prevented the deer from getting out of the water. Eventually he did get out, but he could have been easily shot with a bow while in the water, while getting out, or once he was on land.

It was not done. No trophy is worth doing something unethical. To the true trophy hunter, ethical hunting behavior is paramount.

It is the hunter who decides what is a trophy. For my old friend, Keith Dana of Rock Springs, Wyoming, a trophy antelope is one that has abnormally shaped horns. Me, I want to hunt an antelope that has normal-shaped horns, but Keith will spend all year chasing a buck that has horns that point in directions that antelope horns normally do not. That is a trophy to him.

Some of us will only take big animals with long bows. Others won't use treestands. Others won't wear camo. A big doe might be a trophy to some. Some bowhunters hunt a certain animal all year long, even though it doesn't meet the Pope and Young Club minimums for record book status.

A trophy has different meanings to different people. A few years ago my dear friend Ginger Fausel took her first animal with a bow, and it was a beautiful strawberry blond bear in Saskatchewan. It was not a big bear, but was it a trophy? Absolutely. The bear was a trophy in Ginger's eyes, and was taken in fair chase, by a bowhunter who is ethical in every sense of the word.

Do people cheat in this system? Eaton, in his article on *"The Evolution of Trophy Hunting,"* suggested that primitive man probably cheated on occasion. A hunter would find a dead trophy, and take the horns to be displayed as his kill. Thus, he gained high status in his clan. We have cheaters today. The cheaters of today are the takers. The trophy hunters are the givers. They fight for hunting, and for the animals. They don't need to harvest animals all the time as they search for that one, sometimes big, trophy.

Real trophy hunters are not the problem with hunting today. They are ethical and have an ethical philosophy about hunting. As Bill Krenz pointed out, the philosophy of trophy hunting "aspires to make hunting more perfect." If that philosophy were aspired to by all hunters, than hunting would be healthier.

"The trophy-hunter is the caveman reborn."

Aldo Leopold

Chapter 15

Attitudes And Education Of Public School Students*

Antihunting groups have spent millions of dollars placing animal rights literature and lesson plans into the public schools. It is an attempt to change the attitudes of our youth.

In some respects this is good. Having children who care about animals is positive for society. However, if such education is not based on reality, then it can be harmful to animals, especially wild animals. Children need to understand the complexities of our ecosystems, and they need to have an appreciation for wild animals.

But that is not happening. For example, children today think that most wild animals are endangered species. They are starting to think that it is "bad" to eat meat, and "good" to be vegetarians. They are being led to believe that being a vegetarian means no harm will come to wild animals. Not so, and if these beliefs carry over into adult actions, they can be terribly harmful to wildlife

What follows are some considerations of where children get their attitudes, what those attitudes are, and what are the consequences of such attitudes.

Cartoons Influence Kids.—-Antihunting groups are targeting children. Visit any secondary school in the country and ask a kid if animal rights is OK, and they will say "yes."

Such attitudes carry over as these children grow older. One 1991 Gallup Survey showed that 41 percent of teenagers support animal rights to a high degree, and an additional 26 percent leaned toward its philosophies. Where did this all start and when do children first get exposed to antihunting philosophies?

*portions adapted (with permission) from "Know Hunting" columns, August 1992, December 1992, December 1995, October 1998, December 1998, Bowhunter Magazine

Chapter 15

Since *"Bambi,"* there has been the perception that cartoons can impact children's thoughts on hunting. Gail Blankenau in the August 1995 issue of Field and Stream (*"Children and the Animal Rights Agenda"*) noted that a number of movies aimed at children convey an antihunting message.

Children's books and cartoons do too. HBO's "Seabert the Seal" was just one of many cartoon shows that presented erroneous material on hunting. This show told viewers that hunting caused many animals to disappear from the earth.

Not true, but the message was clear. And "Seabert the Seal" is not an exception. There are many cartoons that carry antihunting messages at one time or another, and what is the favorite type of television show for young children? You guessed it...cartoons.

There are folks who would have us believe that cartoons are just fictitious stories and characters, and kids who watch can decipher reality from fiction. But research seems to suggest that children do not always discriminate fact from fantasy in these cartoons. Studies show that kids of all ages give human attributes to wild animals (the term for this is anthropomorphic, i.e. making animals seem human), and these same children interpret things seen in the wild in anthropomorphic terms.

There was a major study done to determine whether cartoons impact how children perceive nature. Cynthia J. Wong-Leonard, a doctoral student at Michigan State University, worked with her advisor — Dr. R. Ben Peyton — and determined that cartoons have a strong influence on children's perceptions of animals (see *"Effects of Wildlife Cartoons On Children's Perceptions Of Wildlife And Their Use Of Conservation Education Material,"* Cynthia Wong-Leonard and R. Ben Peyton. Paper presented at the North American Wildlife and Natural Resources Conference, March, 1992).

They looked at two age groups; 1st to 3rd graders and 6th to 8th graders. The researchers developed cartoon stories of animal species and authoritative natural history videos of the same species and showed these to different groups of children in various sequences. They asked a number of questions before and after kids looked at the cartoons story. For example, one question was: "Do you think a kingfisher (a bird) makes plans for what it will be doing three weeks from now?" She was asking if birds think about their life-sustaining activities, which they obviously do not.

Maybe it isn't so obvious. Consider whether a robin thinks about eating worms. "If I eat three more worms this morning, I can just relax in a tree this afternoon."

Or, does a barn swallow reason that, "if I don't catch 12 more insects today, two of my nestlings will starve to death." Such reasoning does not go on in the wild. Back to the study.

For both age groups, Ms. Wong-Leonard found that anthropomorphic wildlife cartoons modified the students perception of real animals. If a real animal was made to look like a human in some way in the cartoon (e.g., animals that talk, animals that have human facial characteristics, etc.) the children accepted that as reality.

If a cartoon animal talked, then kids thought they were saying what a real animal would say in that situation. In other words, cartoons nurtured anthropomorphic tendencies. In addition, children accept information from cartoons as accurate. They do not discriminate on the basis of the cartoon nature of the source. If the cartoon said a pine marten (a mammal that spends most of it's life in tall trees) was afraid of heights, and they knew no differently, many were willing to accept that as true.

If you then showed these same children a narrated slide show that portrayed the true natural history of the species in the cartoons, many, but not all of the misperceptions were corrected. These children who saw cartoons first never scored as high on the post test (i.e., were never as accurate) as children who saw the natural history program only or even those children who saw the natural history program before they saw the cartoons. It appears that in the absence of previous, more authoritative information, those children were willing to accept "information" they viewed in the cartoons as reality.

In other words, if in a cartoon you make a deer look and talk like a human, you are probably contributing to the perception that deer have human emotions and are human. Of course this might be modified or even reversed later among those children who are presented with a different view by a source they believe, but many urban children may not have such an opportunity.

The real truth is that most cartoon animals are like Bambi. They look like real animals, but they talk and have human personalities.

Chapter 15

No wonder children believe animals think and feel just like humans. Interesting from the study was the fact that youngsters with direct contact with animals via farming or hunting were less influenced by cartoons. This effect may be similar to the finding that children who saw the accurate, natural history program *first* also tended to be less influenced by cartoon information. This suggests that many children are willing to "learn" from cartoons in the absence of previous, contradictory understanding. These kids understood better what was real as opposed to the fantasy land of the cartoon world.

Several commercial cartoons have presented stereotypes of hunters as the bad guys. The "Seabert The Seal" program depicted hunters as rather dim-witted liars, cheaters, and law breakers who needed to "see the light." In "Beauty And The Beast" the image given of the hunter was one who was cruel, arrogant, shooting at random, a bad guy. Pretty typical presentation. Fairly atypical of reality.

Certainly, if we believed we fit this stereotype, we'd all be leading the antihunting movement. Many children who watch these cartoons do not have a competing perception of hunters. The research by Dr. Wong-Leonard suggests these children would tend to accept this version and their view of hunters and hunting would be influenced.

The message of right and wrong which many children expect to see in cartoons would place hunters on the side of wrong. For sure some hunters possess all the above characteristics, but to broad brush this image to most hunters is not correct. From experience this description is totally atypical of my friends who hunt.

What about the question that asked whether kids were able to separate out facts and truths from the fantasies of cartoons? Did the children think you should learn from cartoons? Over 74 percent of 1st to 3rd graders who were interviewed answered "yes" to that question and it was higher (89 percent) for the 6th-8th graders in the interview phase of the study.

When asked to explain what sort of things they expected to learn, many indicated they expected there would be some message in the cartoon. Their explanations were interpreted as expecting to see some moral message in a cartoon.

It follows then that if kids expect to learn from cartoons, they will be more willing to accept what they see as factual. They will be more willing to believe that wild animals have human emotions, thought processes and that they would respond the way they are depicted if they could in real life.

Having said that it comes as no surprise that antihunting groups are using the cartoon approach in their campaigns to invade the public grade schools. Now we have representatives of a prominent animal rights group dressing up as a fish and passing out antifishing material to grade school children, and sentimental cartoons are also used to make kids feel guilty about eating meat.

The messages presented are subtle but clear. You are moral if you are a vegetarian, but immoral if you eat meat. Your friends will like you more, and you will have more friends, if you do not eat fish.

Does all of this affect the child's knowledge about the real world? Of course it does. Let's look at a 1992 study done by Billy Higginbotham of the Texas Agricultural Extension Service (*"The White-tailed Deer: A 4-H Program For Public Elementary Schools,"* Southeast Deer Study Group Meeting, 1993). He asked 3rd graders questions about wildlife, then presented an educational program, and two days later came back and asked the same questions. He also came back 60 days later to determine how much retention he obtained.

The results of this study are most interesting. Some questions the children knew. For example, 81 percent knew that female deer are called does while the males are bucks, and the young one fawns. After an education program 90 percent knew the answer. But students did not understand some deer biology. Fifty percent felt that bucks keep their antlers for life. After education, 82 percent understood that they do not.

But here is a surprise, especially for students living in Texas where deer are extremely common. Sixty-one percent felt the white-tailed deer was an endangered species. After education, 23 percent felt they were endangered, and 60 days later, 41 percent felt they were endangered. This clearly is a hard fallacy to combat even in a state where deer are as common as ticks. One can only wonder where such a perception was generated.

Did "Bambi" influence children to believe that deer are endangered, and became so because of hunting? Its hard to know, but something caused that perception.

Various groups have filled the press with similar talk about bears and mountain lions. If people follows the animal rights rhetoric on these two species, they get the perception that both are endangered, or soon will be. But they aren't.

It almost seems that people want to believe that American wildlife is in big trouble, when in fact for almost all species, because of wildlife management, things have never been better. A few years ago there were photos of four supposedly endangered species on the back of a cereal box. The problem was that only one of the species was actually endangered. Two were extremely common — pronghorn antelope and mule deer. No wonder kids believe such misinformation because it's everywhere, even in our schools.

When given a choice of the number of deer living in Texas, the students were offered three choices, 3-4 million, 300,000-400,000, and 952. Fifty percent of the students selected the answer furtherist from reality...952. (There are almost four million deer in Texas.)

After education the number of students who thought there were only 952 deer living in Texas had dropped to 11 percent. Even so, this example shows how difficult it will be to institute wildlife management activities for deer, and other abundant species like black bears and mountain lions when constituents believe them to be an endangered species.

When these students grow up, some of the attitudes they have today will carry over; some researchers believe that much of the attitudes will still be expressed.

In response to the question, "the biggest threat to deer is coyotes, hunting or habitat loss," over 60 percent listed hunting as the major threat. After education that dropped to 30 percent while habitat loss jumped from 18 percent to 60 percent. And 60 days later 22 percent believed that hunting was a major threat to deer. Apparently that message is easier to educate than the endangered species concept.

Clearly a good education project can teach kids the facts about wild animals. But most children are not exposed to good wildlife education materials. Instead, most get a significant amount of their "education" from cartoons, children's books, television shows, and antihunting information provided to the public schools by various groups.

Children's Perception of Animals and Hunting.—-Cartoons obviously influence children's perceptions of wild animals. But what are the results of these attitudes, i.e., how do children perceive animals? A major study of 10-12-year old children showed that the humanistic attitude is the most common in children. (*"Youth and Wildlife-Beliefs and Behaviors of 5th and 6th Grade Students Regarding Nondomestic Animals,"* by Miriam Westervelt and Lynn Llewellyn. US Government Printing Office, 1985).

Earlier in this book I noted that the humanistic attitude was the fastest growing attitude in adults. Apparently kids are also exhibiting this attitude. Humanistic attitudes develop from a strong affection for *individual* animals, where one tends to relate all animals to their individual pet. In this study, girls had higher humanistic scores than boys, but both were high.

Children exhibiting humanistic attitudes tend to attribute human qualities to wild animals. A 1977 Michigan study (*"Young People's Attitudes Toward Wildlife,"* Gerri Ann Pomerantz, Michigan DNR Wildlife Division Report # 2781) asked 7th-12th graders if they agreed with certain statements related to what animals feel. For example, in response to the statement "most wild animals fall in love," children responded with 35 percent in agreement, 22 percent disagreement, and 43 percent did not know.

So we have only 22 percent of our children knowing that animals do not "fall in love." While it is true that a few, very few, species mate for life, it is a stretch beyond comprehension to suggest that "most" animals fall in love. There is the real possibility that "no" animals fall in love.

In response to the question "Wild animals feel lonely in the wilderness," 15 percent agreed, 63 percent disagreed and 22 percent surprisingly did not know. For this question with what seems to have an obvious answer that "no," wild animals do not feel lonely, we have over one-third of all children not knowing the correct answer. Even if we consider chimpanzees who do possess some human-like characteristics, the fact that 37 percent of our children either believe animals get lonely, or don't know whether they do is still surprising.

Another study showed that young children feared animals more than older students; 64 percent of 2nd graders believed that most wild animals were dangerous to people. There was a fear of animals. However, that fear dissipates with age.

Chapter 15

Between the 5th and 8th grade, students move from fear to gaining more factual knowledge about wild animals. When they reach the 11th grade they become concerned about animals, and about their welfare. They gain more ecological understanding as well. With that growth in ecological understanding, is there an understanding about the role of hunting in wildlife management, and thus support for hunting?

There have been several studies that measure antihunting sentiment in children. In the 1977 Michigan study 74 percent of 7th-12th graders opposed hunting for recreation, while 76 percent felt it was OK to hunt for food.

In the later 1985 study described above, 83 percent of girls and 74 percent of boys were anti recreation hunting. Hunting for food was more acceptable; 50 percent of girls and 65 percent of boys were in favor (the same as we see in adults; more favor hunting for food than for recreation).

Looking at older school children, 81 percent of 11th graders opposed recreational hunting (that is quite a bit higher than we see in adults). Is it likely that such attitudes will carry over to adulthood, and we will see a growing trend in anti attitudes?

That is not an easy question to answer. The reason is that many suburban people are having animal damage problems which will modify ones attitudes in a hurry. It is one thing to feel sorry for beavers that are being trapped from a local pond. It is another when those beavers are eating your prized, expensive lawn trees. The same can be said for white-tailed deer in urban environments. Citizens will enjoy the sight of deer up to a point.

Once damage to yard shrubs and gardens, and automobiles via crashes, reaches a certain point, toleration for those deer diminishes. Thus, although students may be against hunting at one point in their life, as they grow older and are faced with animal damage, etc., they may change their minds.

In recent years there have been battles over books placed in the public schools that relate to this topic. The Associated Press reported that two animal rights books (*"The Animal Rights Handbook"* and *"Kids Can Save The Animals"*) were rejected for admission to a Bloomsburg, Pennsylvania school library. The School Board felt the books were more propaganda than educational materials.

Here is just a smattering of what your children can read in *The Animal Rights Handbook*. "Many" sheep die of heat exhaustion in the summer because they are bred for thick fur. Sheep farmers will be surprised to learn about this.

It stated that it was the exceptional case where animals should be used in medical testing; only where there are no alternatives and the knowledge sought is absolutely essential. Most doctors and humans believe that almost all medical research is essential and cannot be done nearly as effectively without the humane use of animals.

On hunting, the book stated that hunters killed 100 million animals last year, and that for every one claimed, "another wounded creature died slowly from bleeding, infection, and starvation." I feel that a grade school child from Michigan might read that and assume that because 400,000 deer are harvested each year, in Michigan that another 400,000 were wounded and left to die from infection and starvation in the woods. Where is the science to back up such ludicrous statements?

It doesn't exist.

Encouraging Kids To Hunt.—In recent years many state wildlife agencies have begun programs aimed at getting kids into hunting. If you've gotten this far in my book, you know I believe that hunting has value for modern society. I would carry that opinion to also include properly supervised and trained young people. My limit on a minimum would be 12 years of age.

My guess is these state agencies realize that youngsters today are exposed to cartoons and other media that tend to be antihunting. They also look at the literature that demonstrates that if you start hunting at a younger age, and if you are successful in those early years, you tend to stay in that form of recreation for years to come.

If one starts later, or has no measure of success, that person tends to drop out of hunting. I believe many youngsters would be far better off with exposure to hunting. There is no doubt there are many forms of recreation that kids can do in nature, but the oldest traditional nature activity is hunting.

We know that ethical hunting teaches character, self esteem, patience, and cooperation. It also teaches children the realities of life and death. Jim Swan in his book, *"In Defense of Hunting,"* suggests that "one of the main causes of the violence and lack of value for human life among children today must be their loss of first-hand contact with the life-and-death processes of nature."

At a time when children need the values they can learn in the woods, a few antihunting groups are making a major push to stop state and federal government youth hunting and hunter education classes. Twenty-six states sponsor youth hunts. More are developing all the time.

With the antihunting focus placed by such groups on children, it was no surprise at their reaction to the relatively recent shootings that took place in the public schools. Right after the shootings in Jonesboro, Arkansas, animal rightists claimed that kids who hunt are desensitized toward living beings; claiming that this is what led to the tragedy.

Let's consider those shootings for a moment. First, we must understand the overall objective of groups that blame hunting for such tragedies. Antihunting groups give the impression that their objective is to make kids more sensitive, more caring, better citizens, and better people. But their actions show that the antihunting agenda has nothing to do with helping today's youth.

Nor is it about making things better in this country. The agenda is simple; no killing of animals for any purpose. Hunting and fishing groups have anti drug campaigns, and promote various activities (other than hunting and fishing; examples being raising funds for various children's hospitals and other needy organizations, having blood donor campaigns, conserving wetlands, etc.) that are good for America. Antihunting groups do not do that.

If hunting really caused kids to be callous, non-caring adults, with no compassion for living beings, then we'd expect to find high crime rates in rural areas where more kids hunt. The opposite is true.

My home state of West Virginia has had the lowest crime rate in the United States for 24 straight years, and there are hunters living in over 50 percent of all homes. (An interesting statistic, and I hesitated to bring it up because crime and hunting are not related, but since the point was made, we should at least look at such data).

Most believe the real problems today center around the loss of family values, something that many hunting families, rural families, still have. Most believe our real problems today center around the loss of the moral fiber that once held this country together.

Instead of the values found in the woods, we find talk shows that focus on sick society and sick problems. We find that homicides by juveniles have tripled since 1983; that one of every 10 adolescents will consider suicide today.

In 1994, the U. S. courts handled 1.5 million cases where a juvenile was charged with delinquency (that is a 41 percent increase since 1985), juveniles murdered has jumped by 47 percent from 1980 to 1994. A quick look at these brief statistics shows that America's youth is in trouble, and regardless of what a few antihunting groups may say, hunting is not the problem.

Consider information found in *"Urban Delinquency And Substance Abuse"* (published in March 1994 by the Office of Juvenile Justice and Delinquency Prevention). In the section on gun ownership and delinquency, the authors conclude the following: "The socialization into gun ownership is also vastly different for legal and illegal gun owners (referring to children). Those who own legal guns have fathers who own guns for sport and hunting. On the other hand, those who own illegal guns have friends who own illegal guns and are far more likely to be gang members."

No doubt, many boys own illegal guns. But when gun ownership comes via a hunting family, not only is there little crime involved, there is more family involvement...more family values...more societal values.

As proof of the loss of societies values, consider a recent survey that showed that 20 percent of college students believe society shouldn't judge mass murderers such as those responsible for the holocaust. Whoa.

As convenient and simple as it is to blame hunting for the ills of society, the fact is that children who hunt probably have more appreciation for life than those who don't. Most wildlife biologists in the last 50 years came into their profession after being hunters. Hunting led them into a lifetime of caring for, and an interest in managing wildlife.

Most hunters care deeply about animals, and our ancestor hunters have done so for hundreds of thousands of years. The hunter understands the animal, the ecology, the life and death struggle of nature.

It seems hard for some to understand that hunters, who kill animals, really care about those animals. Dr. Randall Eaton makes this easier to understand (In *"Tell It Like It Is"* cited earlier in this chapter 14) by asking nonhunters a simple question. "Who loves roses more than those who grow them?" Obviously people who raise roses love them more than most citizens.

He follows by then asking, "Who loves roses more than those who pick and kill them?" Same answer...the people who raise roses are the ones who care, and they are the same people who pick the flower and in so doing guarantee it's death. Roses and deer are both sustainable resources. Those with the most direct contact with those species, care the most about them. Relative to hunters, and being one myself, and being a wildlife biologist, I believe this to be true. All of my friends who bowhunt, care deeply about the animals they hunt.

Since the relationship to the animals we hunt is one of caring, then when a hunter takes a child hunting, they are not leading them into some den of unfeeling, wanton slaughter. They are taking them into a history of spiritual relationship with the prey. And when a father and son, or daughter hunt together, there is bonding, nurturing, learning.

The hunter and his/her children have developed relationships that tend to keep kids out of trouble. Would society be better off today if all fathers spent time with their sons in the woods every Saturday from September to December? It's a simple question with an easy answer.

Though some students might miss a day or two of school on occasion during the hunting season, hunting is not the cause of the mass delinquency problem we now find.

Nor does hunting cause large increases in teen homicides nor does it lead to suicide. The causes for teen problems are many and complicated, and no doubt some of the causes are urban or substance abuse related.

This country has obvious major parenting problems on a large scale (half the households now have both members working). When one looks at what is happening to young people today, at what is happening in society today, you almost have to lack an ethical conscience to blame those problems on hunting.

I understand that some organizations do not like hunting, but I do not understand the use of tragedies like public school shootings to promote their cause. I believe it bears repeating; getting kids into the wilds of nature is good therapy. It doesn't cause problems, but it helps cure them.

There is a definite shift in how people look at wildlife in this country. There is a shift from an interest in hunting wildlife to values that are non-traditional...i.e. not hunting. That shift is a function of younger age groups having different values than their parents and grandparents.

At the same time millions of young people are indicating they would go hunting if someone would take them. This situation is an interesting contradiction. A growing interest in animal rights, yet a growing desire to participate in the life and death struggle from whence we evolved.

"I take my kids hunting so I don't have to hunt for my kids."

Ted Nugent

Chapter 16

What The Bible Says About Hunting*

It was Saturday night at the Moxham Church of the Brethren, circa 1950. My family and I were attending a wild game dinner hosted by Reverend Ellis and the church. In fact some of the wild game was donated by my father.

Wild game in our freezer was important, especially from an economic point of view...i.e. we needed the meat. Evidently dad felt the game dinner was important for families in the church, so he made the sacrifice and donated some meat for the occasion. All my buddies were there with their parents; the Blackburns, the Lehmans, the Shaffers, and others.

Our church was no different than many. Wild game dinners were commonly held in churches throughout the area. That's interesting because today some of the attack against hunting is coming from some who say it is an anti-Christian activity. They suggest that hunting violates one of the ten commandments..."Thou Shalt Not Kill."

Reverend Ellis would have been upset with such contrived thinking. He would never have tolerated anything that was close to being against biblical teachings. My reason for writing this chapter is to take a look at the interpretations that allow hunting to be condemned by some who use the Bible for such attacks.

My guess is that nothing I write will settle this argument. Hopefully readers will find something of value in my Christion perspective on this issue.

Thou Shalt Not Kill.—-I grew up in a Christian home, and attended the Church of the Brethren in Johnstown, Pennsylvania. Mom and dad sang in the choir every Sunday morning, and so we had to be at

*Portions adapted (with permission) from Nov, Dec 1993, Jan 1994 "On Your Side" columns in Bowhunting News.

church on time. Sundays found our house in a bustle as all four children fought over the use of the bathroom, then rushed around getting dressed so that we could leave the house at 9.a.m.

To be late for church was to be in trouble with our parents. We could charm mom, but dad, well, you just didn't want to be late with him in charge. During the fall hunting season our weekends were typical for most rural families. Go to the Friday night high school football game, get up at 4 a.m. Saturday to go hunting, get home after dark, clean the harvested game and put it in the freezer, then up and to church on Sunday morning.

There was nothing incongruous about hunting one day and going to church the next. In fact, church and hunting seemed to go together. Apparently the Church of the Brethren felt there was nothing in the Bible against hunting, for many members were hunters.

All of my buddies at church were hunters. There were even church activities that related to hunting. Every spring there was the annual church wild game dinner mentioned above where all the men brought in game, and we ate and had fellowship together.

Many of my high school friends went to other churches, and things there were the same. But somehow, in recent years, for some Christians, that has changed. A few have become antihunters, and I find that puzzling.

Why? Because the Bible is quite clear about man's relationship and responsibilities to animals, and it is so clear most Christians have always supported hunting. In fact, many ministers were hunters, and many still are today.

So what is happening that brings some Christians to think that hunting and other uses of animals is bad? Has a liberalized society and government created an environment that makes theological thinking people see things differently?

It appears so. Consider the following. Dave Roose of Cadillac, Michigan, is a superb fellow and leader in the Christian Bowhunters of America and has received some negative mail from Christians because his group supports hunting. These letters use the commandment, *"Thou Shalt Not Kill"* as the argument against hunting. One such letter stated: "Real Christians know that the Lord watches over all, beasts and humans alike, and I'm sure that He is deeply sorrowed by your torture on fellow creatures." Hmmm.

There were "real" Christians in my church as a kid, and they were hunters too. The Bible hasn't changed either, so obviously the change has been a societal one.

Michael Tobias published an article (*"Hunters: Thou Shalt Not Kill"*) in the November 1991 issue of Trilogy Magazine. In that article he stated: "I hear countless lightweight pieces of diatribe over the right, the need, the rationale for and against hunting. But nowhere do I see hunters or environmentalists, philosophers, theologians, or magazine editors ever debating the most simple and pervasive of all edicts—the one we all grew up with, Buddhist, Jew, Christian, Native American, Muslim, Hindu, Taoist, Australian, Native African, Aborigine, or Martian, for that matter, namely, that "Thou Shalt Not Kill."

Tobias's interpretation of this phrase is not Bible based. The Bible does not give this commandment relative to killing animals.

One can argue ethics, differences of opinion, different philosophies, but what I would like to do here is simply reduce this "Thou Shalt Not Kill" argument to a Biblical context. David Roose wrote a response to the letter he received, and a portion of that response is as follows (published with permission of Christian Bowhunters of America, 3460 W 13th. St., Cadillac, MI 49601). "It is true that one of the Ten Commandments says, "Thou shalt not kill." However, I must remind you that they (the commandments) were given to Moses for the governing of the people. The first four commandments relate to man's relationship to God and what it should be.

The last six relate to man's relationship with each other and what it should be. Obviously then, "Thou shalt not kill" pertains to the taking of the life of another man, and therefore has nothing to do with animals." Seems fairly clear to me.

Now, let us consider the ramifications of this "Thou Shalt Not Kill" commandment if it applied to humans killing animals as some people suggest. Obviously, if this were the case, then farmers and butchers, the owners of McDonalds, and maybe even anyone who eats meat would be sinners for doing so.

However, it makes little sense to suggest that it is a sin for a farmer to kill and butcher animals for others to use. It makes little sense to suggest that all meat eaters are sinners for eating meat.

Perhaps we should look at this "Thou Shalt Not Kill" issue from another perspective, an ethical perspective; what is right and wrong for man to do. The late Dr. Manford Meitzen, former Chairman of the Religion Department at West Virginia University, wrote a paper published in a theological journal on the *"Ethics of Hunting."*

His argument was relatively simple. Meitzen said that man (not animals) is the pinnacle of the hierarchy of life, hence, man is different from animals. He pointed out that "Biblical ethics revolve about man, i.e., man's relationship to God and to other men. Animals are involved in ethical considerations only insofar as they might have a bearing on relationships between human beings or between God and man."

Meitzen said that "ethics" is a human construct. He went on to say that humans cannot sin against an animal, humans only sin against man or God. In Exodus 21, Dr. Meitzen noted that it was the human owner of the ox who had to restitute the owner of another injured ox. Man sins not against the oxen by injuring it, but he sins against the human owner of that oxen.

Meitzen concluded: "Therefore, we have to discount the most common criticism leveled against hunting, for it is a simple appeal to the fifth commandment, "Thou Shalt Not Kill". Sinning against animals is not possible."

According to Meitzen's thoughts, with which I agree, if a poacher shoots more deer than the law allows, then he is being selfish, and he is sinning. But he is sinning against other humans who he robs of having a chance to hunt that deer or having a chance to see that deer.

He is not sinning against the deer that he killed. Meitzen stated that to sin is to be selfish. If a person gets overly consumed with hunting then they "might sin against themselves and society by hunting so much that they dull their own intellectual or artistic lives."

It should not surprise anyone that there are a few hunters who break hunting laws, and who do get selfish and try to kill more deer than the law allows. Selfishness is manifested in human behavior in every aspect of our lives.

There is the race car driver who "cheats" with the rules to win the race. There is the businessman who "cheats" with the rules to make more money or to outsell his competitors. There is the restaurant owner who "cheats" his customers by serving lesser food than is listed on the menu. Teachers who abuse students, policemen who go bad, plumbers who steal from friends, your neighbor who cheats on his/her taxes, people who cheat on their mates, etc., etc. In all human endeavors the basic sin is selfishness, and we all have it somewhere within us. That's the sin.

As David Roose pointed out: "In the meantime I will continue to take my bow which is not violent because it is an inanimate object, and use it to harvest game — which is sound resource management. This will be done within the bounds of proper civil law. And I will use the meat of the game taken, as God gave permission, to strengthen my body. This I will do along with the purchase of meat and other produce obtained from the market place. Isn't God good to provide for our soul and our body in spite of our sin? (Psalm 107:8)."

The Bible teaches that *God created humans in his image and humans are the pinnacle of the hierarchy of life*, and as such, "Thou Shalt Not Kill"" is a commandment that applies only to humans. Having said that, note that this reality does not give humans an unconditional right to abuse animals. Some feel that because man sometimes kills animals for recreation, that this is the real sin. Let's look at this a little closer.

Hunting For Recreation.—-The Bible shows clearly that in fact the fifth commandment refers only to humans and not human's relationship to animals. If that is true, then why do some Christians believe that this commandment refers to hunting?

Tony Campolo in a book entitled *"20 Hot Potatoes Christians Are Afraid To Touch"* (published by Word Publishing, 1988) discussed the question, "Is Hunting A Sin?"

He stated that it is OK to kill animals for food or in self-defense. He acknowledged that hunting is needed to kill overpopulations, but thinning "should be carried out with sadness and not for thrills."

Campolo goes on to say: "I am sure that the psychological motivations for hunting must be complex."

He will get few arguments there. He was also correct when he noted that animals are good for people and that they were put here by God for food. The debate then appears be in his assumption that "to kill such precious gifts from God as a sport must be sin."

Chapter 16

This appears to be the crux of the problem. Some Christians think it is a sin to kill animals for recreation. i.e., it is a sin for hunting to be fun.

Above I discussed the paper by theologian, Dr. Meitzen. Meitzen also addressed this issue and stated that "There is something evil about hunting as there is about most everything we do." Every human being has hostile and aggressive drives which manifest themselves in some form. It is a normal feature of human nature. These drives are manifestations of the fallenness of human nature."

I remember when first reading this that I was upset by the charge that there is something "evil" about hunting. However, if you look at this in the context that sinning is to be selfish, than Dr. Meitzen may well be correct. From that context we humans do a lot of sinning.

My wife wants our yard to look nice (I do too). So, in order to make sure that our yard fits in with the neighborhood, I mow, plant flowers, kill dandelions and other weeds, trim, manicure, fertilize, etc., and the yard does look nice. She doesn't say that she wants our yard to look nicer than the neighbors, but there is no question that it must be at least on a par with others that live nearby.

Trying to outdo my neighbors is being selfish. That is a sin.

When I was a wildlife professor, students taking my tests definitely tried to score higher than other students in the class. That is a form of selfishness. That then is a sin.

We try to earn more money than others, dress nicer, have more things than others, to work harder than others, want our company to do better than competitors, try to make our pies taste better than others, and want our little league baseball team to beat the other team. Yes, in this context, we are all sinners.

Hunters try to get a bigger buck than their hunting companions. Sure, they often help their companions get a buck, but deep down, most hunters have a secret hunting location they protect from everyone. They have a secret hunting technique that they just won't share, selfish rascals that they are.

If sinning is evil, then yes, Dr. Meitzen, there is something selfish about hunting just as there is something evil about almost everything we do. When you reduce life's activities down to the barest minimums, humans are selfish, at least a little bit, sometimes.

However, Meitzen also pointed out that the ethical hunters don't do too badly in all this, simply because most sinning leads to vented hostilities against other humans. But not hunting.

The ethical hunter only takes the legal limit, doesn't break the hunting laws, so even though he might selfishly want to take a bigger animal than another hunter, he is not being aggressive toward another human even though he is sinning against another human for selfishly wanting a bigger animal.

Meitzen stated: "the current increased ethical criticism of hunting is not especially Christian motivated." On what grounds can Dr. Meitzen make this statement?

Because the Bible says nothing in particular about the ethics of hunting. But as a matter of intellectual analysis it can be said that it (anti thoughts) is not a Christian point of view.

Indeed, most Christian scholars understand that "the moral laws directing our relationship to animals and our fellow man are different from man's relationship to animals and the creation around him." (quote from David Roose).

Roose noted that Genesis 9:2-4 "is very explicit about man's permission to kill and use animals. Every moving thing that liveth shall be meat for you; even as the green plants have I given you all things (Genesis 9:3, Deuteronomy 12:15)."

He further pointed out that God did not forbid us to kill or eat animals, but he did forbid us to eat blood (Genesis 9:4, Deuteronomy 12:23, Leviticus 17:13).

Why? For blood is the life. Our animal rights friends forget that life is not in the flesh of an animal, but the flesh is the product of the life which is in the blood. Roose goes on to point out that this is "rightly so, because the life-giving blood is the only hope man has for this life and eternal life to come."

Rev. Roy Steward, a Senior Pastor in the First Evangelical Lutheran Church in Altoona, Pennsylvania noted that man's use of animals for food, clothes, companionship, etc. predates Christianity. "Animals in one account predate the creation of man, but are placed under man's dominion (Genesis 1)."

Rev. Stewart referred to Genesis 3 when he noted that animals are created as helpers for man. He pointed out that the concept that animals are provided for food is not limited to Judeo-Christian thinking. Rather it is present in most indigenous religions from Native Americans to Jews. Animal use, given to us by God, is universal except for Hindu and offshoot Asian beliefs. As Rev. Steward noted: "this universal religious understanding is in tune with the natural order of things."

Does this mean that man can be abusive to animals? Of course not. "He has use of the animals but also, as part of the office of dominion, has responsibility for the well-being of animals, domestic and wild."

This is a critical point, that *man has the responsibility for the well- being of animals.* Maybe this is the crux of the problem for animal rights Christians; they feel that man can manage wildlife without killing them. At least I assume that is what they feel.

If they are Christians, they surely cannot argue with most of the above, most of the Bible thinking here is on animal use for man.

So, I can only assume that they feel that man, in carrying out his responsibility to maintain the well-being of wild animals, can do so without killing some of them, at least not if it involves enjoying the hunt.

Almost all (or perhaps all) wildlife biologists feel that we must view animals as species, as populations, not as individuals. Thus, to manage the species there are times when we must kill some individuals.

Tobias in his Trilogy magazine article believes that man should give "the gift of life to animals. Why not simply stop the killing?"

He goes on: "These (animals) are living beings with their own individual souls and destinies, and abilities to feel, to imagine, to think, to speak, to love. These are animals like ourselves."

This is in total disagreement with Dr. Meitzen's views that animals and humans are different, that they are not equal, that Man is the pinnacle of the hierarchy of life.

The concept that animals have their own individual destinies? I don't think so. The animal rights concept that animals are equal to man? That is not biblical. That value system is not Christian.

Man might have destinies for animals, but animals do not have destinies. Do animals have abilities to feel, imagine, think, speak, or love? Why are we trying to make such illogical, contrived connections between humans and animals here when the facts lead us in another direction?

At the risk of sounding condescending, which I do not want to do, let me question whether animals can "imagine." It seems a real stretch to consider that animals have an imagination, and the power to imagine.

The musings of a deer? "I wonder what it would be like if all oak trees were laden with acorns every fall. Ah then, I would be extremely happy. My chances for survival would increase. I could have more offspring, the health of our deer herd would be so improved. Life would be grand."

No, humans and animals are different and man has been granted the charge of managing animals. Deer cannot think, muse or imagine. Those are human activities.

There is sinning in relishing the kill of animals or in wanting to kill more animals than others and in overly rejoicing and boasting about such. As we noted in earlier chapters about Native American's philosophy about hunting — an almost religious fervor about the hunt—to brag offends the spirit of the animal.

However, humans have a responsibility to manage wild animals, to do so without abuse (I hesitate to use the word humanely..."humanly") and to abandon wild animals to natural forces is an abdication of our Christian responsibility.

Humans And Animals Are Different.—-One book that is as important to some animal activists as the Bible is to Christians is "*Animal Liberation*" by Peter Singer (Avon Books, 1975). Singer felt that "A more enlightened view of our relations with animals emerges only gradually, as thinkers begin to take positions that are relatively independent of the church."

Maybe that sums up the disasters that are taking place in all phases of our liberalized society. We are gradually taking positions on all kinds of things that are independent of the church, and I might add, of the Bible. Indeed, the question of animals being similar to man, and deserving similar rights to man are in debate.

However, based on the Bible, humans and animals are very

different. David Roose wrote at great length about this difference.

"In Genesis 1:26, God is saying, let us make *man* in *our image*, after *our likeness* and give him *stewardship* of all that we have made in the earth (paraphrased). The making of man was God's desire to reproduce His own likeness. In no other creative wonder was that desire expressed."

Thus, and Mr. Roose nicely pointed this out, this alone is enough "to refute any and all arguments that animals are equal with man."

Dr. John Mulder also wrote on this subject. He is a veterinarian and Director of the University Animal Care Unit and Professor of Veterinary Science at the University of Arizona. He looked at this question in a June 1989 article in Synapse. He believed that one key word in understanding the difference of man and animals was the word "dominion." He noted that this word was used 49 times in the Old Testament, and "it is translated from six different Hebrew words found in original Bible manuscripts."

He pointed out that the Hebrew word used in Genesis 1:26 and 28 is "rodoh", which means "domineer."

My Webster's Unabridged Dictionary states that "domineer" means to rule, to be master, to impose one's own opinion and wishes. Mulder stated that this meant that man has full authority over the animal kingdom. I agree.

Bill Parlasca, in an article in the September 1991 issue of Quail Unlimited, noted that nonhunters seem to be uncomfortable with *man's* role of dominance. I think he hit the nail on the head. I suggest that some animal rightists feel guilty about humans acting "dominant" over animals.

Yes, guilt because man survives by using animals, by being dominant over animals. Mr. Parlasca attributes part of the "neurotic guilt" for survival to be the antihunters lack of "the farmer's intimate experience with control over food sources." For more than a few of them (non-hunters), pets are a subconscious expression of benevolence in contra version of their guilt."

In other words, some antihunters feel guilty because they don't understand the life and death struggles of nature and the farm. And they are kind to their pets to make up for the way we humans have mistreated animals.

"I'll be nice to my pets to make up for killing and eating animals for my survival, for putting herbicides on vegetables (so that I can be a vegetarian) grown in areas where wildlife used to live, for using animals in medical research to help my children survive disease and car wrecks and other things that befall man."

That is the possible antihunter reasoning for some people.

Most Christians don't go through such turmoil about using animals. Study the Bible, and you don't need to feel guilty about having dominion over animals. God gave *humans* such dominion.

Everything we humans do impacts our environment and the environment of wild animals. Hunters...nonhunters...vegetarians...our impacts are the same. A vegetarian who drives a car: is he/she having a negative impact on wildlife? Sure because acid rain is a by product of driving a car, and acid rain is bad for wildlife.

The car is driven on a road, and that road was carved out of wildlife habitat and the construction of that road led to the death of animals. Nonhunters who watches birds? Are they having a negative impact on wildlife? Sure because they wear clothes made of oil-based products, and producing those clothes is bad for wildlife.

Everything all of us do on this planet has a negative impact on wild creatures, habitats, and the environment. We do good things for wildlife and the environment too, we manage it. We practice conservation.

Man does have dominion over the earth. Man does have dominion over animals, but with that dominion comes the responsibility to manage the earth and wildlife.

God gave us the abilities to do just that. He gave us the ability to reason, to think, to be compassionate, and to understand. As Parlasca pointed out, "the fact that carrots aren't cute and furry doesn't change the operation of natural law, and animals have no rights under nature's rules." Man is given the right to manage wildlife.

Parlasca also asks the next leading question. What about the charges of "needless suffering?" What is needless suffering? We use pesticides to raise more carrots for humans to eat, but this results in more dead and dying wildlife. Is that needless suffering? We build four-lane highways around cities, but this results in more deer being hit by cars so is that needless suffering? We want growth because that leads to more jobs, but growth results in loss of wildlife habitat so is that needless suffering?

Some people will say yes to all the above, some will say no, and a large group will be somewhere in between depending on the issue. Nothing is black and white, and there are a lot of gray areas here, but not for some people.

Some citizens says the issue is killing. They believe that if we taught all children not to kill under any circumstances, then the world would be a better place. Maybe they do not like the motives of hunters, but we humans have the biblical mandate to manage wildlife.

To abdicate that responsibility, to stop killing some wild animals, would lead to suffering and loss of habitat and species. When deer overpopulate, wild flowers decrease. When deer overpopulate, ground vegetation and the wildlife that utilizes that vegetation suffers. When deer overpopulate, the remaining deer that survive suffer.

All of this has been documented over and over. Man has dominion, the right to manage deer. Killing overabundance is one form of management. Abstinence of killing is not a form of management. In fact not killing may well cause more suffering, and could lead to even more death. And not killing some deer in certain situations can lead to human suffering too.

The Bible tells various stories where animals were killed by man.

Samson killed a lion. Jesus told men exactly where to place their nets in order to catch fish, and they caught more than their nets could hold.

The Bible sets standards for humane care of animals (see Mulder paper; Deuteronomy 25:4, I Corinthians 9:9, I Timothy 5:18, Matthew 12:11, Proverbs 12: 10 and 26:17), but it gives us dominion. Within that dominion each hunter must decide for him/herself whether their behavior is moral.

Each must decide whether they are taking every step to treat animals with respect. In summary, let me again quote Dave Roose: "Should man hunt? I believe he has permission from God to do so (Genesis 27:3, 9:2, Leviticus 17:13). Is killing wrong? To take the life of an animal is permitted by God but not the life of a man (Genesis 9:3, 9:6). Are animals equal with man? No, because they were not made in the likeness of God (Genesis 1:27, 9:6, Ecclesiastes 3:21)."

"And God said, Let us make man in our image, after our likeness: and let them have dominion over the fish of the sea, and over the fowl of the air, and over the cattle, and over all the earth...

And God blessed them, and God said unto them, Be fruitful, and multiply, and replenish the earth, and subdue it: and have dominion over the fish of the sea, and over the fowl of the air, and over every living thing that moveth upon the earth."

Genesis 1: 26, 28

Chapter 17

Conclusions

What a shame that the word "sport" has been used to describe hunting. Dr. Randall Eaton pointed out that "...hunting is not sport" (In *"Tell It Like It Is,"* Bowman's Journal, Autumn 1999). I could not agree more, but hunters and nonhunters have used the "sport hunting" tag for many years. In fact, it has been used for so long, any change is difficult (though I am trying herein, as I've referred to modern hunting as "recreational hunting").

I call it "recreational hunting" because hunting is not sport. The dictionary defines "sport" as, to play or frolic, a pastime, amusement, a game (especially involving bodily exercise), a field diversion (and it mentions hunting and fishing as examples). Even our dictionary definition of sport has adopted hunting under it's umbrella. However, when we consider our roots, and the reasons we hunt, it isn't sport.

Hunting isn't play or frolic. It is not done for simple amusement. It isn't a game.

Sport usually means competition. Hunting is not about winning and losing. Sporting games usually have an audience, hunting does not. Sport can be loud. Hunting is solemn. It is private.

As I discussed in chapters 3 and 4, hunting is instinctive, it's spiritual, it is a ritual. It is not sport and it's time we quit using that very inappropriate term to describe what humans have done for one million years.

I've devoted much of this book in making the argument that we should not discount our evolutionary roots as hunters to accommodate a minority of those who oppose hunting. Shane Mahoney, chief of the wildlife department in Newfoundland, recently talked about hunting in an address to the 1999 Outdoor Writers Association of America conference. He noted that watching wildlife and hunting wildlife are different.

Hunting wildlife pits man as a predator against wildlife, the prey. The hunter participates in evolution, in a million-year past where man is directly involved in the death of animals, where man is connected to nature.

The wildlife watcher, on the other hand, sees animals passing in and out of their view. There is little involvement. (I would add that this is true for most wildlife watchers, but is not true for hardcore bird watchers. Bird watchers study habitat, and get engrossed with the animals as hunters do.

Truth is that bird watching and hunting have similar components. Bird watchers study the bird and habitat. They scout an area, "hunting" for likely locations to see birds. Then they "spot" the bird, and their search is over. Their stalk has ended with the bird sighting. Bird watchers obviously do not kill their quarry, but as a form of wildlife watching, bird watching is serious business.)

There are those who say that things have changed, our past is no longer pertinent, we no longer "need" to hunt. The late Paul Shepherd disagreed and he wrote at length about our evolutionary past.

Shepard believed our genetic history was pertinent to our living today. Early hunters cooperated, and we evolved by such cooperation. Life and death centered on being able to help, trust, and live with our fellow man and our environment. Shepherd believed that the hunter's Pleistocene genetic natural selection couldn't change in such a short time (referring to the 10,000 years since we began to farm and added grains to our diet). He felt our very survival depended on a return to the hunter's natural world.

When I was growing up as a hunter we had hunters contributing toward the conservation of habitat and wildlife. They have always cared about wildlife and provided the leadership in groups that spiritually and financially supported wildlife.

I also saw that in my family and those of my friends, hunting had a special meaning. The necessity to hunt for survival is obviously no longer there, but that cannot erase the eons of our close ties to the life and death struggles of nature. My father didn't have to "hide" the fact that he hunted. It was not politically incorrect behavior.

Even though hunting has been painted with a tarnished brush in

America, nonhunters not only support wildlife management via hunting, but there is a latent interest in hunting. Richard Stedman and Daniel Decker recently showed that over 33 percent of nonhunters believe there is utility in hunting, and 10 percent received benefits from hunting (see *"Illuminating an Overlooked Hunting Stakeholder Group: Nonhunters and Their Interest in Hunting,"* in Human Dimensions of Wildlife 1(3):29-41, 1996).

These researchers found that over 61 percent of New York nonhunters has eaten game meat, while 58 percent shared hunting stories with hunters. The majority felt they received no important benefits from hunting, but nonhunters enjoyed eating wild game and many believed hunting was important for proper wildlife management.

Even with support for hunting, we continue to see a divorce from nature. Shane Mahoney sees this as a major societal problem (In"*The Role of Hunters in the Conservation of Wildlife*". Fourth Governor's Symposium on North America's Hunting Heritage, 1995).

In this paper Mahoney cited the works of mythologist Joseph Campbell. I never had an interest in mythology nor the traditions and religions of mankind. However, I've seen most of Campbell's brilliant lectures on public television, some of them over and over again during the past six or seven years. Public television commonly replays his lectures during their fund-raising campaigns each year. The lectures are captivating as are the ideas.

As Mahoney noted, Campbell's 1959 *"The Masks of God*: *Primitive Mythology,"* (Viking/Penquin Press) clearly spelled out a basic principle of our existence on earth that flesh eats flesh. Man, and his rituals and ceremonies, is historically and prehistorically tied to hunting. Mahoney goes on to say: "Today we have small hope of comprehending ourselves and our world unless we understand that man still, in his inmost being, is a hunter."

Throughout the antihunting literature there is the theme that if we all stopped hunting, if we all stopped eating meat, if we stopped using animals for medical research, we would become a better society. We will become gentler, more loving, kinder people.

The philosophy goes a bit further to suggest that if one doesn't eat meat, nor support using any animals for medical research, and is against hunting, and all other uses of animals, they are "good" people.

If one supports or does any of the above, then they are the "bad."

Bob Mottram talked about the "new reality" we are trying to create in this country (see *"New Reality Enables Animal Rightists To Win,"* in Outdoors Unlimited, Feb. 1988). He points out that kids today grow up not understanding reality. We want to show them a farm,"but we want the animals on it (the farm) to live forever—never mind what *real* farmers do" (referring to the fact that farm animals are raised for human use...flesh eats flesh).

We've also reached a point in this country where small minorities can accomplish their goals by being legally pushy, filing law suit after law suit, by confrontations and demonstrations. Confronted often enough, good causes and the leaders of those causes, back down. It happens to many biologically and ecologically sound hunts every year.

Biologists try to manage wildlife, and in so doing, schedule legal and needed hunts. A few citizens who oppose the killing of animals demonstrate, file injunctions, and get publicity. These continue for months and weary citizens and agencies either compromise or fold.

This is all part of our system. The sad part is that in most cases, wildlife and wildlife habitat suffer. It's the "new reality" that Bob Mottram talks about. How can this happen?

Ted Kerasote has the answer. In his keynote speech given at the Izaak Walton League of America's 1996 National Outdoor Ethics Conference he noted that this new reality comes about not because the animal rightists are doing a good promotion job, and not because the outdoor ethics programs are not doing a good job, but because the values of society are changing.

The change is scary if your job is to manage wildlife populations. Our system of wildlife management revolves about utilitarian use of animals. But the new reality is that societies values are shifting from that use to one of protecting individual animals.

Wildlife biologists are faced with another major challenge. For years the wildlife profession paid little heed to nonhunters. And nonhunters put no demands on the profession. That's all changed.

Today there is increased pressure on state wildlife agencies to answer to the majority of the population, those who are nonhunters. As Dr. Robert Schmidt pointed out, this pressure creates "tension between hunters and nonhunters when it comes to the question of how to manage wildlife" (see *"A Modest Proposal To Assist In The Maintenance Of A Hunting Culture"*, in Wildlife Society Bulletin 24(2):373-375, 1996).

Schmidt noted that we need additional monies to manage nongame species. The hunters agree, and support such efforts, and in fact lead such efforts. At the same time hunters are concerned that if wildlife agencies receive huge monies from nonhunting sources, then they will become disenfranchise from the support they've received from those agencies for many years.

(Note, in recent years antihunters have felt disenfranchised and that is one of the reasons they so strongly carry their arguments forward.)

Schmidt goes on to suggest that hunters must support wildlife programs for nonhunters as this puts them on the "moral high ground." Hunters value wildlife. Supporting programs that benefit nonhunted species proves they do so.

Tom Wood in the March 1990 issue of Outdoors Unlimited (see *"To Use Or Not To Use"*) noted that there is a growing rift between man and nature. He suggested that when we "disenfranchise the very people who still have a direct commitment to the land" (herein referring to hunters, fishers, trappers) we widen the "rift between man and nature."

Who has been disenfranchised of late? Wood mentions the Newfoundland sealers, fur trappers, native people who take one whale a year. Animal rights outcries to these activities have been long and loud. If we add hunters and fishers to this growing disenfranchised list, the rift will grow larger.

Wood goes on to say that in society today, "wildlife is valued only to the extent it is used." I've made this point several times in this book: wildlife is a sustainable natural resource. We use it, and we still have it. But if hunting, trapping, fishing are stopped, then we don't use the resource. Who then will be the protectors of wildlife? Dr. Randall Eaton suggests that *"only* hunting connects us to nature and the creatures, and it is *only* hunting that motivates us to fiercely protect them (animals)."

Some might say the animal rights and antihunting folks will

protect wildlife. Maybe. However, the existing track record there is not good at all. Such folks have contributed almost no money and no energy to manage wildlife. Additionally they have not been strong supporters of legislation that helps manage wildlife. Protect individuals animals....yes. Manage wildlife populations....no.

Wildlife biologists views are not immune to the changes going on in society, and their views are also slowly changing. Some do not support what has been considered traditional methods of managing wildlife.

I believe that part of this change, and the problems it causes wildlife, is that we are now getting some wildlife biologists who neither hunt, nor have any relationship or understanding of hunting. My guess is that Aldo Leopold would applaud the new interest in nongame management. But having numbers of wildlife biologists that cannot relate to hunting would probably cause him much concern. And it does lead to problems for wildlife.

For example, yesterday I read about a U. S. Fish and Wildlife Service proposal to introduce 450 bison into the Valentine National Wildlife Refuge in Nebraska and expanding their numbers in the near future. Not a problem, except that the Nebraska wildlife agency opposes this move.

That gets my attention. The local biologists in a state wildlife agency are concerned about a proposal made by a federal wildlife agency. What do the state biologists know that the federal administrators do not?

This refuge has value for waterfowl, prairie chickens and ground nesting birds. The state wildlife agency feels the cost of fencing this herd is high, and that bison will damage prairie habitat. Local biologists do not want to jeopardize the wildlife on the refuge by adding bison.

The U. S. Fish and Wildlife Service also wants to put elk and bighorn sheep on the refuge. Again, fencing would be required. Finally, they want to stock prairie dogs in the area. Biologists in Nebraska think that the loose sand soils there are not conducive to the clays needed by prairie dogs.

Who knows why the wildlife service wants to stock these species there, especially when state biologists have good reasons to oppose it. My guess is that some federal administrators with little or no field experience in Nebraska (the kind of experience that many Nebraska biologists gain via hunting) are making such decisions.

Will the general public like seeing another huge enclosure full of elk, bighorns, and bison? Probably, but is that in the best interest of this refuge? Probably not.

As wildlife administrators become more removed from our one-million-years of connection to nature we will see decisions harmful to wildlife.

There are places in this world where hunters and hunting are still valued. In Germany they have kept the history of the hunt alive. The jagermeister, the hunting master, holds a prestigious position in society. There the ceremonies of the past are still continued.

In fact, the ceremonies before and after the hunt are very solemn, important occasions. Tradition, ritual, history are important. Those ceremonies teach new hunters about the animal, about hunting. They help older hunters keep hunting and respect for the animal in perspective.

We fail to do that as much as we should in our country. We portray hunters as rednecks and good-ole boys. Our hunting industry does the same. No wonder the general public thinks hunters are dumb, drunken, violators who care little about the animals.

Yes, hunters and hunting needs to change a bit in America. Hunters need to end all the infighting between hunting organizations, the bickering among gun and bow hunters. Although these inter-hunter conflicts have been greatly reduced in the past 10 years, hunters need to do more. The hunting industry and community needs to lead the change, to create that spirit of cooperation, to make hunters a "community" again.

The managing wildlife agencies need to do more as well. Sure, hunters pay the bills of wildlife agencies, but they need to be viewed as more than a commodity.

Richard Haynes and several co-authors published a most interesting paper on the connection between how we manage natural resources and local community well-being (In *"Natural Resource Management And Community Well-being,"* Wildlife Society Bulletin 24(2):222-226, 1996).

Chapter 17

They noted that small communities provide us with a "sense-of-place." Many of us who grew up in small, rural communities can relate to that feeling. Small towns were, and still are, places where people pull together and they know and help neighbors. People feel safer in small towns, and they probably are safer.

As Haynes noted, such communities remind us of the past. Such communities are "sources of fundamental American values," and it is those values that we should strive to protect. The "sense-of-place" that we find in such communities is tied to our natural surroundings. Tied to the local lake, to the woods, to the environment.

Hunting has given me a career in wildlife, a chance to work and help wildlife and wildlife habitat. It has given me thousands of hours in the woods observing and learning about wildlife. Hunting taught me to look for wildlife, it gave me a reason to do so.

When younger, and yes, even today, hunting encouraged me to read. It brought me new friendships. Hunting taught me to be more cooperative, more punctual, more responsible, more patient, more persistent, more understanding. It taught me humility, and to strive for success. Hunting gave me good health, and it helped teach me about eating a better diet. It also showed me that life in the wilds also involved death.

Hunting gave my life spiritual meaning. It taught me about the habits of animals and their interrelationships with the environment. It showed me the value of wildlife and the necessity for protecting it. Hunting gave the woods a "sense-of-place" for me. I care about that patch of bobwhite quail cover, and about that wetland filled with nesting ducks. I will fight to protect it. I care about that farm opening where turkey broods and deer go to feed...and so too the great horned owl. Those need protection too.

Hunters care about that strip of cover between the cornfields where ringneck pheasants seek shelter and red-tailed hawks perch and hunt. I worry that if hunting decreases, these wild places and wild creatures will also decrease.

Dr. David E. Samuel

About the Author

Dr. David Samuel spent 30 years as a professor of wildlife management at West Virginia University. Since 1971 he has been the Conservation Editor of Bowhunter Magazine, where his "Know Hunting" column still appears. His activities on behalf of wildlife are diverse: from starting a local National Audubon Society chapter to initiating the West Virginia Bowhunter Education Program.

He presently serves on several boards including the West Virginia Environmental Quality Board, the board of the Native American Fish & Wildlife Foundation, and the Pope and Young Club. Now retired from University work, Dr. Samuel spends his time writing, bowhunting, traveling and gardening.